Space Warfare

This book considers military space strategy within the context of the land and naval strategies of the past. Explaining why and how strategists note the similarities of space operations to those of the air and naval forces, this volume shows why many such strategies unintentionally lead to overemphasizing the importance of space-based offensive weaponry and technology.

Counter to most US Air Force doctrines, the book argues that space-based weapons don't confer superiority. It examines why both air and naval strategic frameworks actually fail to adequately capture the scope of real-world issues regarding current space operations and how by expanding a naval strategic framework to include maritime activities – which includes the interaction of land and sea – the breadth of issues and concerns regarding space activities and operations can be fully encompassed.

John J. Klein uses Sir Julian Corbett's maritime strategy as a strategic springboard, while observing the salient lessons of other strategists – including Sun Tzu, Clausewitz, Jomini, and Mao Tse-tung – to show how a space strategy and associated principles of space warfare can be derived to predict concerns, develop ideas, and suggest policy not currently recognized.

This book will be of much interest to students of space politics, US foreign policy and strategic studies in general.

John J. Klein is a Commander in the US Navy. He has published extensively on military strategy and tactics and is an advocate of using historical maritime strategy to develop current space strategy.

Space Power and Politics
Edited by Everett C. Dolman and John Sheldon

The *Space Power and Politics* series will provide a forum where space policy and historical issues can be explored and examined in-depth. The series will produce works that examine civil, commercial, and military uses of space and their implications for international politics, strategy, and political economy. This will include works on government and private space programs, technological developments, conflict and cooperation, security issues, and history.

1 Space Warfare
Strategy, principles and policy
John J. Klein

2 US Hypersonic Research & Development
The rise and fall of Dyna-Soar, 1944–63
Roy F. Houchin II

3 The US Military and Outer Space
Perspectives, plans, and programs
Peter L. Hays

4 Chinese Space Policy
A study in domestic and international politics
Roger Handberg and Zhen Li

Space Warfare

Strategy, principles and policy

John J. Klein

 Routledge
Taylor & Francis Group

LONDON AND NEW YORK

First published 2006 by Routledge
2 Park Square, Milton Park, Abingdon, OX14 4RN

Simultaneously published in the USA and Canada by Routledge
270 Madison Avenue, New York, NY 10016

Routledge is an imprint of the Taylor & Francis Group

Transferred to Digital Printing 2006

© 2006 John J. Klein

Typeset in Sabon by Prepress Projects Ltd

British Library Cataloguing in Publication Data
A catalog record for this book is available from the British Library

Library of Congress Cataloging in Publication Data
A catalog record for this book has been requested

ISBN10: 0–415–77001–7 (hbk)
ISBN10: 0–415–40796–6 (pbk)

ISBN13: 978–0–415–77001–9 (hbk)
ISBN13: 978–0–415–40796–0 (pbk)

For all my girls:
Capi, Jacey, and Emme Jo

Contents

Preface   ix

PART I
Introduction and framework   I

1 Where we are and where we're going   3

2 Contemporary space strategies   13

3 Maritime strategic principles   21

PART II
Strategic principles of space warfare   33

4 Space is tied to national power   35

5 Space operations are interdependent with others   44

6 Celestial lines of communication   51

7 Command of space   60

8 Strategy of offense and defense   69

9 Strategic positions   80

10 Blocking   91

11 Space as a barrier   100

12 Dispersal and concentration   107

13 Actions by lesser powers   116

14 Comparisons   127

PART III
Implications and recommendations   **135**

15 Space policy   137

16 Summary and conclusions   154

   Notes   165
   Bibliography   184
   Index   189

Preface

My desire to write this work arose while I was at the US Naval War College in 2003 conducting research as part of the Mahan Scholars Program. During this timeframe, I gained an appreciation for maritime strategy as well as its historical development. The Mahan Scholars Program afforded me the opportunity to investigate the various space power and space control theories, while determining if maritime strategy had anything to contribute to the debate. From this research, the conclusion reached was that maritime theory in fact provides a suitable framework for thinking about broad national security issues and military strategy in and through space. Despite the apparent utility of maritime strategy in developing space strategy, my earlier research failed to fully describe and elucidate the strategic principles of space warfare in a manner the subject deserved. The work here, consequently, is an effort to more fully describe the strategy and principles of space warfare. All of this is done to provide a useful framework for contemplating military operations in space.

This work is primarily intended for two audiences: the warfighter and the policy maker. The developed space strategy is offered to those military professionals who will fight future conflicts and need an understanding of the complexities of space warfare. Chapters 1 and 2 provide the background to contemplate military strategy in space, along with prior methods of thinking about space strategy. Chapter 3 describes the maritime strategy, as developed by Sir Julian Corbett, which is used as a template for considering the strategic principles of space warfare. Chapters 4 through 13 detail the most important concepts and principles of space warfare. These developed concepts and principles are subsequently compared to other highly regarded viewpoints in Chapter 14.

My intent when beginning this work was to shy away from addressing specific policy recommendations, since I viewed policy as beyond the scope of military theory and strategy. Upon further consideration, however, I came to the conclusion that a broad theory and strategy for space warfare could indeed provide insights and recommendations for policy makers. As a result, Chapter 15 includes specific policy recommendations for government and military leaders, based on the implications of the developed space strategy. Chapter 16 represents a summary and conclusion of the entire work. For those who are pressed for time but still desire an overview of the arguments made, I would suggest reading Chapters 1 and 16 to start.

Admittedly, I am neither a historian nor part of the "space cadre."[1] Consequently, I do not claim to be an expert in either history or space doctrine. Nevertheless, what is offered is a strategic framework for thinking about space warfare, based upon the lessons of history. One of the greatest impediments to developing the strategic principles of space operations is the current perceptions of the subject. One perception is that the bulk of any space strategy should deal with the role of weapons in space. Warfare and strategy, when properly considered, must address broader national security issues and not just the tactical employment of weapons. The second perception is that discussion about space warfare is the arena for futurists and those involved in fanciful thought. Yet much of the current innovation regarding warfare involves space-enabled technologies, such as precision weapons that utilize global positioning information, ballistic missile defense programs designed to engage enemy warheads in the lowest regions of outer space, and information operations that utilize orbiting satellites in performing their mission. Moreover, the military professional must be concerned with protecting national interests and is obliged to consider military strategy in any medium, even space. Since space activities are tied to national interests and security, military operations in space deserve to be thoughtfully studied, just as with land, sea, and air operations before.

As this is my first venture into writing a work of this length, I am indebted to many for their mentoring, feedback, and support. John Hattendorf, the Chair of Maritime History at the Naval War College, never tired in trying to educate me on maritime strategy, and he offered repeated encouragement to further develop and amplify my earliest ideas and concepts. Without his prodding, this book would not have been written. The Mahan Scholars Program provided the venue to conduct the initial research that helped formulate some of my early ideas. Vice Admiral Rodney P. Rempt, then President of the Naval War College, provided valuable mentoring and guidance on what "thinking strategically" really means. Carnes Lord and Joan Johnson-Freese, both professors at the Naval War College, also lent a critical eye to my early arguments and suggested comments on how to become a better writer. Pelham Boyer provided sage editorial advice and greatly facilitated getting my first article on this subject printed in the *Naval War College Review*. My fellow Mahan Scholars, Dave Hardesty and Rich Freeman, offered a much-needed critique on the maritime-inspired strategic framework. Additionally, to Tom Brady, Bob Cady, Dominic De Scisciolo, Alex Dornstauder, Rich Morales, Tuan Pham, Ward Scott, and Peter Zwack, many thanks for enduring my repeated discussions on space strategy and for your camaraderie.

Everett Dolman and John Sheldon from the journal *Astropolitics* also graciously accepted a more expanded version of my original thoughts for publication in their journal. John Logsdon of the Space Policy Institute at the George Washington University was kind enough to let me present some of my early policy ideas to the Security Space Forum held at the school. Peter Hays of Science Applications International Corporation waded through several chapters of the manuscript and provided many suggestions, corrections, and insights.

This work was predominantly written while I was the Navy Federal Executive Fellow at the Brookings Institution during the 2003–4 program. Rear Admiral Carl Mauney, then Director of the Strategy and Concepts Division and head of the Navy's Federal Executive Fellow program, provided professional advice on my research efforts and mentoring throughout the fellowship. I greatly appreciate the work of the Brookings library staff – David Blair, Elizabeth Barnes, Sarah Chilton, Eric Eisenger, John Grunwell, and Laura Mooney – who fulfilled my ever persistent requests for articles and books, and who never told me "no." Also, many thanks are given to the colleagues I met there, including Jim Steinberg and Michael O'Hanlon, who pushed me to more fully develop the chapter on policy recommendations. I am grateful to my compatriots at Brookings – Dave Gray, Eric Herr, Sam Mundy, Terry Markin, and Lincoln Stroh – for our countless discussions on military strategy and policy throughout the yearlong program.

Lastly and most importantly, I am sincerely grateful to the naval leadership – both past and present – for their foresight in recognizing the value of educational opportunities such as the fellowship program, which enabled the undertaking of this work.

The contents of this manuscript reflect my own personal views and are not necessarily endorsed by the US Department of Defense or the Department of the Navy.

JJK

Part I

Introduction and framework

Chapter 1

Where we are and where we're going

Since the 1940s, the nature of space operations and the need to develop a space power theory has been debated.[1] In an attempt to formulate such a theory, both theorists and strategists have noted the similarities of space operations to those of air and naval operations. Consequently, many have attempted to derive a theory of space warfare through analogy to either air power or sea control models. By using past strategic frameworks as a guide, the hope was to develop a clearly articulated, all-encompassing strategy for military operations in and through space. Despite these previous efforts to develop a comprehensive theory and strategy of space warfare, it has been observed that such a strategic framework – one encompassing the essence of space operations and associated national interests – has yet to be formulated.[2] This failure is a consequence of the many divergent and conflicting ideas regarding space strategy, since in the end they only offer a menagerie of competing strategies and viewpoints.

This work will look at past air and naval strategic frameworks to see if space operations and associated national interests in space have any analogous parallels to either military operations in the air or at sea. Then, the best historical framework will be used as a guide in developing the relevant strategic principles of space warfare. Since the developed strategic principles will be based on a historical framework, these newly developed principles will need to be tested and compared with contemporary thought regarding military operations in space. Finally, the military and governmental space policy implications resulting from the deduced strategic principles will be addressed.

Through this investigative process, the conclusion reached is that both air and naval models fail to capture the true breadth of pertinent issues regarding space operations and strategy. Yet, by expanding the purview of naval operations to include those of maritime operations, the full extent and nature of space operations can be adequately represented. Furthermore, by using a maritime theory based on the work of Sir Julian Corbett, a suitable strategic framework can be defined and relevant space strategy subsequently extrapolated. The resulting strategic principles, while not entirely in agreement with conventional wisdom, do encompass many of the current observations and ideas regarding national interests and military operations in space.

Laying the foundation: terms, definitions, and current operations

Some pragmatic critics may ask, "Why bother developing a space power theory?", their argument being that the United States has done quite well in developing space systems and operational doctrine, even without a consensus on what a theory of space warfare entails. The rebuttal to this view is the adage, "You don't know what you don't know." This statement may seem trite at first, but it accurately conveys the problem. A theory attempts to make sense of what would otherwise be inscrutable and sets forth "rules of the game" by which actions become intelligible.[3] The Prussian military strategist and land warfare theorist Carl von Clausewitz (1780–1831) praised theory, noting that theory educates the mind so that useful order can be gleaned from an apparently disorderly universe.[4] He emphatically stated: "[Theory] can give the mind insight into the great mass of phenomena and of their relationships, then leave it free to rise into the higher realms of action."[5]

In order to achieve the insight of which Clausewitz wrote, past strategic theories will be compared against one another, and the one best representative of operations and activities in space will be used as a framework for developing the strategic principles of space warfare. The intent is to use past strategic theories as a guide in this endeavor, since such historical understanding and knowledge improves one's ability to solve problems more wisely than arbitrary choice, pure chance, and blind intuition would allow.[6] From the underpinnings of the theory, strategic principles can be developed, which are those concepts that ought to be considered prior to and during the course of war.[7] A distillation of these strategic principles is the major input when formulating any military strategy.

After the principles of warfare, the next consideration is strategy. Strategy refers to the art and science of marshalling and directing resources to achieve some objective. Or, more simply, it refers to the balancing of one's ends with one's means.[8] Strategy can be distinguished further into two types: grand strategy and military strategy. Grand strategy, also called national strategy, applies during both peace and war to all instruments of national power to achieve a state's objectives. In contrast, military strategy typically refers to plans that organize and direct military elements in achieving specific objectives.[9] Below military strategy is battlefield strategy, more commonly referred to as tactics.[10]

Since available technology affects one's means, strategy will change as technology advances. Furthermore, tactics are closely tied to available technology, so they too will change with technological advancement. On the other hand, the theory and strategic principles of any form of warfare should remain unchanged – if they are indeed theory and strategic principles – even with the passage of time and as technology advances.[11]

In trying to conceptualize these different terms and nuances of usage, it is convenient to think of theory addressing *why*; strategic principles addressing *what*; tactics addressing *how*; and military strategy bridging the gap between *what* and *how*. From this hierarchy of military thought, it is understood that from theory we develop strategic principles; from principles we derive strategy; and from strategy we formulate tactics.[12] So, theory is the first and most necessary step in thinking about warfare.

Differing from strategy is policy. Although some within the government use "policy" interchangeably with "strategy," the two are considered different. Both policy and national strategy are interrelated, since a distillation of grand strategy serves as the foundation for policy. Nevertheless, policy, as interpreted here, refers to official government guidance, whether in spoken or written form. Therefore, policy itself is the actual communication of strategy regarding a topic of national concern.

The instruments of national power – whether diplomatic, economic, information, or military – are used to achieve the objectives of national strategy.[13] The diplomatic instrument refers to political efforts used between states in the realm of international affairs. Although sometimes "political" is used instead of "diplomatic," their meanings and usage are mostly the same. The primary difference of "political" is that it refers to the general domestic influence of politicians within a country, whereas "diplomatic" pertains to activities between different countries or regions of the world. The economic instrument refers to the influence of trade, commerce, and financial activities.[14] The military element of national power is the influence achieved through the application of presence, coercion, or force. The diplomatic, economic, and military instruments are the categories of national power most typically acknowledged by other theorists and strategists. Yet other instruments of national power have been suggested also. These include psychological, intellectual, social, and technological.[15] These additional instruments of power mostly pertain to the method of influencing others through culture, values, and information using news and media sources. The best term to describe this instrument of power is actually "information," as it refers to facts, data, or instructions in any medium or form, along with their transfer and meaning assigned by humans.[16]

It is important to realize that all instruments of national power are methods by which one state can influence another, but they also represent reciprocal methods by which one can be influenced as well. Furthermore, while it is mentally convenient to separate the instruments into separate categories, any national strategy or state action may influence any one instrument of power or any combination of them.

This work primarily deals with space warfare at the strategic level, while suggesting possible operational and tactical implementation of the concepts.[17] Even though the subject deals with the theory, principles, and strategy, some comment regarding the implementation of tactics is warranted to lend a greater understanding of the espoused strategic principles, thereby effectively putting "meat on the bones" of the space strategy's skeletal framework. Failure to provide specifics on how to execute a space warfare strategy could potentially impede the formulating of required doctrine, tactics, and future governmental policy. While the strategic principles presented are in the context of general military operations, they go under the label of "space warfare." Although the term "space warfare" may invoke strong passions and bring with it the associated "baggage" that comes from preconceived ideas, the term provides a suitable context for discussing military space operations. Although the focus here is on military strategy, both military and grand strategies are inextricably linked, as changes in one can dramatically affect the other. Therefore, both will be addressed.

What is "space"?

Before comparing past strategic theories of warfare, it must be understood what space is and is not. Such a simple task turns out to be not so simple, as space has been defined in a variety of ways. The report *Space Power 2010* summarizes the difficulty in defining space, by noting:[18]

> If trying to define where space begins for biological reason, one might choose 9 miles above the earth, since above this point a pressure suit is required. If concerned with propulsion, 28 miles is important since this is the limit of air-breathing engines. For administrative purposes, one might find it important that US astronaut's wings may be earned above 50 miles. An aeronautical engineer might define space as starting at 62 miles above the earth's surface, since this is where aerodynamic controls become ineffective. Conventional and customary law defines the lower boundary of space as the lowest perigee of orbiting space vehicles.

Joint Publication 3-14, *Joint Doctrine for Space Operations*, defines "space" as a medium, like the land, sea, and air, within which military activities shall be conducted to achieve national security objectives.[19] For our discussion, "space" or "outer space" will be functionally defined as beginning at the lowest perigee required for orbit and extending out to infinity, since this is in keeping with observed customary law.[20] Although the scope of this work is not intended to describe in detail the intricacies of operating in space or orbital mechanics, some rudimentary information is useful prior to considering a strategy of space warfare.[21]

Current space activities

The United States and the world have become increasingly reliant upon space. Currently in the United States, space-based technology enters homes, businesses, schools, hospitals, and government offices through applications related to transportation, health, the environment, telecommunications, education, commerce, agriculture, energy, and military operations. This has lead to the observation, "The US is more dependent on space than any other nation."[22] As space operations continue to grow, many countries are likely to become even more reliant on space-based assets.[23] Although the range is indeed broad, a state's space activities can be divided into four major sectors – civil, commercial, intelligence, and military.[24]

Civil space activities include those to explore space and advance human understanding. For instance, the National Aeronautics and Space Administration is involved in these. Through human spaceflight missions – like Apollo, Skylab, and the International Space Station – and unmanned scientific missions – like Viking, Voyager, and Mars Pathfinder – space exploration and scientific understanding have been advanced.

Commercial activities are those where private companies and industries provide services with the intent of making a profit. Currently, satellites performing telecommunications services form the most profitable segment of the commercial space sector, and other services that may soon become profitable include global positioning, launch, and remote sensing.[25] The International Telecommunications Union and the Federal Aviation Administration have responsibilities for overseeing and enforcing many of the regulations involving commercial activities.[26]

The intelligence sector includes surveillance and reconnaissance missions conducted by government agencies, such as the National Reconnaissance Office. Through the use of space-based surveillance and reconnaissance systems, the verification of arms control agreements – including those between the United States and the Soviet Union during the height of the Cold War – has been possible. Presently, these systems are frequently used to monitor and gather intelligence leading up to and during combat operations. Whereas these kinds of systems have been historically used at the strategic level of planning, the current trend, especially in the United States military, is to push the information and data provided down to operational and tactical-level warfighters.

Military space activities are those promoting national security through offensive or defensive operations – whether from, into, or through space. Included in this category are intercontinental ballistic missiles, since they typically traverse outer space during their mid-course flight phase. Because of the sensitive nature of these activities, many research and development programs related to the military use of space are classified; yet some of these past endeavors have been declassified, and information about them is readily available in open sources of literature.

Positions and regions of interest

In space there are positions and regions of interest. Some of these positions of interest include those actual systems employed for civil, commercial, intelligence, and military purposes. Currently, many of these space systems include near-earth satellites and a few pertain to systems operating further away from earth, like those used for specialized scientific study and exploration. In the future, if bases were eventually located on celestial bodies, these would also represent a potential position of interest.

Regions of interest also include those near-earth orbits in which satellites are placed. Although outer space in fact includes much more than just near-earth orbits, at present this is where most of our interests in space lie. In describing various types of orbits, they are often classified by their path around the earth. The path is often chosen based on the intended mission and function of the orbiting system, and in most cases orbits are labeled by their relative height above the earth. Higher orbits provide a larger field-of-view of the earth, and offer ground stations wider accessibility to a satellite's data and information. In contrast, lower orbits have smaller fields-of-view, but can provide greater surveillance detail and potentially lose less signal strength through attenuation. There are various classifications for orbits, and some of the more popular include the low-earth orbit, the medium-earth orbit, and the high-earth orbit, which includes the geosynchronous orbit.[27]

When a geosynchronous orbit, which has an orbital period identical to one full rotation of the earth, is located directly above the equatorial plane, it appears stationary from any point on the ground. This type of orbit is referred to as the geostationary orbit. A geostationary orbit is frequently sought after by those placing communication satellites in space, including television broadcast services, since fixed antennae can easily track and access the satellite's information. Because of the high demand for this type of orbit, the International Telecommunications Union regulates geostationary "slot" assignments.[28] The perceived value of geostationary slots is illustrated by the fact that eight equatorial nations declared sovereignty over the geostationary orbital slots above their countries.[29] Additionally, low-earth orbiting satellites are also growing in number, as countries and companies continue to develop and market telephonic services that utilize space-based systems. Because of the increased use of space-based services, near-earth orbits are becoming even more congested.

Space is neither benign nor featureless. Outer space has pockets where radiation levels can be dangerously high, and such radiation can permanently damage electronics, degrade communications, and be deadly to humans if not properly protected. In the vicinity of earth, these concentrated areas of radiation are known as the Van Allen radiation belts. These belts form two donut-shaped regions encircling the earth's magnetosphere that trap charged particles.[30] Since the locations of these radiation belts are well known, passage through them by satellites and astronauts is often avoided or minimized, and those spacecraft needing to pass through the belts are frequently built with more protection against the harmful radiation.

As a result of the many launches of space systems, there are also concentrations of space debris in orbit around the earth. This "space junk" often includes the leftover remnants of rocket boosters, satellites decaying in orbit, or other launch debris.[31] Although these remnants were not placed in orbit maliciously, a high-velocity impact with such debris can degrade or destroy a spacecraft. Because of this risk, a concerted effort exists to track as many pieces of debris as possible, but the size of the debris that can be tracked is limited by the available technology. Because not all debris can be tracked or avoided, spacecraft are designed to withstand the impact of smaller-sized debris and even micrometeorites. For larger, more threatening debris, spacecraft are steered away from the debris's well-known trajectory.

There are also locations in outer space with special characteristics. Some of these points include locations near the earth known as Lagrange points.[32] These points are five locations where the gravitation forces are effectively canceled out, and objects located there can remain fixed relative to the earth and the moon, at least in theory. The three points on the earth–sun line (L1, L2, and L3) are considered unstable. If an object at one of these locations were displaced perpendicular to the earth–sun line, it would return to its original position; yet if it were displaced along the earth–sun line, it would continue to drift away from the Lagrange points. Of the five points, only two (L4 and L5) are considered stable, and these points are located off the earth–sun line. It is speculated that these two Lagrange points hold strategic importance for commercial and military activities, since the energy needed to remain at these points is effectively zero. Even the more unstable points – L1, L2, and L3 – are currently being used. For example, L1 is now occupied by the Advanced Composition Explorer and the Solar and Heliospheric Observatory to monitor the sun and solar wind, since the point proves a superb location for solar study.[33] Always in the earth's shadow, L2 is speculated to be an ideal location for an astronomical telescope, where the earth would act as a shield against potentially damaging sunlight.[34] It is noteworthy that any two-body celestial system has similar Lagrange points, such as the earth–sun or earth–moon combinations.

Moreover, other positions of interest are on the earth itself, such as those ground facilities used to support space operations. Ground stations commonly used as uplinks or downlinks are included in this category, since without them many of the space-based services currently enjoyed would not be possible. Many facilities used to support and manufacture spacecraft and satellites are also positions of interest, because they frequently represent large capital investments and infrastructure, which also make space-based operations possible.

Other positions of interest include those launch locations used to place systems into space. The location chosen for space launch facilities can dramatically affect the cost and efficiency of placing payloads in orbit. Equatorial launch positions hold greater intrinsic value, especially for launching systems destined for geostationary orbit. Since the rotation of the earth can be used to assist in reaching orbital velocity, equatorial launch positions impart a 1,037 miles per hour relative velocity advantage, when compared to those launched at the earth's poles.[35] Space vehicles launched at positions other than along the equator must make up the additional thrust requirement by either decreasing their payload weight or increasing the size of their engines, in comparison to the same launch system at an equatorial location. Therefore, equatorial positions have a relative cost and efficiency advantage when compared to positions north or south of the equator. For example, a European Ariane rocket launched on an eastward trajectory from the French Space Center in Kourou, French Guiana – which is at 5 degrees northern latitude – has a 17 percent greater fuel efficiency advantage over an American rocket launched eastward from Cape Canaveral, Florida – which is at 28.5 degrees northern latitude.[36]

Shared use

Outer space is shared among countries, organizations, and businesses. This sharing includes not only highly valuable orbital positions but also the frequency spectrum used by the telecommunications industry and others for the transmission of data and information. This common sharing is not unique to the space environment, since international waters and airspace also have a legacy of being shared among the world's citizens. Nevertheless, the common use of space has important considerations when developing military strategy and formulating national policy.

International agreements and treaties have attempted to address the equitable usage of the electromagnetic frequency spectrum in and through space, since the frequency spectrum is used for a variety of applications, including radio, television, and telephonic services.[37] Several conventions and agreements have attempted to regulate the shared used of frequencies for both commercial use and for military purposes. For instance, the 1973 International Telecommunications Convention noted, "In using frequency bands for space radio services Members shall bear in mind that radio frequencies and geostationary satellite orbits are limited natural resources, that they must be used efficiently and economically so that countries or groups of countries may have equitable access to both."[38] Because of the pervasive use of and dependency on the electromagnetic spectrum for operations in and through space, countries have warned against any intentional or unintentional interference to one's communications services. Also exemplifying the widely held belief that outer space and its inherent value should be shared equitably is the Preamble of the International Telecommunications Satellite

Organization Agreement that entered into force in 1973. It states the need "to provide, for the benefit of all mankind . . . the best and most equitable use of the radio frequency spectrum and of orbital space."[39] So, as with the oceans of the world and international airspace, outer space is considered a medium that should be equitably shared with others.

What does the law say?

Customary and international law, including the United Nations Charter, have relevance for a country's space activities. Customary law, which is often based on hundreds of years of precedent, serves as the foundation for observed international law. International law includes treaties and conventions, and it provides guidance when deciding what is considered acceptable international behavior and practice. While space law spans only about fifty years, it too draws upon historical customary law and previous international law in forming its fundamental precepts. Although not all new treaties are recognized as being based on customary or international law, if these new treaties remain in effect long enough they can become legal precedent nonetheless.

Much of our recent perspective regarding the rules of outer space is described in four multilateral treaties negotiated through the auspices of the United Nations. The first and most widely cited is the 1967 Outer Space Treaty.[40] The others include the 1968 Agreement on the Rescue of Astronauts, the 1972 Conventions on Liability, and the 1975 Conventions on Registration.[41] Other agreements have addressed specific military issues or have provided a legal framework for acceptable space activities, including the 1972 US/USSR Anti-Ballistic Missile Treaty, the 1973 International Telecommunications Convention, and the 1980 Convention on the Prohibition of Military or Any Other Hostile Use of Environmental Modifications Techniques.[42] Whereas treaties and agreements of this kind have been hailed by some as the model for international agreements and accord, others have criticized them for being conceived in the mindset of Cold War competition.[43]

Despite all the many treaties and international agreements, the one most relevant in shaping our currently held view regarding activities in space is the 1967 Outer Space Treaty. The Outer Space Treaty is more formally known as the Treaty on Principles Governing the Activities of States in the Exploration and Use of Outer Space, Including the Moon and Other Celestial Bodies. As indicated by the length of the title, this treaty tried to reach consensus on a variety of issues involving the use of space. It entered into force on 10 October 1967 and stated broad principles on how outer space was to be used by the international community.[44] Under the Outer Space Treaty, outer space is open to exploration and use by all nations. Additionally, space is not subject to national appropriation and must be used for peaceful purposes. Whereas a number of states maintain that "peaceful purposes" excludes military activities, United States policy has consistently interpreted "peaceful purposes" to mean non-aggressive purposes.[45] As such, international law does not preclude military activity in space. Based on this interpretation, space-based systems may lawfully perform essential functions that facilitate military activities on land, in the air, and on and under the sea.[46] As stated in *Air Force Doctrine Document 2-2*, it has been subsequently inferred from this interpretation that there is no legal prohibition against developing, deploying, or employing weapons in, from, or into space.[47]

Other highlights from the Outer Space Treaty include its legal restrictions on military activities. It banned nuclear and other weapons of mass destruction from space.[48] Additionally, military bases, installations, and fortifications may not be erected, nor may weapons tests be undertaken on natural celestial bodies, which include the earth's moon but not the earth. Military personnel, however, may be employed on natural celestial bodies for research and other activities related to "peaceful purposes," including the ability to perform self-defense or denial measures. Moreover, the Outer Space Treaty contains other important provisions. Brazil was able to campaign for the inclusion of a provision in Article I requiring all countries to share in the benefits resulting from space activities, irrespective of their degree of economic involvement or scientific development.[49]

So the last several decades have provided a useful legal framework for considering what legitimate and acceptable actions in outer space are. Despite this loose framework, not everyone agrees what the framework actually means regarding space strategy. Nevertheless, any future decisions, treaties, or agreements regarding space will draw upon the centuries of customary law and current international law to answer questions on contentious issues. This thought, along with the prevalent use of space by the international community at large, will be critical when formulating a suitable strategic framework for space warfare.

Chapter 2

Contemporary space strategies

Currently there are a variety of competing views regarding space theory and strategy, and the inability to reach a consensus on the issue is not due to lack of vigorous debate. Some strategists have argued for developing a space power theory based on an air power model, while others argue for a space control framework based on the centuries-old precedent of naval strategy. Still others have postulated a space strategy based solely upon specific viewpoints regarding the role of weapons in space.

Because of this menagerie of divergent approaches and viewpoints, it is difficult to determine what exactly our national interests in space are or what kinds of assets are needed to protect those interests. If an overarching and preferably historically based framework could be discerned, a more coherent and meaningful space strategy should result. Without such a framework regarding space, it is to be feared that national resources and military force will be misguided or counterproductive in their application. Depending on which analogy or theoretical approach is selected, a different and distinct space strategy may be formulated in each case. Because of this, the lessons of history will be needed to determine if any of the proposed strategic concepts are indeed salient and useful in the context of warfare in space.

Historical air and sea frameworks

It has been observed that space operations have more in common with the sea and the air than is widely appreciated.[1] For, just as space operations utilize ground facilities, uplinks and downlinks, and the satellites themselves, so naval and air operations also have facilities at home, ships and planes, and facilities abroad. Like international airspace and waters, space is open to all nations, and it is free from the claims of sovereignty and not subject to a nation's appropriation.[2] Because of these similarities, some view the history of sea power and air power as offering true precedents for developing a space strategy.[3] As a consequence of this view, many elements of current space power theory have been derived by handpicking tenets of existing air power and sea power theories.[4]

Air power

While there is no comprehensive and universally acknowledged air power theory on a par with Clausewitz's land power work, Air Marshal Giulio Douhet of Italy is generally credited with developing the first theory of air power.[5] In his book *The Command of the Air*, he contends that aircraft are the solution to strategic and tactical stalemates, and all future wars can be won from the air.[6] The aircraft's superior advantage is said to be its offensive characteristics – freedom of maneuver and speed – which are achieved by operating in the air.[7] Moreover, any defense is futile against the airplane, and "no fortification can possibly offset these [airplanes], which can strike mortal blows into the heart of the enemy with lightning speed."[8] Douhet's final formula for victory included gaining command of the air and then attacking the enemy's industrial and commercial facilities and critical transportation centers and routes, as well as designated civilian population areas.[9]

Albeit Douhet recognized that land, sea, and air forces should cooperate to achieve common objectives, he placed special emphasis on each component achieving results independently.[10] As a consequence, air forces should operate and achieve results "to the complete exclusion of both army and navy."[11] Furthermore, he believed that the airplane could achieve military victory without the efforts of the army or navy, and consequently air forces are "first in order of importance" of all the armed services.[12]

In another view on the proper role of air power, Brigadier General William "Billy" Mitchell stated, "as air covers the whole world, aircraft are able to go anywhere on the planet . . . [and] have set aside all ideas of frontiers."[13] Mitchell assessed that some air operations – such as strategic bombing – can achieve independent results, thereby winning wars by destroying the enemy's warmaking capability and will to fight.[14] Additionally, he believed that the first battles during future wars would be air battles, and the nation that won them was "practically certain to win the whole war."[15]

In a more contemporary view of air power strategy, John A. Warden developed a theory in 1986 that unabashedly asserted the dominance of air power over surface forces. The premise of this theory is that air power possesses the unique capacity to achieve victory with maximum effectiveness and minimum cost.[16] Having an underlying foundation in Clausewitz's center of gravity concept, Warden's theory is characterized by visualizing society as a series of concentric rings. The most important of these rings is at the center and represents the enemy leadership. Because of the leaders' strategic-level decision making ability, military efforts should be directed there, and air power is ideally suited for this mission.[17]

Early thinking about utilizing space forces was based on the assumption that they were merely "high-flying air forces."[18] For example, the term "aerospace" was coined and subsequent doctrine established by just changing "air" to "aerospace" in the US Air Force literature.[19] Credit for this name change is generally given to the Air Force Chief of Staff, General Thomas D. White, who in 1958 first argued that air and space are indivisible, thus the natural environment of the Air Force.[20] White wrote, "In discussing air and space, it should be recognized that there is no division, per se, between the two. For all practical purposes air and space merge, forming a continuous and indivisible field of operations."[21] According to "aerospace integrationists," space power is no different from air power because it delivers similar products to users.[22] As a result, no separate space power theory or definition is warranted, since aerospace power is inclusive of space operations.

Nevertheless, many critics have argued against combining air and space strategic theories, pointing out that propulsive, aerodynamic, and orbital mechanics conditions and requirements make air and space quite distinct media.[23] This thought is manifested by the differing abilities of aircraft and space systems to maneuver and loiter during the conduct of their missions. Disagreements with placing air and space operations under the aerospace umbrella continue. Yet, while implicitly acknowledging that air and space are operationally different, *The Aerospace Force* – the US Air Force's long range strategic plan in 2000 – stated, "Our Service views the flight domain of air and space as a seamless operational medium, and the environmental differences between air and space do not separate employment of aerospace power within them."[24]

Although air and space are different environments, they have an interrelationship and dependency due to shared activities and adjoining boundaries. For instance, no space vehicle can ascend directly into orbit without first traversing the air realm. The history and development of aerospace power theory is therefore a useful example for the derivation of any strategic theory, since it incorporates the interaction between environments and shared activities. Consequently, the lesson to be learned is that any derived theory and strategy of space warfare should consider the dependency between different environments and also be "holistic" in scope, thereby addressing the indirect effects of space operations on other environments, non-space activities, and grand strategy.

Sea power

In emphasizing the similarities between sea and space operations, some strategists have said that the best space strategy may be achieved by simply substituting "space" for "sea" in naval strategy.[25] Yet before we assume that the naval model is indeed applicable for developing the strategic principles of space warfare, what the term "naval" entails must be understood. Naval theory deals with ships, shipbuilding, war at sea, and those military forces associated with navies.[26] Moreover, naval theory and strategy are primarily concerned with the means and methods of employing force at sea to achieve national goals and increase national power and prestige.[27]

Falling within the framework of naval strategy is the concept of sea power. Sea power includes many of the same precepts as the more general naval strategy, but it has a slightly broader scope. Sea power encompasses not only the naval activities listed above, but also the role of auxiliaries, commercial shipping, naval bases, and trained personnel.[28] Sea power is a measure of one nation's ability to use the seas and oceans in defiance of enemies or rivals, and when the term is used in reference to a nation state it means that the state has a high degree of such capability.[29] The roles and missions included within the "sea power" concept have been described as strategic deterrence, sea control, projection of power ashore, and naval presence.[30]

Some have criticized the use of any naval framework for developing a space strategy by saying that the sea–space historical analogy is weak, since ships primarily transport goods and people, whereas spacecraft – with minor exceptions – are built to collect, relay, or transmit information.[31] Granted that this criticism appears to be more valid nowadays, this view fails to recognize that the fundamental tenets of naval strategy were drawn from the Age of Sail, when ships traversed the world's seas and oceans, thereby transporting goods and people and relaying information in the process. A noteworthy example of ships being used to transport information and gather intelligence is when Admiral Nelson traveled all over the Mediterranean Sea looking for Napoleon Bonaparte's fleet. Nelson and his men spent months sailing across the Mediterranean and gathering bits of intelligence, all in the hope of determining the French fleet's location. Eventually Nelson was able to collect the timely intelligence he needed and proceeded to sail off toward Egypt to engage the enemy. As a result of the information gained, Nelson decisively defeated the French fleet at the Battle of the Nile.[32] So while today ships are not used to relay information in the same ways they once were, naval theory and strategy were formulated during a time when they were indeed used for communicating information.

"Schools of thought"

Although air power and sea power frameworks have been used to think about space strategy, other approaches have been used as well. These other approaches are commonly referred to as "schools of thought."[33] The different doctrinal schools of thought correspond to the perceived value of space itself, and from this perception the various underlying precepts of space strategy are induced. Usually, four main schools of thought are given: sanctuary, survivability, control, and high-ground.[34] Even though it is realized that individuals may incorporate one or more of these schools of thought in forming their own personal views, these four different categories prove useful when contemplating military space strategy. Specifically, these schools of thought are frequently referred to when debating whether, and in what manner, space should be weaponized.

Sanctuary

The sanctuary school holds that the primary value of space forces is their capability to "see" within the boundaries of other nations. Since space systems can legally fly high above the sovereign territory of other countries, they can perform treaty verification via their onboard sensors. Additionally, overflight by space systems has not been denied by other states in the past and, accordingly, surveillance and reconnaissance systems provide a stabilizing influence in international relations, especially when verifying arms control compliance between superpowers.[35] Space, therefore, should be designated a war- and weapons-free sanctuary to ensure this stabilizing effect in the future through continued overflight operations.[36]

Survivability

The survivability school is the next doctrinal school of thought.[37] This view emphasizes that space systems are inherently less able to survive than terrestrial assets and forces, and is predicated on three assumptions. The first assumption is that space systems are vulnerable to long range weapons. Second, it is reckoned that space assets cannot effectively use maneuverability or terrestrial barriers to protect themselves. Third, it seems doubtful that states would retaliate over the destruction of a space system because of its lack of political importance. While the survivability viewpoint acknowledges that space is an excellent medium for basing some military systems, space must not be depended upon for essential wartime functions, since space-based systems are not likely to survive hostile attack.[38]

High-ground

The third doctrinal approach is high-ground. Advocates of this school of thought state that domination of the high ground ensures domination of the lower lying areas. Furthermore, since space systems provide a global presence, when coupled with an offensive weapons capability, they can provide a defense against ballistic missiles or deter an adversary's aggressive actions. Consequently, space forces should have a dominant influence during military operations, including the use of offensive weapons and missile defense systems.[39] The high-ground view has been around since the late 1940s and is exemplified by the prevalent belief at the time that the nation that first possessed a space station would be in a position to rule the earth.[40]

Control

The last doctrinal approach is the control school. Control advocates argue outer space's inherent value through analogies with both air and naval strategies.[41] One analogy goes, "Whoever has the capacity to control the air is in a position to exert control over the land and the seas beneath, [and there-fore]. . . whoever has the capacity to control space will likewise possess the capacity to exert control over the surface of the earth."[42] The analogy to sea operations compares space lanes of communications to sea lanes, which must be controlled if a war is to be won. Although the control school model holds that space operations are coequal with those of land, sea, and air, con-trol of space is viewed as essential to ultimately achieve military success.[43]

Limitations of these approaches

Three of the four doctrinal schools – sanctuary, survivability, and high-ground – have serious limitations for strategic thought. Despite their apparent utility in debating the role of weapons in space, each of these approaches fails to provide anything close to a strategic framework for dealing with the many broad and diverse concerns surrounding national interests in space. These different schools of thought are found wanting since they do not address, either explicitly or implicitly, concerns related to diplomacy and econom-ics. For these reasons, the sanctuary, survivability, and high-ground schools prove inadequate to formulate a strategy for space warfare.

At first, the control school approach seems promising. This is because it argues a space strategy, although quite vaguely, through historical analogies to air and naval operations. Since air and naval strategies have the benefit of many years of development, along with the lessons coming from their application during real-world conflicts, the space control approach seems as if it could be applicable. In the end, however, the control school of thought is just a supposition grasping to become a strategy. It is too loose an approach to formulate the needed strategic principles of space warfare, since it lacks a clear understanding of what it is trying to be or say. While "control" is used in its description and refers to ensuring access to lines of communication in space, it does not go beyond this concept to develop other tenets of its strategy and provide a broader strategic context. The control school only hints at a loose analogy to control in air and naval strategies. Yet there is something to be learned from this. Of the four schools of thought, the control school looked the most promising, and it owed its lineage to air and sea strategies. Therefore, a likely guess is that the desired strategic framework for space lies somewhere within either sea power or air power strategies.

Although both air power and sea power have relevant considerations for space operations and activities, they each fail to fully encompass the breadth required to develop a space theory. The air power model, as delineated by the aerospace strategy, takes into account the interrelationships of other forces and environments, which is an important part of the needed "holistic" scope. Its shortcoming is that it primarily has a military focus and lacks considerations for diplomacy, prestige, and commerce. Whereas naval strategy, which includes the sea power concept, addresses some diplomacy, prestige, and commerce issues, it mostly deals with the actions of fleets and consequently tends to have a "sea" and "navy" centered focus. As such, naval strategy does not fully encompass the interaction and dependency of other environments, such as land forces, and therefore lacks the "holistic" scope needed.

It would appear that the previous discussion has been for naught. The two most promising and historically based strategies are found too deficient to enable the formulation of an adequate space strategy. The inadequacies of air and naval strategy – aerospace power primarily having a military focus, and sea power excluding the dependency on other environments and forces – are insurmountable. Nevertheless, there is a strategic framework that incorporates other environments, as aerospace power does, while including diplomacy and prestige concerns, as sea power does. It is maritime strategy.

Maritime strategy

"Maritime" pertains to the overarching activities and interests regarding the seas and oceans of the world. These activities and interests include the inter-relationships of science, technology, cartography, industry, economics, trade, politics, international affairs, imperial growth, communications, migration, international law, social affairs, and leadership.[44] Additionally, maritime strategy is inclusive of the interaction between sea and land. Since many national and local economies have historically depended upon coastal ports for trade and economic well-being, nation states developed the need to protect their maritime trade with fleets. Naval strategy, therefore, is but a subset of maritime strategy. Since maritime strategy appears to more closely match the broad and diverse interests in space, especially when compared to either air power or sea power theories, a maritime strategy will be used to develop a strategic framework for space. The next question to be asked is "What model for maritime strategy will be used?"

A plethora of authors have used the work of Rear Admiral Alfred Thayer Mahan (1840–1914), particularly *The Influence of Sea Power upon History, 1660–1783*, in this effort. Mahan was an American naval officer, historian, and strategist, who has been commonly regarded at the time and since as the most important analyst of sea power. Mahan's work is credited with linking maritime and naval activities to national and international issues, along with laying out principles for formulating naval strategy.[45] His writings cover many areas, including national policy, sea power, sea control, offensive versus defensive operations, speed and mobility, communications, trade, concentration of force, and strategic positions.[46] Indeed, Mahan's work has received high acclaim and has been extensively quoted, especially in the United States, to promote a variety of ideas. Unfortunately, in their search for axioms on strategy, modern-day strategists have used, misused, superseded, broadened, and modified Mahan's original concepts.[47] Properly understood, Mahan's strategic theory insists that the "proper sphere" of the fleet is offensive operations. Additionally, he gives little attention to matters that are outside the direct action of navies and fleets. Since Mahan does not adequately account for the interaction of land armies and the interdependence of other environments, his strategic context is in fact more naval than maritime in scope. So if not Mahan, then who?

Though not in unanimity, many historians have recognized Sir Julian Stafford Corbett (1854–1922) for his coherent and convincing exposition of maritime principles.[48] Corbett was a British theorist and strategist, who was renowned for his 1911 work titled *Some Principles of Maritime Strategy* and is acclaimed as Great Britain's greatest maritime strategist. Corbett gave a series of lectures to the Royal Naval College in Greenwich that involved the relationship of naval strategy to the general theory of warfare and, because of this in part, he became the acknowledged expert on tactics in the Age of Sail.[49] *Some Principles of Maritime Strategy* received notoriety for its "fusion of history and strategy" in discussing maritime strategic principles.[50] Even though Corbett wrote on many of the same issues as Mahan, Corbett's theory and strategies are said by many to be more accurate and complete than Mahan's work, while also being "more logically developed."[51] In comparison with Mahan's work, Corbett's more accurately reflects maritime theory and strategy, since he addresses the navy's interaction with armies and those concerns that are affected indirectly by naval operations. Thus, Corbett's strategic framework provides the needed holistic scope.

Therefore, in specifying a maritime strategy, Corbett's ideas and principles from *Some Principles of Maritime Strategy* will be used. It is noteworthy that Carl von Clausewitz, who wrote *On War*, had a significant influence on Corbett's maritime theory and strategy. Several times in his work, Corbett paraphrases Clausewitz or quotes him directly. It may be asked, therefore, why not use Clausewitz instead of Corbett for a framework of space strategy, since Corbett's work seems to rely heavily on Clausewitz's theory and ideas. While Corbett was indeed influenced by Clausewitz, Corbett provides a strategic context that is unique to the maritime environment and, as a result, Corbett clarifies and elucidates the strategy of warfare where the land and sea meet.

Although it is argued that a maritime inspired framework most fully embraces the strategic issues of space operations, it is not argued that either air or naval strategies cannot be used to develop a space strategy, only that they are not the best strategic frameworks for doing so. Moreover, space is a unique environment, and any historically based strategic framework – whether naval, air, or maritime – cannot realistically be taken verbatim in its application to space strategy. Only the most fundamental concepts of maritime strategy, therefore, will and should be used to derive the strategic principles of space warfare.

Chapter 3

Maritime strategic principles

Since the interests and activities of spacefaring nations are similar to those of seafaring nations of years past, it is presumed that space and maritime strategies will share similar principles also. It is not presumed, however, that operations in space are the same as those at sea, since physical and environmental considerations definitely preclude that possibility. Therefore, although the theory and strategic principles of space and maritime operations may in fact be similar, the operational and technological differences probably necessitate that their tactics will be quite different. The application of maritime strategic concepts to space is nothing new. Some strategists have hinted for years that maritime concepts like chokepoints, mining, and blockades have a place within the strategy of space warfare.[1] Yet as a separate medium for potential conflict, space warfare requires a context and lexicon all its own. Consequently, the application of maritime strategy must be thoughtfully considered before blindly accepting any of its historical principles.

Despite these caveats, the best maritime strategic framework to begin thinking about space strategy, along with the ensuing principles, is still Corbett's work. As hinted at by the title chosen, *Some Principles of Maritime Strategy*, he would probably disagree with any assessment that his work should be used to describe *all the principles* of maritime strategy. Additionally, Corbett wrote the "Green Pamphlet," a condensed version of his strategic principles that was issued to students at the Royal Naval War College. Since this smaller work complements the book and serves as a more direct and succinct format in communicating many of his ideas, the "Green Pamphlet" will also be used in describing his strategic concepts and principles.[2]

Corbett makes it clear that theory and strategic principles are never a substitute for good judgment and experience. Like Clausewitz, Corbett believed that a theory-based strategy helps determine a coherent plan for war, but should not be blindly trusted in action.[3] Individual thought and common sense should remain masters, providing guidance when the situation is uncertain.[4] Furthermore, theory's practical value is its ability to assist in acquiring a broad outlook, whereby the factors of a sudden predicament may be rapidly ascertained.[5] In the end, strategic theory must be able not only to make sense of what has occurred in the past, but also to provide some prediction of what is likely to be in the future.[6]

Corbett's strategic theory and principles cover a wide gamut of concerns. He notes how military operations must support political and national objectives.[7] Corbett believed that offensive and defensive strategies are complementary to each other and that land and sea forces must work toward a common military objective. Also, he states that one's access to and use of lines of communication are the most important factor in maritime operations, and consequently this access and use must be protected. The other principles he describes relate to the methods of protecting lines of communications, as well as the likely actions of an adversary. What follows next are those ideas and concepts Corbett emphasizes most.

National power implications

Corbett writes of the national power implications of maritime operations during both peacetime and wartime. As with Clausewitz, Corbett recognizes that both land and sea operations are influenced by national politics and interests. Corbett observes, "War is a form of political intercourse, a continuation of foreign politics which begins when force is introduced to attain our ends."[8] In emphasizing how warfare and national power are intertwined, Corbett declares that the grand strategy of war cannot be decided apart from domestic politics and diplomacy.[9]

Besides addressing the obvious impact on naval forces, Corbett repeatedly highlights the role of maritime action on trade and economics. Interfering with the enemy's trade is not only a means of exerting economic pressure, but also serves as a means of overthrowing the enemy's "power of resistance."[10] A nation's economy is an important factor in sustaining a protracted war, and he observes, "All things being equal, it is the longer purse that wins" and, as a consequence, naval warfare must attempt to undermine the financial position of the enemy.[11] Moreover, because a nation's commerce and finance capability is a major factor in determining relative power and influence among countries, naval operations must concentrate on the capture and destruction of the enemy's maritime trade and property, whether public or private.[12] Successful naval operations should put economic pressure on the enemy from the start of the war. This is contrasted to land warfare, which he says puts economic pressure on the enemy mostly after a decisive victory.[13] Since economics affects the relative wealth between nations and the object of naval warfare is to control sea lines of communication, particularly those related to commercial and economic activities, Corbett deduces that naval actions can affect the balance of wealth and power among nation states.[14]

Contrary to the popular thought of many of his peers, Corbett thought that even minor fleet actions could affect diplomacy, economics, and the balance of power between states. Since a state's relative standing and diplomatic effectiveness result, in part, from its economic strength and the extent of its commercial trade, minor naval actions that upset maritime trade – especially along trade routes – can affect this balance.[15] For example, Corbett did not view past British naval actions along the European seaboard as a design for permanent conquest, but as a method of disturbing the enemy's plans and strengthening the position of Great Britain and its allies.[16] Such harassing operations may be manifested by small scale commerce raiding – *guerre de course* – or it may include a more sizable "disposal force." In either case, the effect is meant to achieve national objectives at the expense of the enemy.

Interdependence with other operations

Although stating that naval action is indeed important during wartime, Corbett observes that sea and land operations are interdependent, and therefore they must work together toward accomplishing political objectives. The "closest cooperation" of ground and sea forces is necessary, since naval strategy and operations are just a subset of overall wartime operations. As a result, the purpose of maritime strategy is to determine the "mutual relations of your army and navy in a plan of war."[17] This interdependence cannot be overstated. One of the reasons a maritime framework was chosen was because it encompasses a holistic approach, and here Corbett's idea of maritime operations working in conjunction with land forces substantiates the correctness of the decision.

Differing from other maritime strategists of his day, like Mahan, Corbett says it is paramount for naval strategy to work within the overall wartime strategy, since it is almost impossible for war to be decided by naval action alone.[18] Since people live upon the land and not upon the sea, the greatest issues between nations at war have always been decided – except in the rarest of cases – either by "what your army can do against your enemy's territory and national life, or else by the fear of what the fleet makes it possible for your army to do."[19] Therefore, although fleet actions can significantly impact the enemy and his economy, it is unlikely that naval actions will solely determine a war's outcome; for more often than not, a war is only concluded after land forces are put on enemy soil. Because of the "delicate interactions" between the army and navy, they should be effectively considered as one weapon.[20]

Maritime communications

Maritime communications pertain to those lines of communication by which the flow of "national life is maintained ashore" and, therefore, they have a greater meaning and are not analogous to lines of communications traditionally used by land armies.[21] Although maritime communications include lines of supply and trade, they also include lines of communication that are of a strategic nature and are thus critical for a state's survival. Corbett describes three types of maritime communications: the communications to support the fleet; those required by an overseas army; and trade routes.[22] The objective of naval warfare, according to Corbett, is controlling maritime communications for one's own commerce and negatively impacting the enemy's economic interests. By occupying the enemy's maritime communications and closing his points of distribution, the enemy's "national life afloat" is destroyed.[23] Emphasizing the importance of sea lines of communication, Corbett believed in the vital need to protect one's access to these lines of communication, and, if the enemy's fleet is in a position to render them unsafe, the enemy must be "put out of action."[24]

Corbett writes that the lines of communication used in land warfare are quite different from those used in naval warfare. Ashore, the lines of communication of each belligerent tend to run approximately in opposite directions, until they meet in the theater of operations. At sea, however, the lines of communication of each belligerent tend to run approximately parallel or may even be one and the same.[25] Because sea lines of communication between belligerents are often shared, Corbett declares, "We cannot attack those of the enemy without defending our own."[26] As a result, naval strategy has as its primary purpose the control of maritime communications, so the fleet is mainly occupied with guarding one's own sea lines of communications and seizing those of the enemy.[27]

Command of the sea

Closely related to maritime communications is the strategic concept of "command of the sea." Since the inherent value of the sea is as a means of communication, the object of naval warfare must always be to either secure the command of the sea or prevent the enemy from securing it.[28] Consequently, command of the sea is the "control of maritime communications, whether for commercial or military purposes."[29] Despite the prevalent use of the phrase during his day, Corbett believed "command of the sea" was in fact "too loose an expression," and that a phrase that expressed his thought more clearly was "control of passage and communications."[30] To fully understand command of the sea, it must be appreciated that operations on the land and sea are fundamentally different, as the sea cannot be subjected to political dominion or ownership.[31] Furthermore, a nation cannot subsist upon the oceans, nor can others be excluded from it.[32] Key to understanding Corbett's thinking is that command of the sea actually only exists in a state of war.[33] For if one claims command of the sea during times of peace, it is done rhetorically and only means one state has adequate naval positions and a sizable fleet to secure command once hostilities are commenced.[34]

Corbett differentiates the types of command based on the size of the area – general or local – and based on the duration in which it is achieved – temporary or permanent. General command is achieved when the enemy is no longer able to "act dangerously" against one's lines of passage and communications or even to defend his own, and as a result, the enemy is unable to seriously interfere with one's trade, military, or diplomatic activities.[35] On the other hand, local command means that maritime communications are sufficiently protected to prevent the enemy from interfering with passage and communications within a specific and somewhat limited geographic area. In considering the duration for which general or local command is achieved, temporary command means that command is achieved for a specific period of time to accomplish a stated political goal or military objective. In contrast, permanent command means that time is no longer a vital factor in the wartime situation and maritime environment.[36]

In cases when command happens to be both general and permanent, this is only achievable through the annihilation of the enemy's fleet; nevertheless, even in this situation, the enemy can still act. For "no degree of naval superiority can ensure our communications against sporadic attack from detached cruisers, or even raiding squadrons if they are boldly led and are prepared to risk destruction."[37] Therefore, command that is both general and permanent means only that the enemy cannot seriously interfere with maritime trade and naval operations to affect the war's outcome.[38] Whereas offensive operations are needed to gain general and permanent command, defensive actions can be used to gain local or temporary command by concentrating forces where the enemy fleet is weak or not located.[39]

Although gaining and exercising command of the sea is important for protecting one's maritime communications, Corbett observes that history has shown the normal state of affairs is not a commanded sea but an uncommanded one, indicating that command is normally in dispute.[40] When command is in dispute it means that one's own forces have preponderance, the enemy has preponderance, or neither side has preponderance. To effectively dispute command the weaker opponent may concentrate his forces within a local area, for a specified duration, to gain a relative military advantage. Consequently, the weaker force is merely attempting to gain local or temporary command against a stronger opponent.

Strategy of the offense

Offensive strategy, according to Corbett, is called for when political objectives necessitate acquiring or wresting something from the enemy. Because it is the more "effective" form of warfare, offensive strategy should be employed by the stronger power.[41] The stronger power can use offensive actions to obtain positive results, while also attaining the "strength and energy" that comes from initiating attack.[42] Corbett believed offensive operations that seek a decision against the enemy's fleet are key to securing command that is both permanent and general.[43] While nine times out of ten it is better to seek out the enemy's fleet, the most effective way of seeking the enemy fleet is to seize his vital lines of communication.[44] Like other strategists of his time, Corbett thought the attacker gains initiative through offensive operations, thereby attaining the advantage of "dexterity or stealth." Nevertheless, he advised that the offensive must not be confused with initiative itself, since it is possible to seize the initiative under certain circumstances by assuming a defensive strategy.[45]

Despite the advantages of offensive strategy, Corbett warns those naval professionals who might value the offensive at the expense of everything else, by noting that fleets are difficult to replace and should not be "thrown away in ill-considered offensives."[46] Furthermore, a superior force looking for a decisive victory will probably find the enemy in a position where he cannot easily be affected, since throughout naval history attempts to seek the enemy fleet for a decisive battle have been thwarted by the enemy retiring to the safety of his coasts and ports.[47] If offensive action is sought when the enemy is in a readily defendable position, a "heavy cost" will be paid for such action.[48]

Strategy of the defense

More extensively than any other subject on which he writes, Corbett describes and amplifies the proper role of defensive strategy in naval warfare. Defense is called for when political objectives necessitate preventing the enemy from acquiring something or achieving a political objective.[49] Because defense is the "stronger" form of warfare, a defensive strategy enables inferior naval forces to achieve notable results, especially considering that if this same inferior force undertook offensive operations, it would probably result in its own destruction. The main disadvantage of a defensive strategy becomes apparent when it is the sole strategy used during a war, since using only a defensive strategy can be detrimental to the morale of one's forces. Once a defensive strategy ceases to be a means of reducing the enemy's power of attack, it loses its inherent strength and advantage.

Being part of the total war plan, offensive and defensive strategies are mutually supportive and indispensable in achieving ultimate victory. For example, Corbett postulates that a truly offensive strategy cannot be fully achieved without defending one's lines of operation and communication – the very lines that make offensive operations possible.[50] The inherent advantages of the defense are proximity to one's base of operations and supply; familiar surroundings; and the initiative and surprise achieved by an offensive counter-attack, which Corbett views as the "soul" of effective defensive strategy.[51] Because defensive operations are the "stronger" form of war, a weaker navy should use them until becoming strong enough to assume the offensive after reconstituting its fleet or gaining the support of allies.[52] Defensive strategy requires an attitude of alert expectation, and Corbett believed that one should await the moment when the enemy exposes himself. At such a moment, a successful counter-attack should be launched, thereby crippling the enemy fleet and allowing one to take the offensive.[53] Furthermore, by assuming defensive positions in some locales, more forces can be used elsewhere for offensive operations.[54]

Despite the many apparent advantages of defensive strategy, Corbett was concerned that some naval professionals of his time had exalted the offensive into a fetish, to the detriment of the defensive. Contrary to what many naval strategists and officers of his day thought, Corbett believed defensive strategy is a non-passive strategy, since at its heart is the counter-attack.[55] Defensive strategy should not be shunned or avoided, but should be embraced. According to Corbett, an understanding of the nature of warfare indicates that, when the defensive is required, it will be at a critical time.[56]

The power of isolation

Like Clausewitz before him, Corbett classifies wars according to whether the object was limited or unlimited in aims. Limited war is where "we merely seek to take from the enemy some particular part of his possessions, or interests." On the other hand, unlimited war is where a nation seeks to completely overthrow its adversary, forcing it to submit to avoid destruction.[57] Corbett emphasizes that it is critical to determine the nature of a war, to ensure it is not mistaken for, or made into, something it can never be.[58]

Limited wars, he believes, can be successfully conducted when the attacking belligerent has overwhelming maritime superiority and can prevent one's adversary from escalating the war into a conflict that is unlimited. Corbett goes on to say:

> A war may be limited not only because the objective is too limited to call for the whole national force, but also because the sea may be made to present an insuperable physical obstacle to the whole national force being brought to bear. That is to say, a war may be limited physically by the strategical isolation of the object, as well as morally by its comparative unimportance.[59]

Therefore, for island powers or powers separated by seas and oceans, a war with limited intent should be initiated only when one commands the sea to such a degree as to isolate the distant object, thereby making the invasion of one's own home territory impossible. Corbett uses Great Britain's naval history as a classic example of this thought, especially with regards to failed French attempts to invade Britain. Because of the non-escalatory nature of a limited war that remains limited, the state initiating a limited war requires the "power of isolation" to ensure the necessary defense against any potential use of an enemy's unlimited counterstroke.[60] Summarizing this point, he notes, "He that commands the sea is at great liberty and may take as much or as little of the war as he will".[61]

Disputing command

While not calling into question the need to conduct offensive operations and the requirement of securing command of the sea to achieve naval victory, Corbett envisions that less capable naval powers can still achieve substantial political or military results. For when conditions are such that one's relative strength is inadequate to secure command of the sea, it can be quite advantageous to dispute command.[62] It is wrong to assume, he believed, that if one is unable to win command of the sea one therefore loses it, since the normal condition of war is for command to be in dispute. For instance, a less capable fleet can prevent the enemy from securing positive results, and consequently protract the conflict until more forces can be brought to bear and an offensive strategy can be assumed.[63] Examples of disputing command include attacking commerce along sea lanes and coastal raiding against another country's seaboard.[64] Both types of actions are meant to disturb the enemy's plans, regardless of the size of his fleet, while strengthening one's own national power and prestige at the same time.[65] Corbett argues that limited maritime threats and actions could play a significant role in complicating the overall strategic options of a major continental opponent. Harassing and nuisance operations against a more capable adversary may prevent him from gaining command that is either permanent or general in nature.

Also related to this idea of disputing command is the "fleet in being" concept.[66] For a small navy, it is important to avoid a decisive battle against a more capable fleet; therefore, the less capable navy should be kept "in being" until the situation develops in one's favor.[67] Consequently, a defensive strategy for a relatively small maritime power means nothing more than keeping one's fleet actively in being – not merely in existence, but in active and vigorous life.[68] Corbett thought the true advantage of a fleet in being is its mobility and untiring aggressive spirit, and contrary to some interpretations, it does not mean merely keeping one's naval forces in port. By keeping the fleet in being and avoiding large-scale engagements against a more capable fleet, a smaller navy can conduct minor attacks against maritime communications or coastal possessions, therefore thwarting the enemy's attempt to gain command of the sea.[69]

Strategic positions

Like both land and naval strategists before him, Corbett writes on the use of strategic positions. Victory at sea is dependent upon the relative strength of one's force to the enemy's, along with the exploitation of positions. Among "positions," he includes naval bases, maritime ports of trade and commerce, and focal areas where trade routes tend to converge.[70] These strategic positions influence the conduct of either commerce or the execution of naval warfare. If correctly exploited for military advantage, strategic positions allow a naval force to restrict the amount of enemy force to be dealt with, thus creating favorable conditions for battle.[71] Exploiting positions related to commerce has a twofold effect: it affects the enemy's long-term warmaking potential, and it often forces the enemy to engage one's superior force at a desired time and place.[72] Instead of seeking out the enemy's fleet for a decisive battle, it is more effective to control his ports and maritime chokepoints, consequently threatening his commerce and potentially luring his fleet into battle on terms favorable to oneself.[73]

Blockades

In a similar vein, Corbett writes on blockading some strategic positions. Blockades are of two types: the close blockade and the open blockade. The first type closes the enemy's commercial ports or prevents him from putting to sea, and this strategy primarily exhibits elements of defensive strategy, since it prevents one's enemy from doing something. Despite being defensive in nature, a close blockade can also be used to force the enemy fleet to sea to counter this action, and therefore serves as a method of securing command.[74] Therefore, it also has some elements of offensive strategy. Corbett writes, "By closing his commercial ports we exercise the highest power of injuring him which the command of the sea can give us".

The enemy must either submit to the close blockade or fight to release himself.[75] The inherent weakness of the close blockade is its arrested offensive posture or the defensive attitude it assumes.[76] Methods of achieving a close blockade include ships that threaten offensive action, mining, and block ships – also known as "sinkers."[77] If the close blockade is employed successfully, local or temporary command can be achieved.

On the other hand, the open blockade is a means for a stronger navy to force the opposing fleet to put to sea by occupying the distant and common sea lines of communications. Because its intent includes the acquisition of the enemy's communication routes, it is primarily offensive in nature.[78] Corbett notes that it is better to sit upon his homeward bound trade routes, thus costing him trade or making his fleet engage in a decisive battle, since it is difficult to seek out an enemy who habitually retires to the safety of his ports.[79] By forcing a decisive battle through employment of the open blockade, general command of the sea can be attained. Furthermore, utilizing an open blockade allows for better concealment of one's forces and is therefore better for laying a trap for the enemy.[80] In choosing between the close and open blockades, it must be ascertained whether the need calls for a primarily offensive or defensive strategy, along with which type of blockade is more economical and efficient in its application.[81]

Cruisers

Though they receive somewhat scant mention, Corbett writes on the use of cruisers. As established by his maritime theory, the purpose of naval warfare is to control maritime communications, and therefore a means of establishing this control is required.[82] For Corbett, this is achieved through the cruiser. Cruisers are those ships that have sufficient endurance for long, independent deployments to deter and thwart enemy commerce raiding and protect maritime communications.[83] Furthermore, the means of enforcing an open blockade and stopping the enemy's maritime trade are the affairs of cruisers. Because of the expansive area involved when attempting to control passage and communications, Corbett believed cruisers should be built in significant numbers to cover the numerous maritime routes and coastlines.

Corbett bolsters his argument by citing the historical example of Admiral Nelson of Great Britain, who understood the fundamental and necessary role of cruisers. Nelson incessantly called for more cruisers in the Mediterranean Sea, and if he did not have sufficient numbers of cruisers to exercise command he would pull off ships from the battle fleet to perform the cruiser mission.[84] Corbett agreed with Nelson's assessment and believed whole-heartedly that ships should be pulled off from the battle fleet to control maritime communications, even if the fleet was reduced to the minimum allowable force as a consequence.[85]

More remarkably, Corbett theorizes that since the cruiser accomplishes the primary goal of naval warfare, the purpose of the battle fleet is to protect cruisers and the ships that support them.[86] This thought indeed was counter to conventional strategic thought of his day. Because of the primacy of the cruiser's mission, even the battleship is relegated to a position of secondary importance.[87] In countering the argument that "command of the sea depends upon battleships," he notes that, while a battle fleet is needed to counter the enemy's battle fleet, cruisers are nonetheless the means of exercising control of maritime communications and are therefore more vital.[88]

Dispersal and concentration

Cruisers must operate in an expansive maritime environment to control the many routes of passage and communication. To accomplish this, Corbett argues, naval forces must disperse to cover the widest extent possible yet be able to rapidly concentrate overwhelming force when needed.[89] Therefore, navies must be able to cover the widest possible areas, while preserving an "elastic cohesion" to rapidly condense.[90] No matter how much the war plan calls for close concentration of naval forces, commerce protection necessitates dispersal of forces, and this means that concentration is in tension with dispersal at all times.[91] Such a strategic use of concentration and dispersal in warfare allows for the engagement of the enemy's central mass when needed, while preserving the flexibility to control maritime communications and to meet the enemy's minor attacks in several areas at once.[92]

This concept of dispersal and concentration is quite different from the principle of concentration within land warfare theory, which usually evokes the idea of massing or grouping forces.[93] Although naval concentration means assembling the "the utmost force at the right time and place," it includes the ability to stop the concentrating process and rapidly shift the direction of naval forces.[94] In paraphrasing Mahan, Corbett writes, "Such is concentration reasonably understood – not huddled together like a drove of sheep, but distributed with a regard to a common purpose, and linked together by the effectual energy of a single will."[95] Furthermore, by holding back on the massing of ships, there is less indication of how and where the naval forces are to be concentrated, thus denying the enemy the knowledge of the fleet's actual distribution and intention at any given moment.[96]

Weaknesses of using maritime strategy

It is a tenet of this work that, because space and maritime activities have common strategic interests, they probably share common strategic principles of warfare. Despite the apparent strengths of using a historically based maritime framework, there are weaknesses in using such a model for space strategy. The first weakness is Corbett's view of international relations. Whereas he addresses at great length the role of maritime operations with regard to international security, the view he presents is one of "haves" and "have nots." To an inordinate degree, he addresses the dynamic interaction of those states with the most power and capability with those states with less. This bipolar approach does prove useful when considering economic and military activities between competing nations, but it fails to fully elucidate the proper strategy between near-peer competitors or medium powers. This bipolar approach has the tendency to lead to the improper conclusion that "if a maritime power could not do everything in a war, it could do nothing."[97] Moreover, not all relationships between countries have to be adversarial, since international cooperation may at times be in the interest of two or more parties. Depending on one's preferred model of international relations, this weakness in Corbett's view of the world may lead to doubting if his maritime model can be used in today's more multinational and cooperative foreign policy environment.

Another notable weakness in using Corbett's strategic framework is the apparent disparity in technological sophistication between space and maritime operations. It is not implied that naval ships of today are not sophisticated or technologically advanced, but in general they do not compare to the advanced technology within most spacecraft. The technological sophistication required for military space operations seems more commensurate with those of air operations. It stands to reason, therefore, that the tactics and techniques to be employed in space should be closer to those of air operations, rather than maritime operations.

So, if maritime operations seem to have little applicability at the tactical level of space warfare, what good is it to the warfighter? The answer lies in an apparent paradox. At the tactical level of warfare, space and air activities are more similar but, at the strategic level of warfare, space and maritime activities are more similar. This realization may help explain why there has been such past difficulty in discerning a strategic theory of space warfare. While the technological and tactical disparity between space and maritime operations is a shortcoming, there is a benefit from this also. The benefit is that the strategic principles of space warfare can be formulated leaving aside technology concerns and the precedent of tactics, which tend to change with the passage of time anyway. So using a maritime strategy as a framework actually increases the likelihood of deriving an enduring theory and strategy of space warfare.

Part II

Strategic principles of space warfare

Chapter 4

Space is tied to national power

The dearth of historical examples regarding military actions in space makes it difficult to discern a fundamentally sound and thoughtful space strategy. There have not been wars in space, where powers have overtly destroyed another's space assets through offensive action. Although decades of experience in space have provided mankind with some hint of what a strategic framework for space warfare should be, this limited experience is not enough. Yet by observing that the strategic interests of space and maritime activities have readily apparent similarities, maritime strategy can be used as a template for formulating space strategy. Therefore, the ideas that are presented in the following chapters use centuries of maritime experience and thought, while giving deference to what has been already learned to date about our interests and activities in outer space.

The range and pervasiveness of activities in space have resulted in these activities becoming critical, and therefore they have become tied to national power. National power is the ability of a nation to influence others through international diplomacy, economic incentives or pressure, information services, or through the threat or application of military force. More simply put, power is the ability to get one's way. National power is not an absolute, but only has meaning relative to others. Because of the breadth of concerns and issues dealt with, national power is directly linked to one's long-term national security.

Although power and influence are often discussed in the context of internationally recognized nation states, others can achieve some power-like effects through their space activities. Since international diplomacy is influenced, in part, by domestic politics, those who can influence domestic politics need to be considered as well. For example, large corporations and non-governmental organizations frequently can influence space activities, whether by virtue of their extensive roles in space-based business and commerce or by their roles in shaping space regulatory policy.

Ultimately, the focus of this work is on developing strategic thought regarding space warfare. Although it is tempting to jump right into the methods of achieving a military victory in the space environment, such an approach would fail to recognize the actual nature of warfare. War is a political instrument, and consequently considerations that are relevant to policy and politics are relevant to warfare as well.[1] As Clausewitz asserts, "The political object is the goal, war is the means of reaching it, and means can never be considered in isolation from their purpose."[2] The grand strategy of war cannot be considered in isolation, and actions leading up to the opening of hostilities will help define and determine the ultimate military strategy. Space warfare, therefore, must be concerned with events during peace as well as war. If space does in fact have implications for national power as previously stated, then it stands to reason that is should also have implications for each instrument of national power – diplomatic, economic, information, and military.[3] For this reason, it is useful to discuss space national interests according to each of the instruments of national power. In those cases when national objectives can be achieved through non-military means, like diplomatic, information, and economic efforts, this is effectively winning without fighting. Such an achievement, the Chinese strategic master Sun Tzu (fourth century BC) says, is the acme of skill and power.[4]

Diplomacy

The term "politics" applies to the domestic political activities of sovereign states or local governments. On the other hand, "diplomacy" applies to the conduct of negotiations between states or governments. Domestic politics help shape domestic policies, which in turn drive the efforts of diplomacy. Depending on the results of these diplomatic endeavors, politics and policy may themselves be influenced in turn.

The competing activities and interests of countries have always impacted diplomacy, as well as eventually determining which nation states have the most power and influence. Space is no different in this regard. When the Space Age was first burgeoning, it quickly became an arena where nations jockeyed for position. During the late 1950s and through the 1960s, the Soviet Union and United States' race for preeminence in space combined nationalistic fervor and political expediency. Although the reasons frequently given for placing the first satellites in orbit around the earth were ostensibly scientific, it was noted that a state's presence in space provided it with more global influence. During this timeframe, space became a "Cold War battlefield" where engineers and scientists fought for national prestige and global influence.[5] This desire for greater global influence caused both superpowers to increase their presence in space, while attempting to outdo the achievements of the other. Furthermore, the emergence of these two countries as space powers gave them unprecedented influence in shaping international policy concerning the uses of space. For instance, both countries were able to reach an agreement on the permissible uses of intercontinental ballistic missiles, which travel through the lower regions of outer space. Since both had a significant presence in space, these two governments could determine an internationally accepted strategy of mutual deterrence involving the passage of nuclear weapons through space. Although the Cold War has subsequently ended, the lessons from it indicate that those with the largest stakes and interests have the most influence and decision making power.

This same lesson is still relevant. Of late, some countries see the need for an active space industry and commercial capability to ensure that their interests are promoted among the global community. The European Union's program to put in place a constellation of satellites to compete with the United States Global Positioning System (GPS) constellation is a case in point. The European constellation, called Galileo, is to provide similar positioning, navigation, and timing services to commercial and military activities alike. The primary reason given for the program is to ensure the critical services are provided, even if the United States decides to deny their positioning services.[6] Yet, based on the lessons of the past, the reason also includes the desire for more presence in space and the greater diplomatic influence that results from such presence. Because of the increased role of the European Union, those countries involved will have a greater say in negotiating and deciding on contentious issues, such as the allocation of frequencies to be used by space-based communication systems.

Another example of this thought is the Chinese space program. The Chinese government's policy has noted the link between an ambitious manned space program and its national strategy.[7] Their policy has attached great importance to space activities, believing that these activities impact economic, national security, science and technology, and social progress.[8] To achieve its national goals, China's multi-decade plan calls for a manned space program, including the establishment of a space-based laboratory and eventually setting up a permanent space station.[9] Such an increased presence in space is seen as promoting the diplomatic interests of the Chinese government and their national security concerns, all in an effort to garner greater prestige.[10] Whereas some international observers worry that greater Chinese presence and diplomatic influence is the harbinger of the start of another space race, others observe that the race is not with the United States, which is currently too far ahead technologically to really care about China's ambitions.[11] Nonetheless, their plan does suggest a desire for more global influence, and this realization may motivate countries like India to undertake an ambitious manned space program also.

Economic Impact

As with diplomacy, economic related space activities and national power are inextricably linked. This manifests itself in primarily two ways: the first through the development of a high-technological work force and industry, and the second through the commerce and trade that are conducted using space-based assets. Both of these areas have subtleties in how national power is affected and how they ultimately affect if and how war is fought in space.

In today's global economy, having and maintaining a competitive workforce is a critical factor. Because of this, some governments have sought to increase the number of their people who are educated and trained in high-technology career fields. Such education and training are often deemed essential for having a growing and robust domestic economy, especially one able to weather global economic downturns. For instance, the United States' race to get a man on the moon had the added benefit of increasing the interest in engineering and scientific fields of study among college students, while also increasing the overall technical expertise of the available workforce. Along with the sizable influx of government spending for this grand undertaking, there was an implicit expectation to employ and train as great a number of people as possible in the process.[12] Additionally, the National Air and Space Administration built operations and support centers all over the country and hired a workforce to support the national agenda. This expansion in infrastructure and workforce had the spillover effect that allowed the aerospace and commercial airline industry to expand during this time. From an economic perspective, the race for the moon made sense.

In China today, there is a similar understanding that space interests can promote economic interests. A goal of the Chinese government is to improve their domestic economy, and their space program is meant not only to instill national pride, but to create jobs too. The Chinese leadership is hoping that their investment of manpower and resources will have a spillover effect that benefits their budding commercial space launch program.[13] China has a reason for this hope: the commercial satellite industry, both building them and launching them, is expected to continue to increase in the years to come. Much of this growth is expected to support space operations in low-earth orbits, as the telecommunications industry and demand for remote sensing services continue to grow.[14] The Chinese leadership hopes that this investment in manpower and resources will increase future financial revenues, as well as the quality and number of available jobs produced in China.

Besides the benefits to the domestic workforce, there are benefits resulting directly from space-enabled commerce and trade. As exemplified by the size and success of businesses that rely on space-based technology, satellites are able to profitably relay data and information. In many cases, the communication services provided by these satellites are in locales where using fiber optic or telephone lines would prove impractical. Because of the advantages of using satellites, some counties and companies have expanded their available service area for space-based communications to parts of the world that were previously inaccessible to other methods of communication.

A greater competition for "limited" space resources has resulted, in part, from the fact that space can be used and exploited for economic gain. This competition has caused some to seek the most desirable orbital locations for their satellites, such as geostationary orbits. Because the number of the most valuable orbital locations is perceived to be finite, international regulation and oversight are used to allocate geostationary orbital locations, along with some operating frequencies. This is done with the intent to distribute these limited resources equitably.[15]

Information as power

Information activities related to space operations can influence national power and security. The term "information" refers to facts, data, or instructions in any medium or form, along with their transfer and the meaning assigned to them.[16] One method of influencing others results from the positive benefits of prestige coming after a successful space launch or from actual information services being provided by space systems. Admittedly, prestige is not frequently thought of as falling within the "information" category, but the influence within the domestic and international community resulting from any perceived achievement can indeed provide a government with greater influence. In a military context, some might lump prestige into the category of psychological or information warfare, but any benefits coming from prestige can occur just as much during peace as war. So thinking of prestige in the context of warfare alone is incorrect. More commonly understood are information activities that are used to support intelligence gathering activities. Such operations can promote national security – often through intelligence, surveillance, and reconnaissance missions – and these missions are also just as important during peace as during war. Therefore, in considering space-based activities and their role in national power, it is useful to differentiate these activities' impact on prestige from that on national security.

Prestige

The history of the United States in space has lessons for considering the benefits of prestige through accomplishment, along with the repercussions of failure. During the 1950s, there was a strong desire within the Eisenhower administration to be the first to launch a satellite into orbit, and it was said it would be a blow to national prestige if the United States was not first in this accomplishment.[17] This desire for international prestige was said to have special meaning during the Cold War era, since any success would have the associated psychological benefits coming from outdoing the Soviet Union. According to some, the race for space included the notion that the Free World countries could successfully resist Communist expansion only if the United States could launch a satellite into space first. Amazingly, consideration was even given to the possibility of developing an orbiting inflatable balloon that would be symbolic of the "American Star" rising in the West.[18] Yet the United States was not first, and *Sputnik I* was launched by the Soviet Union. Consequently, the antithesis of prestige became relevant to the United States. The Soviet success led some newspapers to report that the Communist way of life and non-materialistic philosophy were superior to capitalism, as evident by the first milestone of the space age.[19] For many within the United States, the failure to be first was seen as national defeat.[20]

In the case of the Chinese space program, the perception that accomplishments in space can enhance national prestige is still evident. Many inside and outside China view their ambitious space program as being motivated by prestige and an attempt to recapture its lost legacy of technological mastery and innovation.[21] Such an ambitious program can have dramatic effects. A national space program that mobilizes an entire nation can increase domestic support for government leadership, and future success will bestow a sense of being on the correct path, either ideologically or politically.

Moreover, these benefits will not be just internal to China, but will be realized within the international community. It is perhaps noteworthy that China has not as yet been incorporated into future plans for the International Space Station, but with their recent manned launch and ambitious space program, other space power nations are taking note.[22] With their heavy lift launch capability, which could provide frequent service to the space station, China can bring a capability that only a few other space agencies can provide. It should be expected, therefore, that China's international recognition as a space power will result in greater influence during negotiations concerning space regulatory policy. Moreover, the prestige that China garners could result in its government becoming more of an equal partner in future space operations, including the International Space Station or the European Union's Galileo program.

National security

In a different application, space-based information services can affect a country's power and promote its national security. Information has long played a critical role in national security and warfare, since early strategists first contemplated how to gain an advantage over the enemy. Sun Tzu acknowledges the importance of information in his enduring work, *The Art of War.* In emphasizing the important role that information and intelligence have in gaining a relative advantage over one's adversary, he writes, "Quantities derive from measurements, figures from quantities, comparisons from figures, and victory from comparisons."[23]

Information gained through space systems has been used by nations as an instrument of foreign policy. During the Eisenhower administration, intelligence and reconnaissance satellites were used to verify the activities of the Soviet Union under the "Open Skies" national policy, and this policy is credited with having stabilized tensions that existed during the height of the

Cold War. In this case, the information gained, in part, through satellites was used to maintain stability between the two competing powers and ensured that each followed arms control agreements and treaties. Had these space-based information services not been available or used in this manner, a direct confrontation between the two would have been more likely, which would have probably diminished both economically and militarily.

During wartime, exploiting superior intelligence leads to better strategic employment of forces and resources, helping bring one closer to victory. The surprise and initiative gained through the use of intelligence have a demoralizing effect on the enemy and often subvert their will to fight, even if just temporarily. Intelligence, surveillance, and reconnaissance assets are frequently used in this endeavor. Also included are positioning, navigation, and timing satellite constellations, which often provide information that is used to help determine the position of oneself and the enemy. The information gained in this manner can then be used to support offensive operations against one's adversary.

Since information is an instrument of national power, there will be some states, organizations, and groups that will try to manipulate, degrade, or deny its use. Such actions will occur during times of relative peace or intense hostilities. For this reason, it is necessary to protect one's interests and security by taking sufficient measures to ensure that information services can be used at all times.

Military actions

With regards to its military utility, space and space-based systems influence national power. The armed forces have recognized for some time the military advantage gained by having assets that can conduct surveillance and communication around the globe. Outer space is presently seen as an environment that supports combat operations on land, at sea, and in the air, because space is the "high ground" for any terrestrial military operations. While space systems that perform information services are of value to the military, there has been, and continues to be, interest in using space for direct hostile actions.

Indeed, since the beginnings of the space age, space has been a medium to be exploited for military advantage. The German military, limited by the Treaty of Versailles following World War I, became interested in rockets and their applications. As a result of their research, the first ballistic missile was developed, the V-2, which carried munitions toward England in the final days of World War II.[24] Even nuclear-tipped intercontinental ballistic missiles have been around since the early days of the Space Age. Commensurate with the view that nuclear warheads could be deployed *through* space was the view that they could be deployed *from* space as well, since it was widely held in the late 1950s that nuclear weapons would eventually be delivered from orbiting weapons platforms against potential terrestrial targets.[25]

There is a plethora of examples about militarized space programs. Within the United States, the first anti-satellite test program was initiated in 1959.[26] Additionally, the Dyna-Soar space-plane and the Manned Orbital Laboratory initiatives of the late 1950s and the 1960s were both intended to deliver a manned military presence to space, although neither of these programs ever came to fruition.[27] The Reagan administration's highly controversial Strategic Defense Initiative of the 1980s ambitiously sought to protect the United States from intercontinental ballistic missiles, and part of this initiative included the Brilliant Pebbles program to build space-based interceptors.[28] The Soviet Union also had weaponization programs during the Cold War, including fractional orbital bombardment systems (FOBS) as well as anti-satellite weapons programs.[29]

The 1991 Gulf War against Iraq was touted by some as being the "first space war." This title was given in recognition of how space systems enhanced the warfighting effectiveness of land, sea, and air forces.[30] The importance of space systems during the war is not called into question, since positioning satellites were used with dramatic success in precision bombing. Yet the label for this war is inappropriate, since the war was devoid of an actual confrontation in space.

World history indicates that states with significant interests will protect their interests no matter where they lie. Space is no different. Increasingly, countries are viewing space as a medium where national power and security are played out. Because some believe that the United States' supremacy in conventional warfare – land, sea, and air – is difficult to challenge directly, space systems are seen as the "irresistible choice" for attack in order to bring about more parity during future conflicts.[31] To this end, there have been claims about the development of "parasite satellites," or orbiting munitions that attach themselves to enemy spacecraft for detonation when deemed necessary.[32] Although verification of such claims proves difficult, as none have ever been reported as being launched, it is noteworthy that the idea is consistent with the notion that actions in space can affect the balance of power between states.

Minor actions

For smaller, less technologically advanced countries, an ambitious space program may not be an option, but they too can still promote their interests and increase their influence over more powerful governments. As before, actions motivated by prestige can achieve modest results. For example, by joining with another country's ambitious endeavor in space, a smaller nation can gain a sense of active participation, and having one's own citizen fly aboard another country's spacecraft will garner nationalistic pride. Furthermore, placing a national satellite in orbit for the first time using commercially available launch services is also a source of national pride because one is now a "space power." These types of activities are all meant to increase the optimism of a populace, and may result in more domestic support for the governmental leaders in power.

It is not suggested that space programs are a panacea for civil unrest or political volatility. For just as success brings benefits to those in power, tragedy can likewise bring adversity. When disaster occurs and lives are lost, inquiry into why such an accident happened and who is responsible naturally ensues. These inquiries and investigations often become emotionally driven, especially if human error and incompetence are involved. Additionally, it is not implied that a nation's populace are mindless automatons, blindly and unquestioningly following their domestic leadership when times are good. Even with successes in space and the increased national pride that results, other events at home or overseas will also influence a nation's popular demeanor.

Less influential states can also achieve modest results through minor hostile actions. Often such minor actions will occur for pure political or diplomatic effect. Politically driven minor actions are more likely during times of increased tension, but short of general and all out war. Since their objectives are limited, minor actions can serve as a warning to prevent a further escalation in hostilities between adversaries, or they may serve to underscore a diplomatic point or to achieve a slight military advantage. The intent of minor actions of this kind is to influence the decisions of others; consequently, the success of these kinds of minor actions is primarily dependent on how these actions are perceived by the recipient. Both Clausewitz and Corbett recognize that military operations are influenced by national politics and interests, and since politics and policy influence war, the converse is likely to be true as well: war influences politics and policy. The lesson learned, therefore, is that hostile actions in space, even minor ones, can have wide-ranging political and diplomatic effects.[33]

When considering the theory and strategy of space warfare, it is critical to fully understand the role of diplomatic, economic, information, and military instruments of national power. These four instruments represent means by which the strategy and principles of space warfare can affect others. But they also represent instruments by which one's space operations and activities can be affected. So while one considers the proper strategy of employing space assets and conducting operations with respect to both friend and foe alike, friend and foe will probably be doing the same in return.

Chapter 5

Space operations are interdependent with others

A government's overarching goals are contained in its grand strategy and, if a government's efforts are properly marshalled, all sub-strategies should work toward those goals during peace and war. Here in the United States, national military strategy serves the national security strategy, which in turn serves the national grand strategy. For this reason, each of the armed services – along with other government agencies – should work toward achieving national goals at all times. During peacetime, the military trains, refines tactics, rewrites doctrine, and rethinks force structure requirements. During wartime, the military protects national interests and attempts to defeat the adversary in order to achieve political or diplomatic objectives. Each of the military services and subordinate commands supports the entire military strategy through its individual actions and contributions. In the end, however, all their efforts are ultimately subservient to the strategy and guidance as laid out by their national leaders.

As a result, each of the military services must play its part in the cacophony of war. Since there has yet to be open hostilities in space, it is difficult to determine what the proper and relevant role of military space operations should be. Nevertheless, there are certain questions worth asking to determine the relationship of space warfare to the other methods of war: can space forces be used to deter and defeat the enemy without the use of land, sea, or air components, or do space forces need to work with the other branches of the armed services to achieve common military goals? Does the answer to the previous question depend on the conditions of the conflict? To answer these questions and determine what the relationship of space forces and operations is to general warfare, an understanding of the relationship of land, sea, and air warfare is required.

Armies

Space warfare appears to have more in common with either naval or air warfare than with land warfare. Nevertheless, the strategy of land warfare served as the impetus for the renowned military observations of Sun Tzu and Clausewitz. Therefore, an understanding of land warfare, along with its relationship to the overall wartime strategy, is warranted in order to understand the most fundamental principles of war. Past masters of strategic theory observed that wars are waged primarily for political and diplomatic reasons. Since people start wars, people must also stop them. Clausewitz masterfully recognizes the interplay between leadership, the military, and the populace in determining the will to fight wars.[1] By negatively influencing the enemy in any one of the three areas – or in combination – victory is eventually achieved. The military strategy to achieve victory is often determined by matching one's own strengths against the enemy's weaknesses, while recognizing that the enemy will attempt to do the same.

During major campaigns today, armies often rely on transport and resupply provided by land, sea, or air transport and logistics. In the United States, before the enemy is engaged with large ground forces, enemy positions and infrastructure are frequently targeted by firepower coming from land, naval, or air assets to reduce the strength of opposing forces prior to a land assault. Consequently, armies commonly require support from the other services to be effective to the maximum extent possible. Although naval and air forces frequently support army operations, can the land forces win a war alone if needed? History is replete with military land campaigns that were fought and won primarily through the use of armies. Examples include the expansion of the Mongol Empire (AD 1204–1405), the Franco-Prussian War (1870–1), and the many civil wars and conflicts in Africa during the twentieth century. Therefore, the lessons of history would suggest that there are times when armies and land forces can in themselves be the sole means of achieving military victory and political objectives.

Nonetheless, history also provides many examples in which victory could not be achieved solely through land warfare. This is typified when one belligerent is the "elephant" and the other the "whale." Albeit Napoleon Bonaparte had a larger and more capable land force than Great Britain, he did not command the seas and consequently was unable to freely transport his legions across the English Channel. This more than anything else prevented Britain's defeat in the war with Bonaparte. Moreover, major conflicts between great land and naval powers go back for centuries. Thucydides wrote of the great conflict between Sparta, with its superior army, and Athens, a naval power. Despite Sparta's superior military prowess and discipline, they failed to quickly dispatch Athenian naval forces. Athens did eventually capitulate, but only after years of conflict and following the ramifications of poor military decisions by the Athenian leadership.[2]

Although armies do not always decide the outcome of military campaigns, more often than not, ultimate victory and enemy capitulation is not achieved until land forces are on the enemy's soil or pose the threat of incursion. This is primarily for two reasons. First, even after a decisive military victory, the defeated leaders and populace are sometimes reluctant to admit defeat, thinking continued resistance is worthwhile, until such time they are presented with the stark reality of foreign troops on home soil. Second, since wars are ultimately about people and their will to fight, most wars must affect the people where they live, which is on land. Military victory and enemy capitulation is best achieved by employing land forces, or at least the credible threat of using them. The army thus plays a pivotal role in determining when and how success is achieved. But then again, so do navies and air forces.

Navies

As described earlier in Corbett's maritime theory, naval operations are an important component of warfare, but they generally do not bring about an adversary's capitulation by themselves. The reason for this is that wars are about people and, to be successful, must ultimately be waged where they live. Certainly, naval operations can bring a war to conclusion more quickly by destroying the enemy's fleet, decimating his maritime trade and commerce, or supporting amphibious landings against his shores. Despite the utility of navies, they are interdependent – except in the rarest of occasions – with other forces to achieve political objectives and enemy capitulation.

In two of the greatest naval victories, Admiral Nelson soundly defeated Bonaparte's fleet at the Battle of the Nile in 1798 and again at the Battle of Trafalgar in 1805. But notwithstanding these great successes, the war between Great Britain and France continued until Bonaparte's defeat at the Battle of Waterloo in 1815.[3] Only through the continued actions of both naval and land forces was Great Britain, along with its coalition partners, eventually able to defeat Bonaparte. Similarly, during World War II, the United States eventually gained naval superiority during the campaign in the Pacific against the Japanese, but American and Allied ground forces were still required to go ashore and secure each island stronghold from the persistent Japanese fighters. Although naval actions were instrumental in achieving the conditions necessary to deal the final blows against the Japanese Empire, these final blows came in the form of air power.

Notable exceptions do exist where naval action alone is able to achieve political objectives, and these are usually the case when there is the threat of force, besides that coming from a naval fleet. These include when power projection through naval actions is able to effect regime change. An example of this is when United States Marines stationed a contingency force off the coast of Liberia in 2003. This power projection force was used to make readily apparent to the world stage the United States' concern and interest in the situation and to put pressure on President Charles Taylor to resign. The Marines' show of force and Taylor's reluctant resignation clearly illustrate how naval presence – without other operations – is sometimes enough to effect regime change. Nevertheless, the reasons for Taylor's resignation also included the threat of domestic revolt, as well as the possibility of the Marines coming ashore to take him out of power by force. It still holds, therefore, that navies must work together with the other forms of warfare to achieve the political objectives of war.[4]

Air forces

Unlike naval power, air power is more likely to directly influence events on land, which is how wars are eventually won. Many air power advocates, including Douhet and Mitchell, have asserted that air forces are the key to deciding the outcome of conflicts. The idea of whether air operations alone are capable of achieving political aims and the enemy's capitulation is germane to the discussion of space warfare, since many possible tactical actions from space bear a striking resemblance to tactical air actions. Consequently, if it can be determined that air forces alone can achieve the political objectives of war, then so too might space forces.

The strategic effectiveness of air power has been and still is a heated topic of debate, with some air power strategists noting that the true role of strategic bombing cannot be determined definitively and satisfactorily.[5] Yet based on the interpretation of Douhet and Mitchell's ideas, air forces have sought to achieve strategic-level effects through bombing, such as the high-altitude formation bombing during World War II.[6] Such bombing attempted to diminish the warfighting capability of the Germans and Japanese, with the selected targets including rail, shipping, petroleum, and munitions facilities. Such bombing is consistent with the thought that military actions at the tactical level of war can have strategic effects.

Based on the US Army Air Corps doctrine at the time, the goal of strategic bombing was to destroy the enemy's industrial facilities and thus decimate their long-term sustainment capability.[7] In the doctrinal documents from the period, there is no mention of attacking population centers to influence the will of the people, thereby affecting the war's outcome. Nevertheless, because of the close proximity of the labor force to the industrial complexes, and the inaccuracies inherent in high-altitude, non-precision-guided munitions, a large number of civilians died as a consequence of the bombing campaigns. The result was that the strategic bombing campaign against Germany "appreciably affected the German will to resist."[8] Although the significant role of air power contributed to Germany's eventual capitulation, air power alone did not decide the war's outcome. Through hard-fought battles and conventional style warfare, the Allied armies reduced Germany's warmaking capability and troop strength. Allied navies were finally able to mitigate the German submarine threat enough to transport personnel, equipment, and supplies across the Atlantic to where they were desperately needed in the European theater. Navies also enabled the crossing of the English Channel by Allied amphibious forces. Consequently, final success in Europe was achieved through the combined efforts of air, land, and sea forces.

In the air campaign against Japan, many civilians were also killed and the Japanese industrial base was devastated. Near the end of the war, only about half of the employees working at factories showed up for work, and many millions fled the cities that were consistently being bombed.[9] Japan eventually surrendered after the second atomic bomb was dropped, and the combination of strategic bombing using conventional weapons and employing atomic weapons played a decisive role in bringing about the war's conclusion. Yet even in this historical example, to get to the point where air power could play a deciding role required the efforts of all the services. While the surrender decision did follow the dropping of two atomic bombs, the potential threat of an Allied land invasion was also weighed in the Japanese leadership's decision to surrender.

Although the war in Kosovo in 1999, which involved the North Atlantic Treaty Organization, is sometimes touted as an example where air operations alone were able to bring a conflict to an end, the war in Kosovo does not suggest this but correctly illustrates the role of air power with respect to overall military strategy. In the alliance's drive to oust Serbian leader Slobodan Milosevic's forces from Kosovo and to deal with the ever-growing humanitarian crisis, the initial strategy was to use a limited air power campaign to bring about Milosevic's capitulation. Yet bombings against Serbian targets occurred and surrender did not result. The air power campaign even escalated to include more coalition aircraft sorties and the bombing of more targets, yet the result remained the same.[10] It was not until the alliance implicitly threatened to move ground forces into the area, along with Russia's diplomatic pressure on Milosevic, that capitulation resulted.[11] So while the coalition chose to use primarily air power to achieve its political aims, this example illustrates that other factors had to come into play – including diplomatic pressure and the potential use of ground forces – to bring the conflict to an end.

Space forces

With only about fifty years of experience to draw upon, history proves some-what wanting in describing the interrelationship of space operations with the other environments of warfare. Admittedly, space-based systems have been used in the past to support military operations, but full-scale hostilities have not erupted in space nor have offensive operations been launched from space. Yet, by considering space warfare from the position that affecting the adversary's leadership, military, or populace will win a war, the interrelationship of space warfare can be ascertained.[12] Moreover, the previous illustrations regarding the utility of armies, navies, and air forces have relevant lessons for determining what is to be expected of space forces, as well as the interrelationship of space forces with the other military branches.

At the strategic level of warfare, space forces and navies have similar interests. So, given the lessons of naval warfare, it is gleaned that military actions in, from, and through space can impact the long-term warfighting capability of one's adversary, by impacting his space-based commerce and trade. Through the impact on commerce and trade, an enemy's revenues will likely decline, and goods and services normally enjoyed by the populace can be denied. Moreover, wartime actions in space can degrade or prevent some of the enemy's communication of military intelligence, thereby negatively impacting his ongoing or future combat operations. Such actions are meant to degrade an opponent's overall warmaking ability, while at the same time impressing upon his populace that continuing the conflict is to their detriment.

Nonetheless, these factors alone are unlikely to affect the enemy's will to fight enough to secure his capitulation. Past conflicts show that hostilities are rarely concluded in a lasting way until land forces are brought to bear against the adversary, or at least the threat is posed. This is because wars are ultimately about people, and to conclude a war with a lasting peace requires affecting a preponderance of the enemy living on land. So, even if the enemy's space forces are decimated, he will probably continue to fight, especially if his land, sea, or air forces are reasonably intact and effective. For as long as an enemy believes he should and can still fight, conflict is likely to continue.

At the tactical level of warfare, space forces and air forces are most similar. Therefore, tactical-level actions using space-to-earth weaponry will in all likelihood bear similar results to those actions of air forces. Drawing upon the lessons of air warfare, individual offensive action in space will be able to achieve strategic effects. These effects may result from targeting enemy leadership, destroying military command and control networks, or impacting people where they live. The destructive firepower coming from space-based weaponry can negatively impact the enemy populace's morale, resulting in domestic productivity dropping off significantly. If space-based effects can impart a sense of helplessness against such attacks, then one can significantly diminish the collective will to fight of the adversary's leadership, military, and general population.

Despite the apparent effectiveness of space warfare, operations in, from, and through space are quite unlikely to determine a war's outcome alone. That is not to say that space operations will not have a dominant or decisive role in concluding conflicts, but history indicates that most wars will require the combined and effective use of all branches of the military. Only in the rarest of circumstances can military space operations be the sole means of achieving victory. Space forces must, therefore, operate in concert with other military forces, since space warfare is just a subset of general wartime strategy and operations. As a result, it is concluded that space warfare is interdependent with the other warfighting methods – land, naval, and air – and the most efficient and effective success is achieved through the coordinated use of all four.[13] Because of the mutual interdependence of space forces with the other arms of the military, along with the need to support political goals and objectives, space strategy must work to support overall national strategy during peace and war.

While space forces will need the support of the other military branches in working toward common wartime objectives, the other military branches likewise need the support of space forces to be as effective as possible. Historical precedent has exemplified where the other branches of the military have supported operations in space. Early on during the United States space program, the Army's Redstone program, led by Wernher von Braun, sought to place a satellite into orbit.[14] Likewise, the Naval Research Lab's Vanguard program was an attempt to access space, even though its December 1957 initial launch attempt failed to achieve the desired political and diplomatic effects.[15] Examples where space operations have supported land, sea, and air forces have been previously noted, but highlights include space-based systems that assist in finding and engaging enemy targets, thereby enabling the use of precision weaponry. Based on the examples of the past, space warfare will support and enhance the operations in the other media of warfare, while also being supported and enhanced by land, sea, and air warfare.

Chapter 6

Celestial lines of communication

Lines of communication are well understood in the context of land and naval forces, in that they are routes for transporting troops, mechanized equipment, ships, or supplies from one location to another. Even in the case of air warfare, air lines of communications are understood as those flight paths used most often for the movement of aircraft that carry personnel, weaponry, or cargo.

An understanding of the use and utility of celestial lines of communication is most important when considering military strategy in space. The inherent value of space is the utility and access it provides, and this utility and access are enabled through celestial lines of communication. Generally stated, celestial lines of communications are those lines of communications in and through space used for the movement of trade, materiel, supplies, personnel, spacecraft, electromagnetic transmissions, and some military effects. By ensuring access to "lines of passage and communication" in space, a nation can protect its diplomatic, economic, information, and military interests.[1] Because ensuring one's access to and use of lines of communications in space is vital, the primary objective of space warfare is to protect and defend one's own lines of communications, while limiting the enemy's ability to use his.[2] As with lines of communications at sea, one's lines of communication in space may often run parallel to the enemy's or may even be shared with him. Furthermore, since celestial lines of communication between belligerents may be one and the same, an enemy's celestial lines of communication frequently cannot be attacked without affecting one's own.

The term "space lines of communication" is perfectly acceptable in conveying the intended meaning of these routes through space; however, when referred to as an acronym (SLOC) – as is often done by military professionals – it can easily become confused with the more widely known "sea lines of communication" (SLOC). For this reason, it is useful to distinguish space communications as using celestial lines of communication (CLOC), especially when using the acronym.[3]

Another important term for the space warfare lexicon is "space communications." Its meaning is subtly different from "celestial lines of communication," but the difference is relevant nonetheless. Space communications pertain to the movement of trade, materiel, supplies, personnel, spacecraft, electromagnetic transmissions, and some military effects along celestial lines of communication, but they also include the means of doing so.[4] Therefore, the term "space communications" refers to the overall activity of communicating into, from, and through space, while "celestial lines of communication" refers to the routes used for such activity.[5]

Conceptually, there are similarities between lines of communication at sea and in space; yet, when considering maritime and space communications, there are fundamental differences. A key difference is that many of the things being communicated in space are not directly tangible in a conventional manner. While the tangible assets, like trade, materiel, supplies, personnel, and spacecraft, may be transported along celestial lines of communication, so can the intangible – like transmissions using the electromagnetic frequency spectrum and those subatomic particles discharged by particle beam weapons.[6] This realization allows for conceptually differentiating space communications as between the physical and non-physical.[7]

Physical communications

Physical communications pertain to the activity and movement of trade, materiel, supplies, personnel, and spacecraft along celestial lines of communication. These communications seem almost commonplace as governments and companies demonstrate their technological prowess by launching satellites and people into orbit. The launch locations used for physical communication are often repeatedly reused, because of the technological complexity and sizable infrastructure required to place large spacecraft and satellites into space. Moreover, those lines of communication used by physical communications are often the same from one space launch to the next. While deviations in launch trajectories are sometimes required, depending on the type of orbit ultimately needed to perform the intended mission, large deviations from their baseline flight path are frequently initiated once the vehicle is in a preliminary orbit around the earth. So, most physical communications going from the earth into space begin at predictable locations and follow fairly predictable paths. This assessment is exemplified by the many spectators who come to watch space launches, knowing ahead of time where to look for the booster rocket's ignition and what path the residual plume trail will follow.

Once vehicles are in space, their lines of communication used are fairly predictable too, especially those orbiting around the earth. The chosen orbit – whether low, medium, high, or even highly elliptical – is determined by the spacecraft's design and purpose, such as some telecommunication satellites taking a geostationary orbit and the Space Shuttle taking a low-earth orbit.

Thus, more often than not, the space routes used by spacecraft are also well known ahead of time. Furthermore, at the completion of their mission, manned spacecraft will frequently follow a predetermined path to their landing location. Even many unmanned systems follow a predetermined de-orbit trajectory after the expiration of their service life. For those satellites not de-orbited in this manner, they may be placed in a predictable orbit that is above those used most by operational satellites, also referred to as a "graveyard orbit."

At present, physical communications along celestial lines of communication primarily pertain to the movement of technologically advanced satellites, astronauts, or other scientific equipment into orbit. This type of communication also includes the regular transfer of items essential for human survival in space, such as food, water, and materiel used for repairs. Considering mankind's nascent use of space and the observation of maritime history, it is probable that someday resources or materials, either found or manufactured in outer space, will be sent back to earth for the purpose of commerce or trade. These transferred resources may include naturally occurring minerals mined from celestial bodies, and manufactured materials may include consumables such as pharmaceuticals. Both of these potential activities will also represent physical communications between outer space and the earth.

Non-physical communications

Whereas the previous discussion addressed the communicating of physical assets into, from, and through space, it is the substantial use of non-physical communications that most distinguishes space from other media. Non-physical communications comprise the transmission of data, information, and some military effects along celestial lines of communication. The movement of data and information pertains to those services traditionally transmitted and received using discrete electromagnetic frequency bands. The military effects that are considered non-physical communications include lasers, microwaves, and any directed energy weapons. Particle beam weapons are also included in this category, even though these weapons do not rely upon the electromagnetic spectrum for the movement of their destructive effects through space. While the electromagnetic spectrum and charged particles are indeed part of the "physical universe," they are categorized as non-physical communications, since the mass and size of those things communicated are not readily observable by humans. Although somewhat simplistic, another way of thinking about the differentiation of the two types of communications is that "physical" refers to the communication of *things*, and "non-physical" refers to the communication of *effects*.

The lines of communication used for non-physical communication can appear stationary or constantly moving.[8] For instance, when transferring data between a ground station and a satellite in a geostationary orbit, the communications route appears not to move, since each location remains "fixed" relative to each other. On the other hand, telecommunication satellites in a low-earth orbit often provide services within a geographic area for several minutes, until the next satellite in the constellation takes over the service requirements, and in such cases the lines of communication appear to move as the satellite moves relative to the ground station.

Also pertinent to understanding non-physical communications are their path and shape, especially with respect to radio frequency-band transmissions. Some of these communications are highly directional in nature, with a very narrow transmission beamwidth, which usually indicates that the data's transmission and reception is optimized along a specified route or direction. Since cost and weight limit the size of transmitters and antennas put into space, tradeoffs are done to determine what kind of signal propagation is most desired. Directional communications tend to use transmitter power more efficiently but restrict which locations can receive the data and information. Omni-directional communications allow more locations along different paths to receive data or information, but transmission range suffers since transmitter power is used less efficiently.[9] Whether a narrow, directional beam is chosen for communications or not often depends on if the location of the ultimate user of the information is known. If not, an omni-directional communication would be more appropriate. When requirements dictate elements of both methods, a combination of directional and omni-directional techniques can be employed.

Unlike the omni-directional broadcast used for some radio communications, lasers are primarily restricted to directional communications at any given instant in time. Lasers, which utilize a highly directional and coherent light source, may be employed to communicate data, information, or destructive effects. Since lasers require line-of-sight between their source and intended recipient, they usually require unobstructed access along their desired line of communication. Lasers may be used for satellite-to-satellite communications, since these space-based locations often have the required unobstructed access between them. When used as weapons – whether ground-to-space, air-to-space, space-to-space, space-to-ground, or space-to-air – lasers are also highly directional and usually rely on line-of-sight access to engage intended targets. Similarly, particle beam weapons, which project charged or neutral subatomic particles, are primarily designed to be highly directional and are most effective when having unobstructed line-of-sight access to the intended target.

Measures of effectiveness

The skeptical warfighter might view the distinction between physical and non-physical communications as arbitrary with no relevance to fighting and winning wars. Despite such skepticism, the distinctions are relevant and have implications for military strategy in space. The relevance has to do with how the effectiveness of these various types of space communications are measured. Depending on what these different measures are, the best suited war plan against the enemy can be formulated. Depending on the particular mission and type of communication, the measure of effectiveness reflects how success is most often determined. The measure of effectiveness of any mission should not be confused with its efficiency, however. Any efficiency is commonly determined by how much output is realized for any unit of input. For example, aerospace engineers may be concerned with how much propulsive thrust is generated given any unit of propellant. For those involved in commercial ventures, the efficiency may be determined by the income generated relative to operating expenses. Although efficiency can under some situations be one and the same as its measure of effectiveness, it is not necessarily so. Consequently, many factors come into play in determining whether any diplomatic, economic, information, or military endeavor is viewed as successful or not. For simplicity, the following strategic considerations are presented, as they most often hold true based on the type of activity and endeavor.

Physical communication's effectiveness

When physical communications pertain to commercial activities, such as the placement of telecommunication satellites in orbit, their overall effectiveness is most often a function of the path they take from one point to another. For example, there is an optimum trajectory for launching a spacecraft from a ground site to the desired orbit, and any deviations from that trajectory result in added cost through the additional propellant and larger boosters used. So, if a deviation from the optimum becomes too substantial, the associated costs may become too expensive to be practical or economical for launch. Although the amount of time it takes for physical communications to travel from one point to another also impacts overall cost, the cost associated with just additional time is considered to be significantly less than that additional cost associated with deviating from the optimal path or trajectory.[10] As a result, space activities for commercial gain most often attempt to take the most efficient and optimal path into orbit, in order to maximize profit potential.

When physical communication is not for commercial gain, the route taken is also related to its effectiveness, but in a slightly different way. The costs associated with any space launch are always important, since fiscal resources are limited, and therefore non-commercial space activities must be cognizant of expenses given the scrutiny of politicians and the public at large. Yet since highly publicized missions – such as launching people into space – are frequently done for national prestige reasons and not for commercial gain, taking the optimal path is highly desirable, but not necessary for success. The gains reaped from accomplishing the intended mission cannot be assigned monetary value, but they can be assigned a value nonetheless. The perceived value of a national prestige mission is a function of the potential risks to anticipated rewards. The failure to get from one point to another, due to catastrophic failure or other problems, impacts the perceived worth of the mission. Losing the crew of a highly publicized space flight, such as with the *Challenger* and *Columbia* space shuttles, has repercussions that can ripple throughout a nation. This holds true for the failure of some unmanned systems as well. The sense of any loss is temporary, however, and perceptions and sentiments can rapidly shift again after the next success in space is achieved. The conclusion reached is that the measure of effectiveness of prestige missions that employ physical communications is determined somewhat by the path taken, but it is more a function of whether the path is successfully taken at all.

Non-physical communication's effectiveness

The measure of effectiveness of non-physical communications is different again. While non-physical communications may in fact use physical systems, such as ground relays or orbiting satellites, this type of communication pertains to the information, data, or effects transferred, and not to the hardware itself. Especially with the transfer of data and information, the method employed frequently uses a distributed arrangement with a plethora of available paths for communication. If any one relay or satellite fails, others can take over the responsibilities. The possible communication routes in many instances seem limitless, and this distributed capability is an advantage of this method of communication. So, unlike with physical communications, the specific path taken with non-physical communication is not the most important measure of its effectiveness. But the most important measure is a function of time.

Since the communication of data and information using space-based technology is in constant competition with other methods – such as land lines or terrestrial wireless technology – the perceived worth of such communication is mostly a function of the amount of time it takes to transfer its information to the desired destinations. In the case of military intelligence, its timeliness is frequently critical to its usefulness. For television, radio, or telephone communication services using space systems, time is not as critical as with military operations, but it is still important. If a significant delay in the communication occurs, or if the transfer rate is so degraded to make the reception quality poor, other methods of communication will seem more worthwhile and effective. Thus time is a factor in measuring its effectiveness, but time itself is only part of this measure.

Non-physical communications are also concerned with the amount of data and information going from any one source to any number of receiving locations. Since broadcast methods, such as omni-directional, can transfer data and information to any number of locations, it is not necessarily the time it takes for any specific piece of information to get from one point to another that matters most but the overall amount of information being received by users. This means that the measure of effectiveness is a function of the total rate of data and information leaving one location and going to one or many locations. For this reason, the effectiveness of non-physical communications is best conceptualized by the amount of communications transferred with respect to time, or more simply the rate of transfer.

Even when considering the measure of effectiveness of weapons effects, like lasers and directed energy weapons, time and the rate of communication transfer are still most important. Obviously, the amount of time it takes any weapons system to engage its intended target is important in determining its effectiveness. Even weapons that physically communicate effects, such as ballistic missiles and precision-guided munitions, will increase their kill probability if they can travel to their target as quickly as possible. Although time is an important factor in any weapons system, it is still argued that time – and specifically the amount of communication with respect to time – is the most important consideration when it comes to the non-physical communication of weapons effects. This is because the communication of non-physical weapons effects often occurs at or near the speed of light. Consequently, the amount of time it takes to arrive at the target is mostly a fixed constant dictated by the distance between the belligerents' assets and forces. Yet the destructive energy delivered with respect to time plays an important role in determining if the target is destroyed or not. For instance, higher transfer rates of imparted heat from a laser or transmitted neutrally charged particles from a particle beam all result in a greater likelihood of damaging the enemy target. Therefore, the destructive effects delivered with respect to time are considered most critical. The same often holds true with physical weaponry. Even though physical weapons must travel to their destination, they must eventually impart their destructive effects upon the enemy target, and therefore the time it takes to get to the target is not as critical as the actual delivery of destructive effects.

Missions employing physical and non-physical communications

For many programs and missions, the object is to employ physical communications to place a system in space and then employ non-physical communications to transmit and receive data and information. This is particularly the case with missions that are for advancing human understanding and scientific study. As in the case of activities that are for national prestige, those with scientific purposes are also concerned with whether the spacecraft reaches its intended destination or not. Especially in the case of unmanned spacecraft, success is also determined by whether any usable data and information can be gathered and sent back to earth using non-physical communications. So in some cases, as exemplified by missions with scientific purposes, the measure of effectiveness is determined by getting to the intended destination and also being able to send useful data and information back. Therefore, it is realized that sometimes the measure of effectiveness and success is dependent upon being able to use and access celestial lines of communication that enable both physical and non-physical communications.

Degrading and denying access

With an understanding of what most influences the effectiveness of the two types of space communication, the warfighter can formulate the best strategy to degrade or deny the enemy his use of space communications. For example, a viable strategy against the enemy's commercial space activities is denying him the most optimal routes into space. An appropriate strategy against his scientific or national prestige activities is to prevent spacecraft from reaching their intended destination. Lastly, an appropriate strategy against the enemy's data and information communications is to minimize the transfer rate of his communications.

History, however, offers few examples regarding the intentional degrading and denial of another's access to celestial lines of communication, yet a few do exist. Americans had failures early on in their race to be the first to launch a satellite and thus outdo the Soviets. This includes the failed attempts by the US Navy Vanguard program to get the first manmade satellite in orbit.[11] Consequently, the United States was not able to achieve the level of international prestige it sought by being the first to succeed in launching a satellite, and as a result Eisenhower's administration received increased criticism. The Soviet Union had its failures too. Even after his country was the first to launch a satellite into orbit, Soviet Premier Khrushchev sought to further increase Soviet diplomatic stature by being the first to send a spacecraft to Mars. Yet in his October 1960 attempt to "boost Soviet political prestige," all three Mars-bound rockets failed to launch, with the third attempt reportedly resulting in an explosion causing the death of many Soviet scientists.[12] Albeit the Soviet launch failures were not caused by the intentional actions of another state, this incident illustrates that the inability to launch these rockets – representing the inability to use physical communications – prevented Khrushchev from getting the diplomatic boost he eagerly desired. There are numerous other examples of launch vehicles failing during or just after launch, and all such failures represent economic losses, due to cost and manpower invested, as well as events that negatively impact the perceptions of the population.

There are limited examples of the degradation or denial of non-physical communications. Examples of non-intentional, temporary denial include those occasions when our sun's solar flare activity is at a peak. Such activity often causes an excessive amount of charged particles entering the earth's magnetosphere, resulting in degraded space-based transmission and reception quality. At times, these charged particles have temporary effects, but if a satellite's protection proves inadequate, these charged particles can permanently damage sensitive onboard electronics. Other ways of degrading space communication can include deliberate methods, such as jamming or distorting the timing and position data coming from GPS satellites. Such systems have reportedly been used in conflicts to date. Russian-built systems were found in Iraq during the combat operations in 2003, used in an attempt to degrade the effectiveness of American precision attacks using satellite position information. The denial measures employed were neither technologically sophisticated nor demanding in the amount of power output required to be effective.[13]

Because degrading and denying another's access to and use of celestial lines of communication are a possible action not only for sovereign nations, any organization or group with an agenda to advance may attempt such action too. In a commercially related example, a corporation involved in the direct satellite broadcast of television communications may be involved in a contract dispute with one of its content providers. If the terms of the contract dispute remain unresolved, the satellite broadcast corporation may deny the transmission of the content provider's services. Although this example involves a dispute between two businesses, it could just as well be between any state's government and a business.

Because of the vital nature of celestial lines of communication and space communications in general, one will need to protect one's access and use of physical and non-physical communications. This recognition leads to the next strategic idea of space warfare: command of space.

Chapter 7

Command of space

The inherent value of space is what it allows you to do. Space serves as a conduit for terrestrial- and celestial-based movement and transfer, and because of its value, those with interests in space will attempt to preserve and promote their continued access to and use of space. This preservation and promotion is accomplished through the concept command of space. Command of space entails the ability to ensure access and use of celestial lines of communications when needed to support the instruments of national power – diplomatic, economic, information, and military. It also includes the ability to prevent or deny the enemy's access to and use of his celestial lines of communications, or at least minimize the most severe consequences an adversary can deliver along them. Since command of space connotes the ability to use space communications when and where needed, it is a measure relative to others.

Command of space is relevant for nations, organizations, or groups. In the case of nations and sovereign states, activities in space can directly influence any or all the instruments of national power. Yet non-governmental organizations or groups without any national affiliation may also have vested interests in what activities in space are conducted, how, and by whom. Examples of those non-governmental organizations or groups that may have critical interests in space, along with the need protect them, include international telecommunications companies, environmental activists, and terrorist organizations.

Especially within the context of maritime strategy, command is normally thought of as being gained and exercised through the use of military might, and is frequently thought of in terms of "control." Although the idea of command of space incorporates an idea similar to that of "controlling" space communications, command of space is inclusive of much more than "space control."[1] Command of space is a concept with subtleties and includes measures achieved outside hostile actions. The concept acknowledges that, by extensively using space for a variety of activities, a nation, organization, or group can play a prominent role in shaping international treaties, regulations, or accepted customary law. Through such efforts, one can ensure greater access to space communications during times of peace or war, thereby achieving a substantial level of command. How nations, organizations, and groups may achieve and exercise command of space may be manifested in three ways: presence, coercion, or force.

Command through presence

Command of space can be gained by having a presence in space.[2] By doing so, a country gains a certain amount of respect and is given more deference when contentious and competing issues arise between those with interests in space. Although some countries have used the terms "spacefaring" or "space power" to describe themselves after launching a single satellite into orbit, not all levels of participation and presence are considered the same. Although having a minimal presence in space and limited vested interest in space-based activities will yield some positive results, those with the highest levels of participation will easily achieve more influence over those with minimal involvement in space. For this reason, those that are able to "show the flag" in space the most are more readily able to gain command through presence.

Gaining command through presence is applicable during times of peace or "relative peace." By being a major player in space, one gets a proportionate level of influence in shaping international treaties and regulations. During the decades of the Cold War, American and Soviet space programs were the most prominent, and consequently both countries were able to forge the fundamental perceptions regarding what was eventually considered equitable and legitimate pertaining to the access and use of outer space. The Soviet Union's launch of the first artificial satellite, for instance, set the legal precedent for the freedom of overflight by satellites in orbit, and the United States reinforced this precedent by not requesting overflight permission from sovereign states when subsequently launching its satellites into orbit.

The international community, especially in the manifestation of the United Nations, holds considerable influence in the writing of international laws and regulations, as exemplified by the numerous resolutions coming out of the international body. Not all resolutions, however, are the same. Resolutions that fail to be ratified by those states having the most sizable presence in space lack the legitimacy required to be eventually regarded as observed international law. Moreover, since so much pertaining to operations in space is relatively new, those United Nations resolutions that incorporate more novel interpretations regarding acceptable practice or behavior in space require some period of time to be considered accepted practice. If, however, the novel interpretation remains in effect long enough and is observed by others, it can become accepted as customary practice. So, by endorsing and sponsoring resolutions and regulations, spacefaring nations have a tremendous capacity to influence what becomes precedent or considered as acceptable practice. Those countries with the most presence in space can disregard contentious agreements or resolutions made by others, thereby nullifying any new interpretation that is against their own national interests. The United States and the Soviet Union, for example, did not ratify the Bogotá Declaration, in which some nations laid claim to the geostationary belt overhead.[3] This interpretation would have limited those countries that already had satellites located in a geostationary orbit and would have required getting prior permission from those countries along the earth's equatorial belt when using the geostationary orbital slots above their country. Since two of the most powerful space nations publicly disregarded the treaty, it failed to become accepted practice and is now widely discounted. The lesson to be learned is that those with the most active presence and participation in space have a commensurate ability to promote their interests and influence the international legal basis for accessing and using space.

The European Union's Galileo program exemplifies how intended future presence can gain oneself more influence in determining the use of space. The Galileo constellation is ostensibly for the purpose of providing another independent means of positioning, navigation, and timing services for everyday civilian and commercial applications. Much of the service to be provided is redundant to that already provided by the United States GPS and the Russian Global Orbiting Navigation Satellite System (GLONASS) constellations.[4] Early designs for the European program called for "overlaying" some of the same communications frequencies that the United States was planning to use in future military upgrades of its GPS constellation.[5] Intense discussions and debate ensued to resolve the frequency impasse, and European and American counterparts were eventually able to come to a mutually agreeable solution. This example has shown that an intended future presence in space – one that provides competing services and potentially overlaps in signal bandwidth – is sufficient to bring the world's sole remaining superpower to the bargaining table.

Even China's recent endeavors in space illustrate what command through presence affords. Albeit the Chinese government's likely reason for its current space program is to instill pride in its populace, as well as make the international community take note of its achievements, the mere fact that China is only one of three countries to have a manned presence in space gives China substantial leverage in negotiating future space treaties and regulations. While China's technological prowess in space does not yet rival that of the United States, China's achievements have brought and will bring a certain amount of respect and deference from the international community. As a consequence, the Chinese will enjoy greater opportunities to ensure their continued access to celestial lines of communication in order to meet their future national security and domestic needs. These future opportunities may include the Chinese having a greater say in how the most desirable communications frequencies and geostationary orbital slots are assigned and used.

Command through coercion

Differing from command gained through presence is command exercised through coercion. This method of command differs from merely having a substantial presence, because coercion is employed though one or several non-offensive measures in an attempt to change another's strongly held view or position on a subject. Coercion occurs short of open hostilities, but may be the result of the implicit or explicit threat of some detrimental action, including the potential use of force. To be effective, any nation, organization, or group attempting to coerce another should have a significant capability to make the one being coerced seriously weigh the consequences of his or her actions. For this reason, a prerequisite for exercising coercive command is gaining presence within the same area of activity in which coercion is to be attempted. This means, for example, in order to coerce another through economic space-based activities one first needs an established presence of commercial or trade related space systems.

Most often, coercive action is focused toward the opponent's leadership to compel acquiescence in some demand, cause a reversal on a prior decision, or decide in favor of something that is not in their best interests. Coercion has long been used between nation states to influence the decisions of other countries or groups, and the most readily apparent examples have been through the movement or threat of military forces. Armies marching to the border of an adjacent country for some desired effect, navies taking station off another's coast in an effort to project power ashore, and air forces operating near the national airspace of an adversary are all manifestations of coercion. In the case of space operations, the movement of military assets is indeed one method of exercising national power; yet, considering the broader implications and recognizing all the instruments of national power, there are three other areas to consider too: diplomatic, economic, and information.

Diplomatic coercion

As described previously, having a significant presence in space activities bestows a measure of command that causes others to heed – or at least consider – one's viewpoints and desires. Any nation having such a presence in space, or any other noteworthy capability for that matter, can coerce others through diplomatic means. These include international agreements, United Nations resolutions, and unilateral pronouncements on the general conduct of space operations. For instance, the 1967 Outer Space Treaty was passed by a United Nations resolution and ratified by many of the space nations of the time, including the United States and the Soviet Union. The treaty prohibited nuclear weapons from being placed in space or the building of offensive military installations on the moon. Because of its long standing, its provisions are considered the normal state of affairs. In the future, some states might decide that it is in their interest to contest the treaty's provisions and choose to put nuclear weapons in space. In such an event, the international community, possibly led by European, Chinese, Russian, or American delegates, would probably rebuke the offending state to protect the space and security interests of the majority of member states. If those countries with the most notable presence in space were to reiterate their insistence on upholding the provisions of the Outer Space Treaty – including the possible use of "punitive measures" against any offending state – those intending to disregard the conventional interpretation of the Outer Space Treaty would be more likely to reconsider their position on the matter. In this way, command of space exercised though diplomatic coercion would cause others to weigh how much they stand to lose against what they hope to gain.

Economic coercion

Similarly, economic coercive pressure can be applied as well. Space-based technologies play a substantial role in the conduct of everyday commerce and international trade and, because of the growing demand, the number of satellite launches per year is expected to grow in the future. Those that launch the largest number of satellites – including Russia, the United States, the European Space Agency, and China – have the greatest control over scheduling whose satellite is launched and when.[6] If these countries saw it in their best interests to act collectively, they could postpone the launching of a country, organization, or group's space system. If the delayed system were a telecommunications satellite, this could adversely impact business or financial activities. While such collective action is merely denying one's physical communications, non-physical communication can be denied through economic coercion also. This thought is analogous to what others have called economic warfare.[7] This would be possible by threatening to withhold access to space services that enable commerce and trade, like the movement of data and information. Depending on the severity of the action, this can negatively impact those against whom the action is directed, consequently resulting in capitulation over some contentious issue.

Information coercion

The final method of coercion is through information. Since space-based assets are used to communicate information, this information can be used to apply pressure on decision makers or leaders to decide in favor of something contrary to their natural inclination or tendency. Such information may be transmitted through commercial media outlets using satellites into another's nation or geographic area, and the intended audience may include the other's leadership, populace, or military.[8] Coercive communications present those viewpoints and information in a context favorable and beneficial to those sending the information, and the actual information communicated may range from the factual, through the biased, to the blatantly false.[9] Those attempting to coerce another through information should carefully consider the method chosen, since blatant falsehoods may achieve short-term effects but, once discovered to be false, they will be counterproductive, since future communications, whether true or not, will probably not be trusted. Because of this, the best long-term effects can be achieved through coercive communications that are factually based and can be corroborated through independent means.

The role of global media services during the Cold War illustrates the influence of coercive communications. Even though non-space systems were used by media services during this time, satellites were commonly employed to communicate news and information around the globe during the second half of the Cold War. Whether intentionally or not, much of the information broadcast by Western media outlets tended to demonstrate the advantages of democracy, capitalism, individual liberty, and an open society. Although this form of coercion frequently worked in conjunction with diplomatic, economic, and sometimes military actions, information played a substantial part in the eventual breakup of the Soviet Union and its move toward the ideals of Western societies.[10] By the mid-1980s the Soviet Union's economy was languishing, and in an effort to improve economic growth rates Mikhail Gorbachev took action to restructure government bureaucracy and move away from centralized control of the economy. Despite Gorbachev's initiatives, the Soviet economy deteriorated further. With the improved access to global information, the Soviet public was empowered to weigh the current state of Soviet life against the capitalist and democratic way of life as presented by media and news outlets.[11] The access to such coercive communications contributed to a greater realization that it was in the best interest of the Soviet people to ultimately move away from a communist form of government and economic system and instead to move toward democracy and more open markets. This realization, along with the failing economy, directly contributed to the dissolution of the Soviet Union.

The global pervasiveness of Western media is also useful in highlighting the downside and unintended consequences of some space-based information technologies. Although the American mainstream media do not have as their primary goal the coercion of others, a backlash has occurred in some Islamic nations against the "Westernization" of their culture, and such a move is seen as in direct conflict to traditionally held religious beliefs. In some areas of the world, a growing animosity has arisen, with some complaining that the United States has more effect on their daily lives than their own governments. In many instances, incessant communications may be unwelcome and viewed as "coercion" even though such communications are not intended to change another's beliefs or views. Although freedom of speech and open media sources are viewed as being an inherent right of all peoples according to traditional Western beliefs and morals, cultural differences and sensitivities between those sending the information and those receiving the information should be duly considered to avoid or minimize the most significant and negative repercussions.

Command through force

Differing from command gained by presence and command exercised by co-ercion is command through force. In this subcategory, force may be used to *gain* as well as *exercise* command of space, and this type of command pertains to operations or assets that employ force. The primary difference between command through force and command through presence or coercion is that command through force includes the use of overt hostile actions. Such hostile actions may entail offensive operations at the strategic level of warfare or may include localized offensive operations, while assuming a strategic defensive posture elsewhere. Therefore, using force to attain command of space commonly occurs during a time of conflict between opponents. Since the value of space is as a means of communication, space warfare should always be directly or indirectly aimed at either securing command or preventing the enemy from securing it.[12] Command through force attempts to ensure one's use of both physical and non-physical space communications, thereby allowing for the movement of trade, materiel, supplies, personnel, weapons effects, data, and information. Thus, one's own access to celestial lines of communication is ensured, while that of the enemy is denied or minimized. When referring to "command of space" within a general context, "command through force" is most often implicit in its meaning.

Through established international law, outer space cannot be subjected to dominion or ownership, and consequently command of space through force is not equivalent to command exercised during land warfare, where nations have sovereignty and communication routes can be occupied with armies. Because of this difference – along with the realization of the vastness of outer space – even after gaining and exercising command through force, it is next to impossible to prevent one's adversary from using celestial lines of communication for some limited objective or purpose.

Since space is indeed vast, where and when command of space is gained and exercised through force is also important. As in maritime strategy, command can be differentiated based on where and for how long it is achieved. For space warfare, this means that command can be either general or local and either persistent or temporary.[13] General command of space is achieved when the enemy is no longer able to act in a significant or dangerous way against one's use of celestial lines of communication, and it also means that the enemy is unable to adequately defend his own. With only minor exceptions, general command enables the unfettered use of space for diplomacy, trade, commerce, information services, or military operations. Local command applies in a similar way, but the region where command is gained or exercised is less than the total region where one's interests in space lie. Local command is less than optimal but is a suitable recourse for less capable space powers. Furthermore, gaining local command allows for the protection of one's space communications through offensive or defensive measures, while one's adversary is potentially unable to adequately use his communications within that same limited region. The reasons for striving to attain local command can include the desire to gain prestige among the international community, garner domestic political support, protect one's economic interests, or gain a relative military advantage within a specific region of space. The region in which local command is gained will often be determined by the location of those celestial lines of communication considered of greatest importance.

For how long command is to be achieved is a consideration. Whether command is general or local, it may also be either persistent or temporary. Persistent command means that, despite the adversary's attempts, the element of time is no longer a significant strategic factor in the execution of warfare into, from, and through space. When command is both general and persistent, it does not mean that the enemy will not act, but that he is severely weakened to a point where his efforts are unlikely to affect the war's outcome at the strategic level. When command is local and persistent, it means that one's celestial lines of communication are protected within a specified region for the foreseeable future, yet the final outcome of the war or conflict is still not assured.

Temporary command means that either general or local command is gained for a specific period of time to achieve either military or non-military objectives. A less capable space force can often achieve command that is local and temporary by concentrating assets where the opponent is not, and it can also be achieved by taking a sizable defensive posture for a period of time or within a certain region. Such a defensive posture can prevent a stronger space power from operating uncontested within a specific region.

The highest level of command that can be gained and exercised is one that is both general and persistent. This condition is most likely following the decimation of the enemy's space fleet or assets. Even when command is both general and permanent, the enemy can still act adversely and may attempt to achieve command that is either local or temporary. This is true since no amount of military superiority in space can ensure against sporadic attack, especially if the adversary is willing to assume great risk and possible destruction.

Contesting command

Since assets and the fiscal resources that enable space operations are finite, efforts to gain some form of command in space require choosing the desired level of presence, coercion, or force within specific regions of space. Likewise, an opponent may choose to concentrate his efforts within specific regions as well and, if this is done where superior forces are not located, a less capable adversary can gain local command. By contesting command through the concentration of effects or forces within a localized region and for a specified duration, a relative advantage can be gained. Moreover, the methods of contesting command include the use of presence, coercion, or force. Contesting command of space is an option regardless of one's level of capability; therefore, it is applicable when oneself has preponderance, the enemy has preponderance, or neither side has preponderance in space. Moreover, the precedent of maritime history reveals that the normal condition will be for command of space to be in dispute.

Because space-based technology advances rapidly, any recommended tactics or procedures for contesting command will probably soon become outdated. Nevertheless, examples are helpful to illustrate what contesting command means in its greater context. To dispute command through presence, an inferior space power can increase the number of its space-based systems, thus gaining greater say in shaping future international regulations about space activities. While it is not implied that the primary intent of the European Union's Galileo program is to contest the command of the United States GPS constellation, this has in fact been a result and exemplifies the concept of contesting command through presence. By proposing and moving toward implementing the Galileo program, the Europeans have been able to collectively increase their bargaining and diplomatic influence in deciding matters related to space. Contesting command through coercion can be achieved by placing in orbit those space systems having some offensive capability. For instance, if microsatellites were placed in a nearly collocated position to one or all of the satellites used by Galileo, GLONASS, or GPS, then those launching these microsatellites could exercise a coercive effect to contest European, Russian, or American command of space. Finally, command contested through force can employ offensive actions to eliminate or minimize the enemy's threat, and such offensive actions may include the use of kinetic weapons, lasers, or electromagnetic pulse effects to attack another's space-based systems.

Chapter 8

Strategy of offense and defense

The most important guidance for military operations is a nation's grand strategy, and consequently any wartime strategy should work under the purview of grand strategy to achieve its political or diplomatic objectives. Being the two elements of military strategy, both offensive and defense strategies must also be subservient to grand strategy. Although it is easier to discuss offensive and defensive strategies separately, they are mutually dependent on each other and so intertwined that, in actuality, one is ultimately not successful without the other. As the conduct of warfare throughout history has shown, to successfully employ offensive attacks, the lines of resupply and the bases of operations must be protected through defensive means. As a result, any wartime strategic plan should include both offensive and defensive strategies. Some critics may counter with the adage, "the best defense is a good offense," or misapply Clausewitz that the "destruction of the enemy" is the key to victory, thus implying that offensive operations are the supreme consideration in war.[1] Granted that an offensive strategy during military operations is a necessary requisite to achieve final victory, defensive strategies in some locations allow for more effective and subsequently more successful offensive measures in other locations.

Merely addressing the role of offensive strategy in space presumes that force is in fact a suitable course of action; yet the weaponization of space, which enables an offensive strategy, is still currently being debated. Consequently, one could argue that it cannot be presumed that offensive weapons are indeed appropriate to space strategy. To determine the role of weapons and the use of force in space, a historical and legal basis of warfare is needed. This basis is established by customary and international law, especially what is commonly regarded as the Law of Armed Conflict.

The law of armed conflict

The Law of Armed Conflict has been defined as "that part of international law that regulates the conduct of armed hostilities."[2] It generally encompasses international treaty law and customary international law regulating the methods of warfare, and it has implications for the conduct of space warfare and developing its strategic principles. Serving as the foundation of the Law of Armed Conflict is the inherent right of self-defense. This right applies during peace or war and stems from customary international law dating back at least three hundred years. Furthermore, this right is delineated in Article 51 of the United Nations Charter, which states, "Nothing . . . shall impair the inherent right of individual or collective self-defense if an armed attack occurs."[3] This well-recognized right of self-defense is one of the several reasons that offensive operations should be considered appropriate when another nation's interest or sovereignty is threatened.

Pertaining to the application of force, the Law of Armed Conflict calls for using only that degree and kind of force required for the partial or complete submission of the enemy, while considering the minimum expenditure of time, life, and physical resources.[4] Often referred to as "military necessity," this principle is designed to limit the application of force to that required for carrying out lawful military purposes. Sometimes, this principle is misunderstood and misapplied to support the excessive and unlawful application of military force, since military necessity could be incorrectly argued to justify any mission accomplishment. While the principle of military necessity recognizes that some collateral damage and incidental injury to civilians may occur when a legitimate military target is attacked, it does not excuse the wanton destruction of lives and property disproportionate to the military advantage to be gained.[5]

Also of relevance to the application of force is the principle of lawful targeting, which is based upon three underpinnings.[6] First, a belligerent's right to injure the enemy is not unlimited. Second, launching attacks against civilian populations is prohibited. Third, distinctions between combatants and noncombatants must be made, to spare injury to noncombatants as much as possible. Consequently, under lawful targeting, all "reasonable precautions" must be taken to ensure that only military objectives are targeted, so damage to civilian objects (collateral damage) and death and injury to civilians (incidental injury) are avoided as much as possible.[7]

Therefore, the Law of Armed Conflict addresses many of the general concerns regarding the reasons to go to war, along with what is considered appropriate and inappropriate uses of force. Although self-defense is a time-honored justification for going to war, another reason is frequently used as justification as well. Under Article 51 of the United Nations Charter, collective self-defense may be invoked, meaning that, if a state being part of a cooperative defense agreement is attacked, then those other states included in the agreement can act against a belligerent, even though they themselves were not attacked.[8] Such collective defense agreements have been used between nation states for centuries. Besides the Law of Armed Conflict, more specific guidance is often given to the armed forces concerning the conduct of war and the application of force, and in the United States this guidance is contained within its Rules of Engagement.

Rules of engagement

Since the Rules of Engagement have a bearing on the general conduct of war, they will also have a bearing on the conduct of space warfare. As the United States is presently regarded by many as having a superior military capability, it is worthwhile to look at the United States Rules of Engagement in particular. These rules spell out specific interpretations of the right to self-defense, and they can be considered in two sub-categories: Standing Rules of Engagement and Supplemental Rules of Engagement. Standing Rules of Engagement provide overarching guidance for the application of force during peace and war.[9] In contrast, Supplemental Rules of Engagement are issued for the accomplishment of mission objectives during specified hostilities or other military operations.

The Chairman of the Joint Chiefs of Staff promulgates the United States Standing Rules of Engagement, reflecting the inherent right of self-defense. Furthermore, these rules divide self-defense into three categories. The first category, national self-defense, applies to the United States, its forces, and, in specific circumstances, its nationals and their property. The second category, collective self-defense, applies to designated non-US forces, foreign nationals, and their property. The third major category is unit self-defense and applies to a particular force element – including individual personnel – and other forces in the vicinity.[10]

Supplemental Rules of Engagements, on the other hand, are only issued to provide guidance for the accomplishment of specific mission objectives under specific conditions. Additionally, Supplemental Rules of Engagement usually delineate what is considered mission essential equipment, which applies to equipment or property considered vital for the accomplishment of mission objectives. Because of its importance, mission essential equipment is deemed necessary to protect by force.

Alas, weaponization

What is gleaned from looking at the Law of Armed Conflict and the Rules of Engagement is that offensive and defensive actions are appropriate activities to protect one's security and interests. Furthermore, under the right of self-defense, the leaders of sovereign nations have a duty and obligation to protect and defend their interests in space, even if this means the application of force. While the Law of Armed Conflict does place some restrictions on the application of force, so as to minimize the harm to civilian property and the lives of innocents, no indication is given that applying forceful measures in space is not allowed based on hundreds of years of international treaty law and customary law. Moreover, based on the United States Standing Rules of Engagement, weaponry may be allowed in space to protect and defend national security, one's allies, and military personnel. Perhaps even more noteworthy, the Supplemental Rules of Engagement allow for the protection and defense of physical property that is considered vital for mission accomplishment. This idea could easily be applied to strategic assets – like satellites used for positioning, navigation, and timing – which the military presently uses extensively when coordinating and executing precision attacks. Overall, space warfare must observe the same restrictions and considerations when deciding upon and applying force as is already done with warfare on land, at sea, and in the air.

Many critics of space weaponization, such as those embracing the sanctuary or survivability camps, may not be happy with the observations made above, as some have argued that space should be considered differently from land, sea, and air to preclude the use of weapons in space. Specifically, it has been argued that there is a historic and legal precedent for considering space as international commons that obviate the need for weapons in space: this precedent being the Antarctica Treaty. Antarctica has been recognized in the past by several states for its natural resource potential. Seven countries made preexisting claims of sovereignty on the continent: Argentina, Australia, Great Britain, Chile, France, New Zealand, and Norway, with three of the countries having overlapping claims.[11] The United States has refrained from making any formal claims on the continent, but based on early expeditions by Wilkes, Byrd, and Ellsworth and having sustained its manning of observation posts, the United States has a strong legal case for claiming territory if it chose to exercise its prerogative as well.[12] The treaty went into effect in 1961 after ratification by the twelve original participating states, and its preamble says, "[I]t is in the interest of all mankind that Antarctica shall continue forever to be used for peaceful purposes."[13] Moreover, the treaty prohibits "any measures of a military nature, such as the establishment of military bases and fortifications, the carrying out of military maneuvers, as well as the testing of any types of weapons."[14] It does not, however, prohibit the use of military personnel or equipment for scientific research or for any other peaceful purposes.[15] Because of the treaty's success in having the continent of Antarctica viewed as international commons for over forty years, the treaty has been used as a proposed model for thinking about international space activities. Such a model, it is argued, could also allow nations to consciously refrain from formally enforcing sovereignty claims or permanently basing weapons in space.[16]

To understand what, if any, potential applicability or implications the Antarctica Treaty could have for strategic thought in space, one must first review the underlying argument. Outer space is a medium, like the land, sea, and air. The continent of Antarctica is but a region on the earth, or a defined region that comprises the land medium, while also involving air and sea media also. If the precedent of the Antarctica Treaty were properly applied to space, it would in actuality only mean that a region within the space medium could successfully be considered international commons where military measures, installations, and weapons testing are prohibited. Military equipment and personnel would be allowed for any "peaceful purpose." While this treaty may indeed prove to have a certain applicability toward setting policy and strategy in space, the implications coming from the hundreds of years of observed customary international law bear more relevance than a treaty just a few decades old. In weighing the precedent of the Antarctica Treaty against customary international laws, the conclusion reached is that the protection of some national interests may necessitate the use of force, wherever those interests are located. This includes outer space.

It is indeed a current political reality that weapons in space are regarded differently from weapons on land, at sea, or in the air, and this has had the effect of inhibiting some research and development of space-based weapons.[17] Some advocates of placing weapons in space may ask what is the great concern about space weaponization, noting the many past militarization and weaponization programs. These include the Dyna-Soar, Manned Orbital Laboratory, anti-satellite, and Strategic Defense Initiative programs of the United States, as well as the fractional orbital bombardment systems and anti-satellite programs of the Soviet Union.[18] Nevertheless, permanent space-based weapons and space-to-space attacks have not occurred yet, so ongoing debate on formulating international and domestic policy will probably continue. While there is historical precedent for using force to defend one's interests, policy must eventually address where and in what manner force is to be applied in space. While acknowledging that future space policy will continue to be formulated, an understanding of the roles of offensive and defensive strategy in space is vital to both warfighters and policy makers alike.

Offensive strategy

History has shown that when nations expand their interests – like commercial ventures – to new regions, military capabilities to protect these interests follow suit. For instance, the expansion of trade and commerce along sea lines of communications had the effect of tying the viability of many seagoing nations to their successful maritime trade. Consequently, the need to build fleets to protect this trade and commerce arose. As interests and activities in space continue to increase, it is expected that space will be no different in this regard.

Offensive strategy is called for when political objectives necessitate wresting or acquiring something from the enemy. The need for such a strategy in space, along with its military operations, comes from the necessity of protecting one's interests and ensuring access to celestial lines of communication. It is to be expected that a combination of offensive strategy, operations, and tactics will all be necessary ingredients to obtain general or persistent command of space, thereby ensuring one's access and use of space. As Clausewitz and Corbett have noted, the offensive is the more "effective" form of war and, as a matter of general practice, should be attempted by the stronger space power. Offensive strategy can obtain positive results, in addition to boosting morale and imparting a psychological advantage to those who initiate attack. Also, the initiative gained through offensive operations is beneficial thanks to the increased likelihood of surprising the enemy.

Despite the advantages coming from initiative, offensive operations should not be considered synonymous with "attacking first" or "taking the initiative." To be truly effective, offensive strategy must incorporate those elements that are its primary benefits. For merely attacking another when the opposition knows where, when, and in what manner the attack is coming imparts little if no advantage to the attacker. Consequently, offensive strategy should keep its intentions and methods unknown to the enemy in order to be most effective. Also illustrating the reason that the offensive is not merely just attacking or taking initiative is the fact that self-defense actions and general defensive operations can exhibit these characteristics also, especially during the counterattack phase.

Moreover, the strategy of the offense is not a substitute for sound wartime strategy. Albeit Clausewitz writes "the destruction of the enemy forces is admittedly the purpose of all engagements," caution must be heeded when considering offensive operations, otherwise systems and forces may be "thrown away in ill-considered offensives."[19] A superior force looking for decisive victory through offensive strategy in space will probably find the enemy in a position where he cannot easily be affected. For, as in the case of maritime history, attempts to seek a decisive battle against the enemy will be met with the enemy being in or moving to a position of relative safety. If one attempts offensive action against an enemy that is in such positions of safety, a heavy cost will likely be paid for such action.

Defensive strategy

Despite the advantages of offensive space strategy, the utility of defensive strategy is not lessened, since offensive and defensive strategies are mutually complementary, as any successful war plan must have characteristics of both. Defensive strategy is called for when political objectives necessitate preventing the enemy from achieving or gaining something. By their inherent nature, the defense is the "stronger" form of war and should be used extensively by less capable space forces until the offensive can be assumed. Clausewitz writes on the superior strength of the defense, although he admits that the attacker might enjoy considerable advantage during the opening phases of hostilities. He writes, "So in order to state the relationship precisely, we must say that *the defensive form of warfare is intrinsically stronger than the offensive.*"[20] He concluded that a defensive strategy should be assumed when one is weaker relative to the adversary, and a defensive strategy should be abandoned once one is able to pursue the offensive.[21] Some strategists have commented that defensive strategy is not always the stronger form of war in space, saying that it depends on the kind of orbit the satellite is in. Thus, depending on the orbit, the offense may in fact be the stronger form of warfare. Specifically, it has been said, "In space, defense probably is the stronger form of waging war in the mid earth or high earth orbits, but probably not in low earth orbits. There is some safety in sheer distance (in most cases, equal to time)."[22]

Despite space warfare being different from the land warfare theory of which Clausewitz writes, the defense is the stronger form of war . . . *always*. To appreciate this, it must be understood what a defensive strategy and posture entails. Clausewitz believed that the defense meant "awaiting the blow," with the goal of preserving one's forces and assets.[23] However, at the operational and tactical level of warfare, he observes that the advantages of defense include those benefits coming from waiting and from position. Similarly, Corbett says, "If either by land or by sea we take a position so good that it cannot be turned and must be broken down before our enemy can reach his objective, then the advantage of dexterity and stealth passes to us."[24] So implicit in taking a truly defensive strategy is the idea that the position being held has some relative advantage. A unit of soldiers stationed behind a fortification is such a defensive posture. To have these same soldiers lined up abreast in an open field to await their turn in trading volleys of musket fire with the adversary, however, is not assuming such a defensive posture.

The defense also has other advantages that contribute to making it the stronger form of warfare. One advantage is that, once an enemy's force attacks, it often gives away its position and potential disposition, if previously unknown. With the enemy's location and disposition known, one's follow-on counterattack is more likely to succeed. Additionally, after an enemy attacks, he often indicates his strategic intentions, and with this information a sound military strategy can be formulated to thwart his aggression and prevent him from achieving his desired aims.

Although at the operational and tactical levels of warfare, defensive strategy includes awaiting the blow from a position of advantage, that is not all it includes. When assuming the defense, one frequently waits for the opportune moment when the enemy falters or displays uncertainty in his actions. At that moment, a counterattack is launched. Such a counterattack takes advantage of the inherent advantages of defensive strategy, while at the same time attempting to achieve positive results against the enemy. In this manner, one is more likely to deal a serious blow against one's adversary.

What does this mean for space warfare and defensive strategy? This means that defensive strategy is still the stronger form of warfare, but to successfully assume a defensive posture, an advantageous position must be held. Placing space-based defensive systems in an unprotected, highly vulnerable location – as in a near-earth orbit – without any kind of relative advantage is not the strategy of the defense but is the *strategy of the ludicrous*. The conclusion reached, therefore, is that employing a truly defensive strategy in space means holding a position with a relative advantage when attacked. This kind of relative advantage can be obtained, for instance, by employing onboard self-protection systems or by placing space assets where they prove more difficult to attack.

Furthermore, to fully comprehend the advantages of defensive strategy, it is important to consider defensive strategy in its broadest sense, and not just militarily. When considering the defense accordingly, it is useful to think of it in terms of *strategic defense*. Strategic defense pertains to assuming a defensive posture, along with all the benefits of doing so. In contrast, operational and tactical defense pertain to the advantages realized during traditional military actions at the operational or tactical level of warfare. The advantages realized by these two areas are sufficiently addressed by the previous discussions on defensive strategy, including "awaiting the blow" from a position of advantage. The strategic defense, on the other hand, is not explicitly addressed by the writings of either Clausewitz or Corbett. Yet by employing the posture of the strategic defense, benefits can be achieved that the operational or tactical defense alone does not impart.

These benefits of the strategic defense come about from one's inherent right of self-defense. Thanks to this time-honored and internationally recognized right, when one is attacked by an unprovoked adversary, all the advantages and benefits of the inherent right of self-defense are enjoyed. These advantages and benefits include the moral authority that one can defend oneself and retaliate through military actions, and it also includes that one's aims of defeating the attacker are considered legitimate and just. When one is attacked by an unprovoked belligerent, international security agreements and collective self-defense clauses may be invoked so others may come to one's aid and defense. Thus, other states are more apt to unequivocally and expeditiously lend support to defeat one's attacker.

While the general strategy of space warfare is the topic of discussion of this work, it is possible to suggest operational- and tactical-level implementations of an appropriate defensive strategy. These suggestions include using self-protection methods that employ passive shielding against ballistic, laser, or other offensive attack. Other passive methods include incorporating materials that minimize radar, infrared, or optical detection, thereby lowering the probability of enemy detection and subsequent attack, since it is difficult to attack something that you do not know is there. Also included in defensive strategy is the employment of self-protection methods using active space-based or ground-based weapon systems that directly counter the enemy's own offensive weaponry.

Although outer space is vast and seemingly empty, positions can be taken that provide some defensive advantage. Satellites with adequate shielding against charged particles can take station within the Van Allen radiation belts to protect against hunter–killer satellites that might slowly and almost imperceptibly move alongside an unsuspecting space-based system prior to attack, assuming that the enemy's satellite lacks the same shielding against the charged particles. Another example would be taking a position within a known orbital debris field, or even being collocated with a larger piece of space debris. Positions of this kind include those non-operational satellites placed in "graveyard" orbits after their service life has expired. If such a system was small enough to avoid detection by taking such a position, it could potentially operate relatively free from the enemy's attack.

Perhaps the best defensive position is obtained by taking station where the enemy would not dare risk attacking. This would be achieved by locating space systems in close vicinity to high-value or national assets of a neutral or enemy state. For example, parasitic microsatellites could be physically attached to each of the satellites in a positioning, navigation, and timing constellation. If offensive weapons were used against these parasitic satellites, the positioning satellite would also be likely to suffer irreparable harm, thus rendering it useless. In such a situation involving the GPS constellation, the United States may be reluctant to destroy the enemy microsatellite for fear of destroying its own GPS satellite. This example demonstrates that, if a position of advantage is taken, the defense is indeed the stronger form of warfare. If an attack is subsequently launched against the parasitic satellites, the attacking systems can be more readily located and targeted for counterattack, since the application of force often gives the attacker's position away. Such locating and targeting to support a counterattack need not be done with space-based assets, but can employ any combination of land, sea, and air assets to accomplish this as well. So a counterattack to a space-based attack need not be in kind. Once the location of the attacking system is determined, the enemy can await the most opportune moment to conduct his counterattack, thus taking advantage of the benefits coming from defensive strategy.

In a similar vein, a defensive strategy – specifically a posture of operational or tactical defense – can be successfully assumed by designing spacecraft that negatively impact others when attacked. A design of this sort can include using a satellite that fractures into thousands of small pieces when hit with a ballistic weapon, thus fouling a region of that orbit. The design may also include the generation of a strong electromagnetic pulse when attacked, with the result of disabling all electronic systems of foe and friend alike within the pulse's effective range. Under both conditions, an attacker would have to seriously weigh the rewards against the risks of attacking these kinds of space systems, since their own access and use of space could suffer as a result. Space systems that incorporate such designs provide a deterrent against attack, and consequently they may provide a stabilizing effect on the escalation of hostilities. A notable exception to this deterrence is when terrorists desire the fouling of near-earth orbits or the disabling of anyone's satellites, since terrorists may in many cases not care about their own access to and use of space.

Even though space-based systems seem highly vulnerable to offensive weapons, this is a transitory state of affairs within the latest technology cycle. As demonstrated throughout the course of military history, with every offensive technological advantage, defensive technology has evolved to counter it. As the Prussian master of strategy noted, "If the offensive were to invent some major new expedient . . . the defensive would also have to change its methods."[25] So the caution to be heeded by any space power who advocates a strategy based solely on offensive actions is that the defense is still the stronger form of war, and an unfounded overreliance on offensive weaponry is in itself a foolhardy strategy.

Offense and defense combined

In the end, space strategy must recognize that offensive and defensive strategies are mutually dependent on each other. This is not a new observation, since land, sea, and air warfare have long histories of protecting and defending their lines of attack, operation, and supply through defensive strategy. Without defending these lines, an offensive strategy against the enemy would probably not be as effective or efficient as possible. Similarly, to employ offensive effects from space-based weapons requires the ability to communicate these effects through the medium of space. Therefore, one needs to protect and defend one's access to those celestial lines of communication that enable offensive effects. In a tactical example, firing a space-based laser at another's orbiting spacecraft may require a line-of-sight view of the targeted satellite, and consequently one would need to defend against having one's laser interfered with or prevented from having line-of-sight access to the intended target. Because celestial lines of communication are frequently shared between belligerents, attacking the enemy's lines may result in denying one's own access and use too. So when implementing an offensive strategy – like with the tactical employment of electromagnetic interference or pulse generation – one needs to defend one's own access to the very same lines one is attacking.

Likewise, the offensive helps the defensive. Admittedly, a purely defensive strategy is unlikely to defeat the enemy or cause him to acquiesce on a diplomatically contentious issue. In most cases, an effective offensive strategy is needed to win a war. Yet when one has inferior forces, minor offensive attacks can be used to dispute the enemy's command of space, thus "buying time" to reconstitute a superior force or gain the support of allies. The effect of "buying time" is to protect one's interests and prevent the enemy from accomplishing some aim; it therefore incorporates elements of defensive strategy. It is too simplistic, however, to think of offensive and defensive strategy within just a military context. Since diplomatic, economic, and information instruments of power are also at one's disposal, these too can be effectively used in war. Therefore, regarding the buying of more time through minor offensive actions, this concept includes using diplomatic, economic, information, or military actions against the adversary to improve the conditions of one's defensive strategy, until such time as an aggressive and successful offensive strategy can be undertaken.

Chapter 9

Strategic positions

The idea of strategic positions in space has been extensively written about, perhaps more than any other concept regarding space strategy. As with using battlefield high ground for artillery fire in land warfare, using narrow straits that choke maritime communications in naval warfare, and bombing at altitudes high above the reach of most anti-aircraft guns in air warfare, there are advantageous and valuable strategic positions in space warfare as well. Strategic positions are locations that impart some relative advantage from operating there or hold value due to the importance of the activities performed there. Since the inherent value of space is as a means of communication, it then follows that most strategic positions in space are related to accessing and using celestial lines of communications. As such, strategic positions are often located where it is better to have communication routes or where communications already tend to congregate. Those positions dealing with physical communications are used in the movement of space vehicles, equipment, materiel, supplies, and personnel. Those positions dealing with non-physical communications are used in the movement of some weapons effects and electromagnetic transmissions.

Although it is convenient to think about strategic position in purely military terms – like determining those specific locations by which the enemy's forces must transit – the idea is indeed broader than just a military context. This is because non-military interests also come into play regarding the use of outer space, and each of these interests has ramifications when contemplating those locations in space having strategic advantage and value. By definition, strategic positions impart some advantage or hold some measure of value, and therefore diplomatic efforts may be required to regulate or limit access to such positions. States, organizations, and groups may desire unlimited access to the most desirable positions in space and, due to the competition for limited locations, some will probably have greater access to these positions than others. Because of this competition, any entity having access to a strategic position, and able to prevent others from using it, has an advantage that can be used for diplomatic or political gain. As with diplomatic interests, strategic positions in space can affect economic interests as well, since there are regions and locations that benefit commerce and trade in and through space. Such positions can include those that are most advantageous for the movement of data and information for economic activity. Lastly, strategic positions can pertain to information activities, since there are locations or regions that hold value due to the importance and amount of information collected, scientific data gathered, news relayed, and media services broadcast.

Choke-points

Sea power and air power theories provide examples where the movements of ships or airplanes tend to converge or have focal points of operation. Although choke-points are conventionally thought of as those communications routes that converge, hubs of activity like ports and airfields also share this characteristic of convergence, since they represent facilities where a proportionally significant amount of ships and aircraft travel. So, as with ports, airfields, and narrow straits, space operations too should have such locations and regions. Space activities are, however, different from naval and air operations, since space activities presently deal more with non-physical communications than do either naval or air activities. This is not to suggest that data and information do not move through naval or air choke-points. For many centuries the ships of the high seas were used to relay news from distant lands, but in current times this type of activity has substantially lessened. Aircraft, along with the people they transport, have been used to move mail and news, and even serve as a communication relays for voice or data transmissions. Despite the use of naval and air assets to move data, news, and information, space-based systems are used more extensively for the movement of non-physical communications.

The choke-points for non-physical communications are commonly thought of as ground-based uplinks or celestial-based downlinks and crosslinks, which are all used to transmit and receive data and information. Yet the concept of choke-points incorporates an understanding that these are locations where communications tend to converge more than in other areas. Therefore, if a space-based communications network has sufficient redundancy with multiple communications paths for any given task or operation, the movement of the data and information may occur in an almost equally distributed manner across the network. Thus, a meaningful convergence of communications at a few positions does not in fact exist. This kind of distributed path of communications is indeed the case with many telecommunication systems that use a constellation of satellites that continuously transit above a geographic area on the earth when providing services. If one satellite becomes inoperative, there might be a temporary gap in the services provided but, once the next satellite moves into the coverage area, service is restored. The same idea of distributed systems and networks applies to ground stations having several redundant backup locations where, if one becomes inoperable, another station picks up the required tasks. In redundant and distributed systems such as these, some might consider each of the nodes of the communications network a choke-point, since some inconvenience and degradation occurs if any one of the stations or satellites is lost.[1] Nevertheless, applying the term "choke-point" to such networks and distributed systems diminishes the term's meaning, since not every hub of activity should be called a choke-point. It then follows that non-physical choke-points are locations or regions where there is a proportionally significant concentration of communications emanating from or going through them. If the ability to use such a choke-point is lost or denied, the movement of data and information is significantly restricted as a result.

The concept of "positions" and "choke-points" of non-physical communications extends to areas not commonly regarded as such. For there are regions of the electromagnetic spectrum that are more desirable or more predominately used. One example of such a region is that comprising the radio frequencies, since a preponderance of current communication services utilizes this frequency region. The visible light spectrum could similarly be considered such a region, even though its access and use are frequently regarded as commonplace. Other desirable frequency regions include those having lower attenuation losses when traveling through the earth's atmosphere. Therefore, from a strategic viewpoint, positions and choke-points in the electromagnetic frequency spectrum can be exploited for advantage. But, as with those sea lanes used for trade and commerce, these frequency spectrums are often shared, even among belligerents. This fact can be to one's detriment or advantage, depending on the strategic posture chosen.

The next type of choke-point pertains to physical communications. As in the case of non-physical choke-points, if there are many different hubs of activity for moving launch vehicles, equipment, materiel, supplies, and personnel in and through space – and little degradation occurs if use of one these hubs is lost – then it seems dubious that in such cases a choke-point in fact exists. Physical choke-points are, therefore, those hubs that significant concentrations of communications emanate from or go through, and if their use is denied then movement of physical communications is severely restricted. Currently, some states and large corporations have only a few locations to launch their systems into space or return them to earth. In the United States, Cape Canaveral, Kennedy Space Center, and Vandenberg Air Force Base; the French Space Center in Kourou, French Guiana; the Russian Tyuratam and Plesetsk launch sites: these locations represent physical communications choke-points.[2] Other choke points of this kind would include space stations that are a hub for scientific, commercial, logistical, or military enterprise. If such a station were lost, specialized activities or services would be dramatically curtailed, as well as potentially having serious political and diplomatic repercussions. Moreover, permanent stations on the moon or on other celestial bodies are likely candidates for becoming future physical communications choke-points, especially if such stations provide unique services or capabilities.

Strategic positions related to space-based communications can have a military value and, based on the precedents from naval and air warfare, choke-points can be exploited for military advantage. Consequently, space warfare must be concerned with maintaining the use of one's own choke-points and denying the enemy the use of his. If correctly exploited, choke-points allow one to restrict an adversary's movement along and use of celestial lines of communication, thus improving the overall conditions for military operations.

Choke-points of military value include those on earth and in space. Since fiscal constraints limit the number of the most capable and sophisticated launch sites that can be built, terrestrial-based choke-points can be exploited to diminish the enemy's ability to use any one of his few launch facilities. Furthermore, during times of open hostilities in space, if one is able to destroy a number of an adversary's satellites, he will probably want to replace these systems quickly. Yet if one is also able to exploit his launch facility choke-points, an adversary may not be able to act in a responsive manner to get replacements into orbit. Methods of denying or minimizing another's launch capability can be accomplished by destroying the actual facilities or support elements that are used in launching payloads into space.

Non-terrestrial choke-points may also be exploited for military gain. One example includes exploiting a space vehicle's antipodal choke-point – which is a position through which each satellite must pass about a half revolution after its launch based on the antipode of its launch site.[3] Some have suggested exploiting such choke-points by employing anti-launch weapons at these positions to deny the enemy's ability to place payloads in orbit.[4] Additionally, choke-points may be specific orbits. Being analogous to heavily occupied airways or sea lanes, some of the most desirable orbits have become more congested with satellites than other regions. The low-earth and geostationary orbital regions are two locations that have extensive activity, and therefore they could be considered as choke-points. Excluding Russia's propensity for using highly-elliptical orbits, these two orbital regions are where about 90 percent of today's satellites operate.[5] If one is able to exploit the most congested of these orbital regions, while preserving one's own use of them, a military advantage can be realized.[6]

This thought is further exemplified by the pervasive use of space-based systems for military command and control, which orchestrate various actions at the strategic, operational, and tactical levels of warfare. By denying or restricting the enemy's use of command and control communications at his orbital choke points, one can severely limit his ability to give timely orders, thus impacting his overall warfighting effectiveness. If a few low-earth satellites are used as the primary means of command and control, significant amounts of critical military information will converge at these locations. Consequently, these represent locations that can be exploited for advantage. The same would hold true for other mission areas, such as satellites used for intelligence, surveillance, and reconnaissance missions.

High-value positions

Whereas choke-points are locations or regions that can be exploited for military advantage, other positions may also hold strategic value without actually being choke-points. These high-value positions are commonly space-based systems performing valuable or unique services, whether for commerce, information, or military uses. Albeit high-value positions may also represent choke-points for space communications, this is not necessarily always the case. Examples of high-value positions include those satellites making up global positioning and timing satellite systems, such as GPS, GLONASS, or the future Galileo constellation. Because these satellite systems are designed to have about two dozen satellites in each constellation, a loss of a single satellite does not result in too critical a loss of capability, and therefore any single satellite does not represent a choke-point in itself.[7] So, while these positioning satellites are not considered choke-points, they are nonetheless considered high-value positions with strategic value. If an adversary is able to successfully attack and destroy enough of these positioning satellites to make the constellation's services ineffective, commercial transportation industries and military weaponry that rely on the positioning and timing information could be seriously degraded. For this reason, space warfare is concerned with protecting one's high-value positions and attacking or degrading those of the enemy.

Other high-value positions include those hubs of activity used for scientific and commercial purposes. Since they will probably be limited in number, most space stations or bases will be high-value assets – representing a substantial financial investment and performing difficult to replace services. Therefore, such positions hold value due to the importance of the activities performed there. Many high-value systems confer national pride and prestige coming from the accomplishments these facilities make possible or even those accomplishments they promise to make possible in the future. Moreover, when compared to other space systems, high-value systems frequently provide unique services or functions that other satellites and spacecraft do not provide. As a result, if one attacks these positions, their destruction can potentially decimate an entire service sector, along with having a demoralizing effect upon the state, organization, or group to which the system belonged.

Certain orbits have been recognized for years as being advantageous when performing certain functions and services. This is indeed true of geostationary orbital positions used by many communications satellites. Since space systems located in a geostationary orbital position can provide continuous coverage and communication services within a specific geographic area, they have become highly sought after by states and businesses. Since the number of such orbital geostationary slots is considered finite, those attempting to gain access to a geostationary position can have intense disagreements with those attempting to keep their position. Indeed, there have been such disagreements over geostationary slots. The Bogotá Declaration highlights the perceived value of geostationary orbital positions. In the declaration, eight equatorial nations claimed sovereignty of the geostationary belt above their countries.[8] Although the Soviet Union and the United States rejected these nations' claim, the case does illustrate that others have recognized the need to ensure their future right to ownership of and access to these strategic positions.

By using such high-value positions, while denying the same use to others, a relative advantage is achieved. This advantage can lead to fortuitous diplomatic, economic, information, and military results. On the other hand, it is to be expected a foe will attempt to do the same, thereby attempting to limit one's own use of high-value positions.

Since geostationary orbital positions lie along the equatorial plane in outer space, it follows that there might be strategic positions along the same equatorial plane but on *terra firma*. This is in fact the case. Equatorial positions on earth have an advantage over others due to the more efficient launching of payloads into orbit. The equatorial boost from these positions imparts more kinetic energy to achieve a higher vehicle escape velocity, and this in turn allows for larger payloads to be placed in orbit (given an equivalent launch vehicle or rocket) when compared to launch positions at other latitudes. Launch facilities along the equator, therefore, represent high-value positions based on their ability to more efficiently place systems in space.

Finally, the Lagrange points potentially represent high-value positions. These positions have special attributes and subsequently hold the potential for strategic advantage. These points occur between any two celestial bodies, like the earth and moon, and allow an object placed there to remain almost perfectly stable and in a fixed position relative to the two bodies. The scientific community, in studying the sun's solar activity and periodic cycles, has already exploited this phenomenon.[9] Because of their characteristics, it is expected that some of these Lagrange points can be exploited for military advantage as well, especially since space systems located there require little expenditure of precious onboard fuel.

Space as high ground

Outer space, especially near-earth orbits, has been touted as the "ultimate high ground" for some time. Like terrain used by artillery overlooking enemy formations or the high altitude flown by bomber aircraft, assets in space similarly have a superior view of the earth and therefore may enjoy a strategic advantage. This advantage is realized when measured against comparable terrestrial-based systems, since space-based systems will – in theory – enjoy a commanding view of the battlefield.

There are two general benefits of placing satellites or weapons in space: their field-of-view from space and the energy benefits gained from the earth's "gravity well." Intelligence, surveillance, and reconnaissance satellites have long used the extensive field-of-view that comes from having systems in orbit around earth. Depending on the type of orbit and its height above the earth, surveillance systems can be optimized to observe specific terrestrial features or geographic areas. Those advocating that outer space should be a "sanctuary" recognize this. Since the primary value of space, according to sanctuary school advocates, is the ability to "see" within the boundaries of other nation states, space systems may legally fly over other countries and perform treaty verification via their onboard sensors. This commanding view from space is said to have a stabilizing influence, especially when used to monitor terrestrial activities and verify arms control agreements. Although not included as part of the sanctuary school of thought, weapon systems also gain this same field-of-view benefit from operating in space. First detecting and then tracking their intended target, space-based weapons can be used to engage enemy ballistic missiles, armored vehicles, and troop formations. The relative advantage between any two adversaries – one having an effective space-based weapons capability and the other not – may under certain conditions tip the scales in favor of the one having the superior space-based weapons capability.

The second benefit of using the high ground of space comes from the energy advantage it naturally imparts. Because of the earth's gravitational pull and the potential energy coming from operating high above the earth, this energy can be imparted to kinetic energy warheads. Since the energy of any impacting kinetic weapon is a function of its mass and velocity, basing kinetic weapons in space seems to hold some promise of military advantage. Additionally, a side benefit coming from operating high above the enemy's terrestrial-based weapons is that it may take more time for the enemy's ground-based weapons to impact or hit space assets when compared to closer assets on land, at sea, or in the air. Thus, space-based weapons may under some circumstances enjoy more time – although the additional amount of time might be considered insignificant – to take evasive action or employ counter-measures to thwart an adversary's offensive actions. Admittedly, any additional time benefit coming from a greater distance between terrestrial and space-based systems can just as well translate into an equivalent advantage for the enemy.

So the advantage realized by high-ground is a relative measure, often used between space-based and terrestrially-based assets. It is worth emphasizing that this advantage is not realized between two space-based weapons with similar capabilities. Therefore, if asking if high ground is in fact a strategic position, the answer is "it depends." When compared to many ground systems, those in orbit have distinct advantages in military utility. Yet against a comparable space-based asset the advantage and benefit is nullified. Many of today's national security concerns involve activities and interactions between states, organizations, and groups on land, and, because of this, military operations will be in the near-term predominantly concerned with affecting these land-based activities and interactions. Therefore, when the military focus is on events on land, space-based systems potentially hold a strategic position through high ground. If the political and policy objectives change where the most important activities and interactions are in space, the military focus will probably shift to events in and through space. In such cases, space-to-space military strategy will enjoy few benefits coming from high ground. The theory and strategic principles of space warfare should be timeless if they are in fact true, and consequently they should have just as much relevance today as when national interests and activities move outward from just terrestrial-based and near-earth orbit concerns. So it appears quite dubious that an entire strategy founded around a single central theme – such as the high ground of space – will be an enduring strategy in the end.

It is noteworthy that the sanctuary and high ground schools of thought are both acknowledged through the concept of strategic positions in space.[10] Although the conclusions reached by each are different – the sanctuary school concluding that space should be weapons-free and the high ground school concluding that offensive weapons should have a dominant role in space – the underlying assumptions that led to these differing conclusions are considered sound. So while the strategic framework provided here for space warfare does recognize the benefits coming from a greater field-of-view and the energy benefits coming from the earth's gravity well, the interpretation on the role of weapons in space is distinctly different from those reached through the sanctuary and high ground schools of thought.

Positions of negative value

The term "strategic positions" in the context of "choke-points" and "high ground" denotes a region or location with a degree of relative advantage or having inherent value, which is realized when compared to other regions or locations that do not share the same beneficial characteristics.[11] So, although strategic positions like choke-points or high ground give those holding such positions a substantial advantage when compared to those not holding similar positions, it is possible to realize this same relative measure through other means. For instance, if one opponent's position is considered "neutral" in value, while the other opponent is required to use a position considered "negative" in value, then the same relative outcome is achieved: one has access to a position that is better than another. As a consequence, positions of negative value are those regions or locations where a relative disadvantage is realized. As with strategic positions, positions of negative value are best understood in terms of accessing and using celestial lines of communication.

Our current understanding of outer space has allowed us to glean the information that some regions seem more inhospitable for conducting routine space operations and services. For example, potentially hazardous areas for satellites include the Van Allen radiation belts. Although operating spacecraft and systems within the earth's radiation belts is not precluded, it is often not suited for optimal system performance and frequently requires additional shielding to protect sensitive electronics. Other potentially hazardous regions include those with excessive orbital debris. This debris may either be man-made, such as the remnants of previous space launches, or it may occur naturally, like micrometeorites. Larger pieces of orbital debris may often be successfully tracked, and consequently spacecraft can usually be maneuvered to avoid colliding with them. However, smaller pieces of debris, especially within more congested debris regions, are not as easily tracked. Subsequently, spacecraft often attempt to avoid or minimize passage through such regions of space. So positions of negative value include regions where space vehicles and satellites tend not to congregate, since operating there is frequently seen as being a disadvantage.

Depending on a satellite's mission and purpose, some orbits – including some low-earth and geostationary orbits – are often deemed more valuable than others are. If this same satellite could not use the most desirable orbital slot, for whatever reason, the orbit eventually chosen could result in a less efficient launch or in less effective on-orbit operations. For example, one country may desire a specific geostationary orbital slot for its communications satellite in order to provide service within a geographic region. Yet if that country is unable to secure the slot through the International Telecommunications Union, the use of a less desirable orbit may result. A position of negative value like this may require additional satellites to provide the same communications coverage and services, as compared to the more desirable orbital position.

For these reasons, having to operate at positions of negative value may entail more cost or be less effective or more hazardous than operating at more advantageous strategic positions. So, if one can coerce or force one's adversary into operating at negative positions, a relative gain can be realized without oneself actually holding a strategic position.

Time as a strategic "position"

Although it is quite a theoretical and abstract question, an inquisitive strategist may ponder the implications of when "time" itself is the "position" of advantage. Previous discussions regarding positions have concentrated on actual locations, physical assets, and even regions within the electromagnetic spectrum. As understood, such positions have inherent advantage when compared to other positions that do not share the same characteristics. The primary reason that the defense is the stronger form of warfare is that a truly defensive strategy ought to employ a strategic position that imparts some military advantage. Yet what about military scenarios where neither side gains a relative advantage with regards to these kinds of positions? What if the element of time is the only advantage that one side has? What are the resulting implications for warfare?

In such situations, using the element of time to advantage equates to using surprise and taking the initiative. These are the traditional traits of the offense.[12] The advantages of initiative and surprise – as well as their relationship to offensive strategy – have long been recognized, especially within the writings of Clausewitz and Mahan.

The skeptic of defensive strategy may ask, if offensive strategy has inherent advantage, why is the defense still the stronger form of warfare? The answer lies in the implicit understanding that defensive strategy awaits the blow of the offense, albeit with a position of advantage. Consequently, a sound defensive strategy must recognize that those strategic positions taken must be able to "absorb" an enemy's offensive strategy that employs initiative and surprise. If the defensive strategy is unable to do so, it is unsound, and the offensive attack will most likely succeed. In cases when offensive surprise and the initiative have an equivalent advantage to those defensive positions taken by the other adversary, the outcome is less sure. In such cases, chance and uncertainty – which are always present during war – come into play to affect the eventual outcome.

Implications for space warfare

For all of this theoretical- and strategic-level discussion, what does it mean to the warfighter? Since, at the strategic level, space warfare and maritime wartime have striking similarities, it was deduced from the idea of command of space that it will prove difficult to force an adversary into a decisive engagement. Consequently, it is better to control his strategic positions and threaten his commerce and military operations, thus forcing one's adversary to battle on terms favorable for oneself. This goes back to the lesson that one's opponent is unlikely to risk the destruction of his space force on ill conceived offensive operations but will only risk a probable defeat when something of value, such as celestial lines of communication or strategic positions, is threatened. Therefore, by threatening choke-points or high-value positions, one's enemy can be drawn into battle. If this is done successfully, one can disrupt the enemy's lines of communications and "national life" in space.[13]

The concept of command of space has implications for the role of positions in space strategy. The inherent value of strategic positions are not in themselves, but in the benefit pertaining to space communications. As such, strategic positions are understood within the context of the movement of physical and non-physical communications along celestial lines of communication. Some positions can impart an advantage to this movement, while others impart a disadvantage. Sometimes communications tend to concentrate or exclusively go through these choke-points and high-value positions.

If one is unable to gain a sufficient number of strategic positions or threaten the enemy's, it is best to force an enemy to operate in and through positions of negative value. This can be accomplished by fouling the orbits that the enemy uses for commercial and military purposes. For instance, if one can create a large enough debris field, the field may be able to cause an adversary's space systems to fail or be degraded. This has a historical precedent – even though the residual effects were unintentional – in that the Soviet Union conducted an anti-satellite weapons test in the 1960s that left debris in orbit that is still a hazard today.[14] Despite the apparent utility of fouling orbits to create positions of negative value, many near-earth orbits are shared between belligerents, and consequently fouling these orbits or lines of communications may have the same detrimental effects for oneself as for one's adversary.

Although debris fields can be considered as holding negative value, much of military strategy is involved with turning negatives into positives. Consequently, supposedly "negative" positions can be in fact used to an advantage. This would be the case when some locations or regions have extensive amounts of space debris, thereby causing others to presume that these regions will be avoided because of their potential hazard to space systems. Thanks to the excessive amount and smallness of some of the debris pieces, the technology used to track this debris is unlikely to be able to track all of it. This means that one could potentially deploy small satellites within close proximity – or even attached – to some larger pieces of debris, thus preventing their location from being detected and tracked. In such a case, a position within a supposedly disadvantageous region can be used to provide a level of advantage, because it will prove difficult for most offensive weapons to engage and destroy such small, undetected satellites.

Chapter 10

Blocking

In the previous chapter, it was noted that the enemy's choke-points and high-value positions can be exploited for military gain to force him into battle on terms favorable for oneself. Such exploitation usually attempts to disrupt, degrade, or deny the enemy's ability to use his celestial lines of communication. Because the inherent value of space is the access and utility it provides, space warfare must embrace a strategy that attempts to deny the enemy's ability to use celestial lines of communication in any significant or meaningful way. This chapter addresses the methods of accomplishing this strategy.

Throughout naval history, blockades have been used to prevent the enemy from leaving port or to interfere with his maritime commerce and trade. Blockades recognize the need to prevent the enemy from using his sea lines of communication. If enemy shipping attempt to leave the protection of their port that is under blockade, they often put themselves in an unfavorable predicament whereby they will suffer significant loses by the blockading force. Despite the apparent advantages of blockading an enemy's port, any fleet attempting to enforce a blockade near the enemy's port or harbor entrance will probably be met with coastal artillery fire or other defensive measures to thwart such a blockading action. So instead, blockading the enemy's distant sea lanes of communications is sometimes used to avoid the threat posed by coastal and harbor artillery fire. Yet blockading the distant sea lanes also has its downside. The enemy vessels can attempt to circumvent a blockading fleet or attempt to use escorts to engage those ships enforcing the blockade. Developing a sound naval strategy requires determining where, when, and in what manner to enforce a blockade against the adversary's fleet or maritime trade. If the strategy is successfully executed, one's adversary has to accept the conditions of the blockade or fight to release himself under unfavorable conditions.

The strategy of space warfare must also determine where, when, and in what manner to disrupt, degrade, or deny the enemy's use of celestial lines of communication. Despite the similarities between the strategic concepts of naval and space warfare, the strategic concept of blockading is not directly transferable to military operations in space. Naval strategy is primarily concerned with blockading the movement of physical communications, such as ships and items of trade. Like naval strategy, space strategy is also concerned with blocking the movement of physical communications, but space strategy must also consider the blocking of non-physical communications, such as data and information. Space warfare, therefore, requires a different context and terminology for this strategic concept, and as a result, the term "blocking" will be used instead. Blocking is the act of disrupting, degrading, or denying an adversary's ability to use his celestial lines of communication, thus minimizing the movement of spacecraft, equipment, materiel, supplies, personnel, military effects, data, or information. When using the jargon of the warfighter, the expression "blocking CLOCs" is suitable to describe this concept.[1]

Methods of blocking may include military actions, such as using weapons that cause permanent or temporary disability; however, methods may also include non-military actions, such as withholding services that enable enemy access and use of celestial lines of communication. Since the strategy of blocking is concerned with impacting the movement of communications in, from, and through space, a blocking strategy will frequently need to exploit strategic positions, including choke-points and high-value positions. If a blocking strategy is ultimately successful, it delivers the most harmful outcome possible in space warfare: denying the enemy his access to and use of space.

Relationship to offense and defense

Blocking celestial lines of communication incorporates elements of both offensive and defensive strategy. Offensive strategy is used when political objectives necessitate taking or acquiring something from the enemy, and defensive strategy is used when political objectives necessitate preventing the enemy from achieving or gaining something. In blocking, the intent may include wresting lines of communication away from the enemy, thereby taking them for oneself. Thus, the intent here is more offensive in nature. Additionally, lines of communication in space are often shared, and one may initially enjoy equal access to the same lines of communication as one's enemy. In such cases, one's purpose would not be to acquire access to these lines of communication, but only to prevent the enemy from using of them. Therefore, when one initially shares the same celestial lines of communication with the adversary, the blocking strategy is more defensive than offensive in nature.

A blocking strategy should be used with the knowledge that one's adversary will probably retaliate to regain access to his lost lines of communication. Consequently, blocking is a strategy that looks for a fight. By taking on a posture of defensive expectation, blocking can be used to force a fight on terms favorable for oneself. In the end, there are three reasons for blocking an adversary's celestial lines of communication: acquiring the enemy's lines of communication, preventing or degrading the enemy's access to and use of space communication routes, and forcing a military engagement on favorable terms. If the communications lines are already shared and taking the enemy's lines of communication is not needed, then only the last two reasons apply. By blending elements of the "more effective" and "stronger" forms of warfare, blocking takes advantage of both offensive and defensive strategies.[2]

Through the exploitation of strategic positions, a blocking strategy can be enforced at those locations that impart a relative advantage to a blocking force. These strategic positions can include locations with commercial advantage, such as choke-points and high-value positions, or they can include those that are more easily defendable, such as high-ground positions. Since celestial lines of communicate are used to move non-physical communications like electromagnetic transmissions, a successful blocking strategy does not necessarily entail the use of military assets or physical systems. For instance, if one currently provides commercial communications services to another, these services can be withheld. Such an action will accomplish the goal of blocking – denying another the use of celestial lines of communications. Efforts like these can be used to enforce an embargo of sorts, thereby preventing or degrading another's access and use of outer space.[3]

It follows that, because non-military actions can be used to enforce a blocking strategy, non-military actions can be used to counter it also. Those having their communications blocked have non-military options for "maneuvering" against and "engaging" those enforcing a blocking action. These options include the use of diplomatic, economic, and information measures. Since one's adversary has both military and non-military instruments available to oppose blocking, it should be expected that he will attempt to free himself using the most readily available and most effective instrument as his disposal. Consequently, pressure and condemnation through international organizations, economic sanctions, and disparaging media reports all represent possible means for retaliating against one who blocks another's lines of communication in and through space.

Regardless of the potential military advantage to be gained through blocking, the strategic idea of command of space highlights that one's enemy is never totally helpless. As a result, the most successful blocking strategies are unlikely to prevent an enemy's sporadic use of physical and non-physical communications, regardless of a superior force's capability in space.

Types of blocking

The strategy of blocking is simply an attempt to disrupt, degrade, or deny another's ability to access and use celestial lines of communication. Unlike the use of blockades in naval warfare, blocking another's space communication routes does not necessitate an antiquated strategy of opposing fleets within close proximity to one another, since the objectives of blocking can be achieved using either space-based or terrestrial-based systems. This is because land, sea, air, or space assets may be employed when blocking a foe's celestial lines of communication. Furthermore, the fundamental precept of blocking does not require the actual destruction of the enemy's forces and systems, but only that he not use or move along lines of communication in space, under the threat of retaliatory action. As a result, a credible and coercive threat of force that results in the enemy not using his celestial lines of communications is considered equally effective, since the same result is achieved as through the actual application of force.

Drawing upon the lessons of maritime strategy, blocking can be considered in two general categories: close and distant.[4] The two categories refer to where blocking is employed relative to hubs of activity or points of distribution. Yet space warfare is different from naval warfare, especially since activities in space pertain to the movement of things tangible and intangible. For this reason, blocking may be subdivided further by whether one is attempting to block physical or non-physical communications. Therefore, blocking the movement of physical systems means obstructing the movement of launch vehicles, satellites, ballistic missiles, personnel, or orbiting stations. Blocking non-physical communications means interfering with the movement of communications that use the electromagnetic spectrum, including data, information, and lasers. It also includes interfering with the movement of sub-atomic particles, such as those used by particle beam weapons.

Close blocking

Close blocking is obstructing or interfering with space communications within the proximity of uplinks, downlinks, crosslinks, launching facilities, or any hubs of activity. The methods of implementing a close blocking strategy are the realm of tactics and current technology, and both of these areas are likely to change dramatically with the passage of time. Despite this, possible methods of implementing close blocking may be proposed. When denying the movement of physical communications, a possible method includes the threat or use of conventional ballistic munitions against spacecraft before or just after their ground-based launch or their departure from a space station. Any of these methods may include the use of weapons that are land-, sea-, air-, or space-based. Other less overt methods of implementing a close blocking strategy include using electromagnetic interference against a space system's sensitive electronics, sabotaging the enemy's launch systems, and modifying flight control software algorithms.

The close blocking of non-physical communications – like news and media services – employs a similar strategy. As in the case of denying the adversary's movement of physical communications, the purpose here is also to deny the movement of non-physical communications in any substantial or meaningful way. As such, terrestrial or space-based communications may be blocked, and this may be achieved by using munitions against the signal's transmitter or by jamming the communications signal itself. Depending on the method chosen, the effects of blocking non-physical communications may be either permanent or temporary, and if one's goal is to acquire the adversary's celestial lines of communication, the best method is often to make the effects temporary. By blocking non-physical communications and making any damaging effects temporary, one will be able to rapidly access and use those same celestial lines of communications taken from the enemy.

Two examples in particular illustrate this idea. The first example is the 1996 dispute between Tonga and Indonesia. Both nations claimed rights to the same geostationary orbital slot. But Tonga placed their national communications satellite in the disputed orbital slot first and prior to the disagreement's resolution. Although Indonesia quickly responded with a formal protest, it appears they did more than just protest. It has been reported that the Indonesians jammed the communications signal of the Tongan's satellite.[5] The second example is the occasion on which local-area jammers were used with very limited success in blocking the positioning, navigation, and timing of GPS signals within a small area during the war in Iraq in 2003.[6] In both cases, the close blocking strategy was conducted in the vicinity of the end-user, and the strategy proves to be a viable option when competing national interests are at stake.

It is important to remember that some communications transmissions are becoming more narrowly focused and directional. This is particularly the case with communications using high-frequency radio signals or lasers. Because these highly directional, non-physical communications generally require line-of-sight access between any two stations – including the potential use of intermediary relay stations – it is possible to block such communications near either the transmitting or the receiving end.[7] An implementation of this blocking strategy could entail using microsatellites that physically attach themselves to a satellite's antenna or optical receiver, thus blocking any radio or laser line-of-sight communications.[8]

Distant blocking

Besides close blocking, the other option is distant blocking. Distant blocking is the denial or disruption of space communications far away from the hubs of distribution, but still along celestial lines of communication. The intent of this strategy is to acquire the enemy's lines of communication – if they are not already shared between belligerents – and deny the enemy's future use of them. As with close blocking, the enemy will frequently decide to fight to re-lease himself from distant blocking, and therefore this strategy also attempts to force the enemy's retaliation on terms favorable to oneself.

Distant blocking may be enforced against either physical or non-physical communications. Distant blocking of physical communications is the interdiction of an adversary's space systems. This action is appropriate against launch vehicles, thereby preventing them reaching the final intended orbit. Also, it is appropriate against satellites already established in an orbit, thereby forcing them to deviate or risk destruction. Methods of employing distant blocking include the threat of force or actual use of munitions that impact space systems. Possible scenarios include placing man-made debris into the orbital path of a satellite, thus causing its destruction if it passes into the fouled orbital region. Similarly, the implementation can equate to a kind of "orbital mine." Still yet another implementation of distant blocking includes using electromagnetic interference to cause another's space system to wildly deviate from its desired flight path, and this kind of electromagnetic interference may employ either destructive or non-destructive techniques to achieve the desired result. The advantage of the destructive method is that a more lasting result can be achieved, but non-destructive method is potentially more covert and is less likely to escalate hostilities.

When used against non-physical communications, particularly transmissions using the electromagnetic spectrum, distant blocking is meant to disrupt the enemy's ability to use and access lines of communication far away from the primary hubs of activity. When requirements dictate the need to block the enemy's narrow or highly directional transmissions, then distant blocking necessitates obstructing the communications signal between the transmitting and receiving locations. Tactics and techniques to accomplish this could include the utilization of a large expandable panel that remains stationary relative to a satellite and a receiving station. Obviously, such a tactic would prove technologically challenging when attempting to block transmission between satellites and ground stations, because different heights above the earth normally necessitate different orbital velocities or paths. Thus, designing a satellite with a "station keeping" capability may prove quite difficult in this instance. Because of the challenges of geometry and orbital mechanics, implementing this tactic will probably prove easier when attempting to block the line-of-sight crosslinks transmissions between systems in similar orbits.

When compared with methods attempting to obstruct or block line-of-sight communications using an expandable panel or other device, methods that use non-physical means to block non-physical communications might indeed prove easier. Possible methods include interfering with the enemy's communications signals between his transmitting, receiving, or relay stations. By using a technique that distorts or overpowers an existing signal, an enemy's ability to use space communications may be denied or degraded.[9] To be most efficient in its application, distant blocking usually requires knowing specifically where the adversary's celestial lines of communication are. But this may prove difficult with respect to non-physical communications, since multiple paths potentially exist. For this reason, blocking distant lines of communication may necessitate causing interference within a wide region of space, since one may need to deny any number of possible communications routes. Of course, the size of the region and the number of lines of communication that can be denied to the enemy are frequently dependent upon the power output of the jamming or blocking transmitter. More important, however, is that, since one often shares celestial lines of communication with one's adversary, denying a foe's use of non-physical communications in this manner may deny one's own use too.

Close versus distant blocking

In choosing between using close and distant blocking, there are several considerations. It must be determined which method will be most effective and efficient, while considering one's available resources and the amount time necessary to enforce the blocking strategy. Yet, most importantly, it must be determined what one hopes to achieve through blocking, since that will indicate whether the objective is more defensive or offensive in nature.

In the current state of space operations, launches are often from fixed locations and the timing of these launches is frequently known well in advance. For this reason, a close blocking strategy against an adversary's ground launch facilities appears to be a reasonable military objective for many opponents. Additionally, if the goal is to prevent one's adversary from placing systems into space, then this goal is compatible with a defensive strategy. For a less capable space power in particular, a defensive strategy using close blocking is an appropriate method to block a more capable power's use of his launch choke-points.

One the other hand, enforcing a distant blocking action requires greater military prowess to be successful. Consequently, such blocking is an appropriate course of action for those already exercising general and persistent command of space. Additionally, if one's objective is to deny the enemy's ability to access his distant lines of communication and subsequently take them for oneself, this objective is more commensurate with offensive strategy. A space power, therefore, who exercises a substantial level of command should be more inclined to fully embrace an offensive strategy along an adversary's distant celestial lines of communication.

Criticisms of blocking

Even though blocking in space warfare would appear to have tremendous benefits, this strategy is open to criticism. Since the strategic concept of blocking in space is akin to blockades at sea, the same complaints leveled against naval blockades may apply equally to blocking in space. Sir Julian Corbett notes the limitations of the naval blockade due to its "arrested offensive" posture.[10] While Corbett recognizes the utility of a blockade once assumed, he notes that it does not impart the same performance and morale boost coming from the initiative gained through traditional offensive operations. Moreover, there have been critics throughout naval history who believed traditional fleet-on-fleet offensive actions against an enemy are always the best method of securing command of the sea – critics including Alfred Thayer Mahan. Since it is better to seek a decisive victory through dominant offensive actions, so the argument goes, the naval blockade should be relegated to a minor role within the strategy of naval warfare.

Similar criticisms could be leveled against blocking celestial lines of communications as well. Blocking would seem to lack the benefit of initiative that comes from seek-and-destroy operations. Additionally, warfighters performing blocking missions will garner little glamour or prestige, when compared to their counterparts performing purely offensive missions. Despite these perceptions, blocking allows one to gain something that was not held before – the enemy's lines of communication and a position of relative advantage. For this reason, this method of warfare does impart some of the advantages coming from offensive strategy. Because of the benefits gained – along with its relationship to offensive and defensive strategies – blocking does indeed have its place within a broad strategy of space warfare.

The applicability of even using a naval blockading analogy to develop space strategy has been called into question, since space is not the high seas. How can "blockades" be applied to space, since space services are frequently delivered using a distributed system of satellites and the satellite providing services now may not be doing the same a few minutes later?[11] To answer this question, it must be realized that the strategic concept of blocking is fundamentally different from the strategy of the naval blockade. Naval blockading was often conducted against the enemy's sea lines of communication at fixed locations, such as ports and positions along maritime trade routes. Lines of communication in space, especially those used for data and information transfer, may be constantly moving. This is exemplified by the many satellites in orbit that continually pass service responsibilities along to the next satellite coming over the horizon. The main difference between naval and space strategies in this regard is that blocking in space is conducted against the enemy's celestial lines of communication, wherever they are and however they move. Because lines of communication between a satellite and its receiving station may move as the satellite moves, a blocking strategy in space may be conducted against physical communications, like satellites or receiving stations, or against the non-physical communications, like the electromagnetic frequency spectrum through which most signals are transmitted.

Yet another likely criticism against blocking it that it is too overtly aggressive and will lead to escalating hostilities between adversaries, even when such an escalation is not intended. Such an argument may be postulated because blowing up an adversary's ground station or destroying his satellite may lead to the most visceral of retaliatory reactions. This is a valid concern, since any military strategy should be flexible enough to be useful during either minor skirmishes or major conflicts. When deciding upon how to implement a blocking strategy, its potential effectiveness and efficiency must be determined.[12] In cases when one already shares the enemy's lines of communication and one only wants to deny the enemy's use of them, it may be best to block his space communication without the enemy knowing it.[13] This can be achieved by placing errors within his information and data transmissions, resulting in the enemy's discounting the accuracy of the information or doubting the data's utility. So non-destructive and non-invasive blocking actions have great utility in denying another's use of and access to celestial lines of communication, while minimizing the potential for escalating hostilities. Consequently, the strategy of blocking is flexible enough to be useful in a variety of different situations.

Chapter 11

Space as a barrier

From an understanding of command of space and the concept of blocking, it is realized that physical and non-physical communications are readily accessible to those who exercise command; yet space becomes a "barrier" to those who cannot. This thought is based upon maritime strategy, where those having command of the sea are able to deter and prevent their opponent from freely moving along sea lines of communications or from threatening one's coastlines. Corbett writes that, while the sea has a positive value for national life, it has a negative value too, since it can also become a barrier. Yet, by winning command of the sea, one removes that barrier from one's own path, thereby enabling one to impact the enemy's national life ashore through military intervention.[1] This strategic concept was borne out by Napoleon Bonaparte's unsuccessful attempts to move his legions across the English Channel to wage a land war against the British. Bonaparte's inability to do as he wished was due to Great Britain's dominating navy and ability to exercise command within the English Channel.

Like the oceans of the world, space too can become a barrier. Since outer space is an unnatural environment for people to live in – where an army cannot merely march to meet another on the field of battle – moving along or accessing celestial lines of communication is not a simple matter. One's ability to access and use these lines is paramount, and only by doing so can the advantages of operating in space be realized. If such access and use are not possible – whether one is being denied access to lines of communication in space or one's technological capability is insufficient to launch space vehicles into orbit – then space effectively becomes a barrier. Those with the strongest and most effective forms of command of space are able to more easily move material, trade, supplies, personnel, spacecraft, military effects, data, and information along celestial lines of communication; however, to those without a sufficient level of command, these same lines of communication are more likely to become an obstacle to such access and use.

Because space is interdependent with other media of warfare, space can be made a barrier by any combination of land, sea, air, or space assets and actions. So any of the other warfare areas may be employed to deny the enemy's use of space communications. This has implications for those warfighters concerned with space warfare, since they must be knowledgeable in all media of warfare and not just that of space. Such warfighters, consequently, should be versed in those strategies, operations, and tactics that will enable the achieving of political and military objectives in space. Conversely, these same warfighters must also be able to support and advise soldiers, marines, sailors, and airmen in achieving their objectives as well. For space strategy is but a subset of general military strategy, and military strategy must itself support the overarching national strategy.

There are generally three strategic intentions for wanting to effectively make space a barrier. First, it can be for defensive intent, such as wanting to deny the enemy's ability to launch an overwhelming surprise attack. Second, it can be when one has limited intent. This would be the case when one plans to conduct hostile actions for limited aims against another, but one also desires to prevent the enemy's ability to escalate the conflict. Third, it can be when one is conducting an unlimited war with unlimited objectives, such as the unconditional surrender of the enemy, and one desires to prevent the enemy's unlimited counterattack from, into, or through space.

Defensive intent

When exercising command of space, such as through the blocking of physical communications, one can effectively make space a defensive barrier that protects one's space-based assets and prevents an adversary's ability to communicate through space. This may include preventing the movement of another's launch vehicle, which is achieved through using offensive weapons that cause the enemy vehicle's catastrophic failure. Such a result may be achieved when building a missile defense program to block the movement of intercontinental ballistic missiles – along with their warheads – from their launch point to their intended target. A missile defense program of this kind simply attempts to make space a defensive barrier against attack.

The Strategic Defense Initiative of the 1980s was a program that was designed to make space a barrier and its intent was defensive in nature. Although this United States defense program never reached fruition, its purpose was to destroy enemy intercontinental ballistic missiles carrying nuclear warheads from reaching their intended targets.[2] Since such ballistic missiles travel through the lower realms of outer space, this program was indeed an attempt to make space a barrier of sorts. Like the Strategic Defense Initiative of the past, some still suggest scenarios whereby space-based weapons – such as lasers, particle beams, or kinetic energy devices – are employed to destroy enemy assets in space.[3]

Moreover, other current initiatives within the United States are also attempts to make space a barrier. The Theater Missile Defense program, whereby sea-based or land-based anti-ballistic missile systems are to be designed and employed to counter long-range ballistic missiles, likewise attempts to protect and defend against attack. Also, some authors and strategists have proposed using the air medium in a similar manner. Of late, some of the most widely written about scenarios include using airborne lasers to attack enemy ballistic missiles during mid-course guidance or using airborne lasers to attack commercial satellites while in orbit. The difference in these examples is that the land, sea, and air media are used instead of the medium of space itself in making the barrier.

Similarly, one may want to make space an obstacle to non-physical communications. When done for defensive intent, the purpose is most often to deny the enemy his ability to move data and information that may cause either direct or indirect harm. This may include denying the movement of news and intelligence that would be considered harmful to military operations. Granted, what is considered harmful is a subjective assessment, but that is the nature of warfare. Methods of making space an obstacle to non-physical communications include the concept of blocking, like the jamming of electromagnetic frequency spectrum or shielding either the transmitting or receiving stations of space-based communications.

Limited intent

The concept of using space as a barrier is pertinent even when one's strategy is not purely defensive in nature. For instance, those that exercise command of space to the greatest extent can initiate a war having limited political objectives, without fearing the enemy's ability to escalate the conflict into a space war with unlimited political objectives. Conflicts with limited aims include those only attempting to acquire certain lines of communications in space or ensuring one's access within a region of space, but they do not include the overthrow of a sovereign government. Unlimited aims, on the other hand, would include the unconditional capitulation of the enemy's populace, military, and leadership.[4]

So when one's aims in space are modest and the total defeat of the enemy is not needed, the act of making space an obstacle to an enemy can help control any potential escalation in hostilities. This kind of effect will help keep one's limited political aims in line with both limited military and non-military means. Consequently, in such cases, one is able to more accurately predict and allocate those resources needed to achieve one's strategic objective, since the conflict is less likely to spiral out of control into a war of unlimited aims and means.

The means and methods of making space a barrier when one's intent is limited in nature are similar to those previously described. This is because making space a barrier normally denotes establishing command of space that is both general and persistent. For, when one has such a level of command, thereby making space a barrier, one has great freedom in choosing whether one's intentions are defensive, limited, or unlimited in nature. For the result is the same: the enemy cannot adequately respond in using space as a medium of attack. In understanding this thought, it is appropriate to paraphrase Corbett's insight: "He that commands space is at great liberty and may take as much or as little space warfare as he will."[5]

The warfighter might well ask whether a limited level of command is sufficient in making space a barrier when one has limited aims and plans to use limited military means. Under most circumstances, the answer is "no." This is because most often command that is both general and persistent is required to effectively make space a barrier to one's adversary. It is possible, however, to successfully employ military means that are limited in nature, after this highest form of command is achieved and space is made a barrier, in order to achieve limited aims and objectives. The observation that limited means can be used to achieve limited aims makes sense, because if one's intentions or ends are limited then the military means employed should most often be limited in nature too. When one's means and ends are not the same – whether limited or unlimited – then a strategy mismatch has occurred, and most likely one's strategy needs to be reassessed and realigned.

Just because one's intent may be limited, it should not be presumed that it will be a simple task to achieve the required level of command or that this kind of intent is a "shortcut" to making space a barrier. There are, as with many things, exceptions to this rule. Such would be the case when one is able to sufficiently achieve local command within a region, thereby locally dominating a space power that is normally considered as having a greater level of command. The danger of making space a barrier in such a manner is that a more powerful adversary will probably attempt to muster his forces and assets in order to "surround" the region where one's command of space is gained and where space has been made a barrier against his use. Thus, such a condition of making space a barrier may in the end not endure for long. Also, under the rarest of occasions, command that is temporary may achieve enough effect to make space a barrier. But because of the transitory nature of command that is temporary, this method is not usually desirable except by those with few means or options in space.

Achieving command that is either local or temporary may in fact be the only choices open to less capable space powers to make space a barrier, even though it is acknowledged that the result is not optimal. So, under some circumstances, lesser powers may be able to make a "weak" barrier that enables the achieving of some limited objectives. These lesser powers will not be able to thwart an unlimited counterstroke, if the more capable power chooses, but nevertheless a lesser space power may be able achieve specific political or military objectives when its intent is limited in nature.

Unlimited intent

When one's aims are unlimited in nature, the implications for using space as a barrier are different again. When one nation pursues a war with unlimited aims, often it employs unlimited means to achieve its strategic objective. In such cases, the greatest amount of national power – including the use of military force – will frequently be leveled against the adversary. In response to an unlimited attack having as its goal the unconditional capitulation of a sovereign government, those attacked will often reciprocate by employing unlimited means as well. Additionally, those attacked may reach the conclusion that their national survival and way of life depend on the capitulation of the attacking nation as well. Thus, their aims become unlimited in response to an unlimited provocation. Regarding space warfare, if a level of command can be attained that is both general and persistent, this normal dynamic of unlimited wars can be changed. By exercising command and subsequently making space an obstacle to one's enemy, it is possible to block the enemy's unlimited counterattack into, from, and through space. When space can be made a barrier in this way, one can initiate a war with unlimited intent and have sufficient protection against the enemy's most devastating response using the medium of space.

As when done for defensive intent, a sufficient level of command can prevent the enemy's ability to communicate physical assets and, in doing so, one can prevent his unlimited counterattack. This would be appropriate when attempting to obstruct the successful movement of intercontinental ballistic missiles, whether carrying nuclear or conventional warheads. Methods of achieving this condition include programs like the Strategic Defense Initiative or Theater Missile Defense. Likewise, this kind of strategy may be employed to prevent the movement of space-based weapons, including kinetic energy weapons or other munitions. Methods of achieving this may include using land-, sea-, air-, or space-based weapon systems that attack enemy platforms in space. This includes the employment of physical weapons or non-physical effects to destroy the enemy's space-based systems. Although the concept of command of space has shown that one's enemy is never helpless and that minor successful attacks are indeed likely to occur no matter how capable one's defenses are, space can become an obstacle to the movement of the most devastating and detrimental methods of attack.

In cases when space is to be made a barrier to the enemy's non-physical effects in order to prevent an unlimited counterattack, there are several possible applications. These include blocking the effects of some space-to-earth weapons effects, such as lasers and particle beam weapons. Also included are blocking less overt, but equally devastating, methods of attack. These methods include electromagnetic frequency attacks on those lines of communication used for commerce and trade. Any hostile attacks along celestial lines of communication that are used for commerce and trade have the potential of crippling a nation's economy and affecting their long-term sustainment capability for fighting a protracted war. Because of the detrimental effects of these kinds of attacks, those that can prevent them should make every effort to do so.

Tradeoffs and other considerations

A maritime framework has illustrated a little-known strategic concept for space warfare. Admittedly, it may seem counterintuitive to think of space as an "obstacle" or "barrier," especially since outer space is often thought of as a great void of emptiness. But taking the concept of command of space, along with that of blocking, to its natural conclusion has indeed led to this observation. More fundamentally, the previous discussion highlights that outer space becomes a "maneuver space" to those that command it and an obstacle to those that cannot.[6] So space is a medium of potential warfare, where the allocation of forces and resources must be considered and where strategic advantage must be sought.[7]

When deciding upon a strategy to make space a defensive barrier, it must also be remembered that one frequently shares the same lines of communication with one's enemy. When attempting to deny another's access to and use of celestial lines of communication, if one chooses to take military action against an adversary's systems or communications in space, ample consideration should be given to whether such action will result in a significant denial or obstruction in one's own use and access of space. For instance, when employing weapons against an enemy's satellites in orbit or ballistic missiles traveling through space, thought must be given to the amount of space debris resulting from these weapons. When such residual debris does result, the region affected may become an obstacle to oneself as well to one's enemy. This is also the case when making space a barrier to non-physical communications, such as preventing the adversary's movement of intelligence, data, and electromagnetic weapons effects through space. Depending on the method chosen to make space a barrier to non-physical communications, such as employing wide-area jammers against the enemy's radio frequency band, the unintended result may be to deny space to oneself.

Admittedly, command is most influential in the specific medium where it is gained. So, while command of space can be used to make space a barrier for defensive, limited, and unlimited intent, it has less influence on conflicts on land, at sea, or in the air. Therefore, even if one is able to effectively make space a barrier, one's enemy may be able to successfully conduct a surprise attack, escalate hostilities, or conduct a counterattack using the land, sea, or air medium if command is not achieved there too. The lesson to be learned is that, to truly protect one's interests and activities, a sufficient level of defensive capability is needed in all media of warfare.

The possible military methods of implementing a strategy that makes space a barrier to either physical or non-physical communications may seem limitless, yet for those concerned with the strategy and theory of space warfare there are other considerations. These considerations include making space a barrier to space communications, without the overt use of military force. By applying the other instruments of national power, a state or non-state actor may be influenced in such a manner that it decides for itself not to develop the technology that results in contesting one's own command of space. So, whether using diplomatic, economic, or information measures, pressure and influence can be applied that results in one's foe choosing not to develop the technology needed to communicate harmful weapons or effects through space. Such a conscious choice by one's foe may be effectively equivalent to the end state reached through traditional military methods. Whereas the end state is the same – the enemy not using space as a medium of attack – the method of achieving it is substantially different. Both the strategic planner and the warfighter alike have a duty and obligation to consider those other methods of achieving the desired strategic end state, besides the all too commonly considered application of force or military effects. In many situations, the use of these non-military methods may be the best and most appropriate choice, since employing hostile and overt force often results in the most visceral reactions by those being attacked or denied access to space. In fact, some of the greatest advantages are realized through these non-military means, because diplomatic, economic, and information measures are frequently reversible in nature and may not cause irreparable harm to another. Employing non-military methods gives one more flexibility in controlling the pace and potential escalation of any conflict; as such, all the instruments of power can be employed in making space a barrier.

Chapter 12

Dispersal and concentration

Because many nation states have critical interests in space, these interests will need to be protected and defended. Therefore, under certain circumstances, the use of military force may be required. For this reason, it is worth discussing the methods of achieving military goals and objectives in outer space. This is particularly important, since space is vast and any military strategy will be implemented with finite resources. If these resources – like space-based weapon systems and the funds to procure them – were unlimited, then there would be little concern over how to distribute assets that protect celestial lines of communication, because they could be spread equally throughout the realm of space. Alas, such is not the case, as resources and available means are finite. As a result, a suitable method of employing and distributing assets in space must be determined. This is the purview of strategic inquiry, since it is necessary to balance one's ends with one's means.[1]

With most military strategies, assets are allocated in a manner that recognizes how, where, and when they are most needed. Because of the breadth of issues involved, all of the strategic concepts discussed so far must be considered when determining the distribution of military assets and forces in space. Some of the more relevant concepts needed in this endeavor are command of space, offense versus defensive strategy, and celestial lines of communication. From these diverse considerations, the next strategic concept – dispersal and concentration – results.

Dispersal

When considered by itself, the need for dispersal arises from the finite nature of resources, when compared to the far-flung regions where one's interests lie. Many operational planners and military strategists frequently allocate resources where one's security interests are greatest and where conflict with the enemy seems most likely. In land, naval, and air warfare, this idea frequently means placing a greater number of forces where offensive operations are called for, such as in forward areas, and placing a lesser number of forces where defensive operations are expected, such as in rearward areas and along lines of supply. One of the primary considerations in where to allocate forces is determining where one stands most to gain or most to lose. In space warfare, this is no different.

The strategic concept of dispersing assets and forces where and when needed is in keeping with one of the most fundamental principles of general warfare, the principle of economy. The principle of economy pertains to the efficient and effective allocation of both resources and forces where and when needed.[2] Also sometimes referred to as "economy of force," this classic concept of land warfare theory is widely regarded by military planners and is included in United States joint service doctrine. But in the context of space warfare, especially when related to the need to protect interests along celestial lines of communication, the term "dispersal" is more meaningful and so will be used instead.

The strategy of space warfare will necessitate the distribution of both forces and assets wherever one's vital space interests are located. Dispersing forces to the widest extent practical bestows upon oneself those benefits coming from military presence and the potential coercive effects that result from military presence. By moving and placing space systems and forces within a certain region, influence can be gained and interests can be protected, even when actual force is not used.

Less capable space powers should use dispersal as a general practice. This is so that a superior force that exercises command of space is not able to decisively defeat the lesser during a single engagement. Such a strategy is frequently employed by insurgent forces, since keeping forces grouped together increases the likelihood of being found and subsequently attacked by an enemy with superior numbers. Mao Tse-tung realized this during his protracted conflict against those loyal to Chiang Kai-shek, and he understood that, as long as one's foe has strategic advantage, a successful guerrilla strategy depends upon dispersing forces. Even so, Mao also realized that a strategy of dispersing forces was ineffective when one was ready for the counteroffensive. Thus, he concluded that another principle of war was called for during operational- and tactical-level actions, even including guerrilla ones, and that is the principle of concentration.[3]

Concentration

Even though dispersal is called for, it should be expected in many cases that significant amounts of resources will need to be moved to where offensive operations are anticipated or where the potential threat of attack would be most damaging or likely. Such a movement refers to the concentration of forces, assets, and effects. Indeed, the principle of concentration has been expounded upon by many land strategists, such as Mao and Clausewitz. For Clausewitz, the principle means concentrating military forces against the enemy's decisive point. He writes, "It thus follows that as many troops as possible should be brought into the engagement at the decisive point . . . This is the first principle of strategy." [4] Even during guerrilla actions, the principle of concentration proves relevant. Mao advises against striking with two "fists" in two directions at the same time but to concentrate military efforts when attacking.[5] Underscoring this point, Mao writes, "concentration of troops is the first and most essential" condition for military victory.[6] Since space strategy falls under the hierarchy of general military strategy, it is expected that concentration – in some form or another – is applicable for military operations in space as well.

In the context of space warfare, concentration means that firepower, or other desired effects, should be focused to defeat an adversary, defend against his attack, or neutralize the threat the enemy poses. This firepower or neutralizing effect can originate from military systems that communicate force into, from, and through space. Examples include ground-based lasers, air-launched anti-satellite weapons, and space-based weapons. The principle of concentration, therefore, tells the warfighter that, when offensive actions are imminent or necessary, the most force that is practical should be concentrated against one's enemy.[7]

Despite the apparent benefits coming from the concentration of military force, concentration as a principle unto itself is incomplete within a space warfare context. This thought can be readily understood by recounting that there are definite similarities between space and maritime strategic interests and, because of this, many strategic military concepts of the two are similar also. From maritime theory, as described by Corbett, concentration has a significant role in naval warfare, but, contrary to Clausewitz's theory of land warfare, it is not the first principle of strategy at sea. Corbett thought that concentration as a general practice was problematic for three reasons. First, concentrating naval forces at sea has the effect of causing the enemy's fleet to avoid a decisive battle, especially under conditions where their destruction is likely. The maritime strategist writes, "[I]f we are too superior, or our concentration too well arranged for him to hope for victory, then our concentration has almost always had the effect of forcing him to disperse for sporadic action."[8] Second, the more one concentrates naval forces, the fewer are the number of the sea lines of communication that can be secured and controlled.[9] Third, the more one concentrates a superior force, the more difficult it is to conceal one's whereabouts and intents.[10] Because of these problems, a truly applicable and ultimately successful strategy of space warfare requires a balance between dispersal and concentration.

Dispersal and concentration as one

The deduced principle of dispersal and concentration in space warfare denotes "continual conflict between cohesion and reach."[11] Therefore, the application of either dispersal or concentration must be understood as one and the same, not as separate and discrete principles of warfare. This necessitates that assets be distributed, while linking together their "effectual energy" as if of a single will and with a common purpose.[12] For space warfare, this means that space forces and systems, in general, should be dispersed to cover the widest possible area, yet retain the ability to rapidly concentrate force when needed. The "effectual energy" mentioned by Corbett can further elucidate this idea. While Corbett was probably thinking about the dispersal and concentration of ships and fleets when writing about his strategic concept, space warfare pertains not only to physical communications – represented by spacecraft and satellites – but also to non-physical communications as well – represented by data, information, and some military effects. Consequently, dispersal and concentration can be thought of in two very different ways: those pertaining to physical *systems and assets* and those pertaining to non-physical *effects*.

Applying this principle to systems and assets means that resources should be dispersed as a general practice of warfare. By doing so, celestial lines of communication can be protected and defended to the maximum extent possible, and the enemy is less likely to determine one's military intent. Moreover, dispersal mitigates the likelihood that the enemy can conduct a surprise attack against one's large concentration of forces, thereby reducing the chance that a foe can achieve his military aims through a single decisive victory. Yet when the time comes for offensive actions, one can concentrate forces rapidly against the enemy's decisive point to achieve the most successful results possible. Through flexibility of dispersal and concentration, the utmost application of military power can be applied at the right time and the right place. This flexibility enables the rapid shifting of assets, thus giving military planners the ability to respond to emergent needs and requirements.

The concept of dispersal and concentration of non-physical effects, on the other hand, has totally different implications. As with physical systems and assets, the ability to use non-physical effects should be dispersed across the largest region feasible and yet should maintain the ability to concentrate applied force where and when required. Nevertheless, the method of achieving this is significantly different. Non-physical communications, like weapons that use the electromagnetic spectrum, will mostly originate from physical assets. This means that space-based weapon systems that employ directed energy weapons can remain dispersed, while the effects that these systems deliver can be concentrated when needed. Such an admission may come as a great relief to space system designers and engineers, whose designs are often constrained by limited onboard fuel for maneuvering and propulsion. Therefore, any strategy that is sympathetic to conserving precious resources, such as onboard fuel, is usually most welcome.

A critic of this strategy could rightly point out that the act of leaving space systems in place, while concentrating their offensive effects, is the same method employed by many terrestrial-based systems and proposed space-based kinetic munitions. Using a strict interpretation of the previously defined terminology, however, ballistic and kinetic weapons are still considered physical assets that must ultimately be concentrated against the enemy's assets. So the difference here is that assets communicating non-physical effects can remain dispersed, even while their destructive effects are concentrated at the enemy's decisive point. Thus this idea is fundamentally different from the principle of concentration used in land warfare, since the concept here deals with the concentration of effects, as distinct from the concentration of mass.[13]

It is perhaps worth reemphasizing that non-physical communications pertain to data and information. So, when considering the theoretical principle of dispersal and concentration, this concept applies to what is called "information operations." Information operations deal with using news and intelligence to serve one's one purpose, whether for military or non-military aims. In considering such operations, they too should be employed in a dispersed manner, until it is time to "engage" an adversary.

The savvy warfighter might question how one knows when to move from dispersal to concentration. Dispersal as a general practice is most advantageous when one is not actively employing force. In contrast, concentration is most advantageous only when employing force against one's adversary and not beforehand. For these reasons, the warfighter should move from dispersal to concentration once the time to act and employ force has arrived. By delaying the concentration of forces or military effects as long as possible, one enjoys all the strategic benefits of dispersal. However, moving toward concentration once offensive actions are called for imparts the most strategic benefit when engaging the enemy.

"Cruisers" and policing systems

The object of space warfare is to ensure one's access and use celestial lines of communication, and therefore a means of doing this is required. Since this endeavor necessitates protecting lines of communication in space, an equivalent concept is needed to the naval "cruiser," whose mission is to patrol and protect sea lines of communication. These space "cruiser" equivalents should be built in significant numbers to protect and defend the expansive communications routes that are considered vital. Furthermore, these "cruisers" will need to operate where space communications tend to congregate, like choke-points, but will also need to disperse along the most extensively used lines of communications. Because of the primacy of this mission, space systems that perform purely offensive operations – those with negligible influence on celestial lines of communications – are of secondary importance.[14]

The term "cruiser," however, does not seem to really fit within the context of space warfare and operations. A cruiser within the maritime historical context was a vessel of great speed and operational range and was used along sea lines of communication or at other significant locations. By understanding the principle of dispersal and concentration, it is realized that ensuring one's use of space communications can be achieved by employing either assets or effects. Exemplifying assets are those systems that rapidly traverse celestial lines of communication to defend one's interests, or may entail systems that escort high-value space assets to protect them from attack.[15] Since effects may be used with similar results, space "cruisers" do not actually need to rapidly traverse great distances, but their effects do. So spacecraft performing this essential mission do not need to move relative to their intended point of action, since weapons effects that cause minor degradation or major destruction can be used instead. Because of the application of both physical and non-physical methods to this strategic concept, analogous naval terms such as "cruiser," "frigate," or "escort" do not seem appropriate, nor are they useful in describing this mission. It appears then that some other descriptive term is needed instead.

By understanding that a space "cruiser" is meant to patrol vast regions of space, while protecting and defending one's interests, a better term can in fact be discerned. Presence, coercion, and force will be required elements in ensuring one's access and use of lines of communication in space. Furthermore, the specific missions of these essential systems include patrolling celestial lines of communication, escorting high-value assets, and employing force when needed. These are all missions traditionally performed through policing activities. While the term "policing," as used in the context of "the police," is frequently thought of with a civilian significance, policing is in fact a more general function that can be applied during times of peace or war. So in the context of space operations, "policing" refers to maintaining order, protecting assets, ensuring access, and enforcing laws and regulations; consequently the best descriptive term for these essential space systems is "policing systems."[16]

What does all this mean?

Many of the previous discussions could be considered quite abstract, with little real utility for the warfighter or military strategist. Since the subject here is the theory and strategy of space warfare, operational and tactical applications are frequently needed to fully comprehend such strategic concepts. The ultimate design these policing craft eventually take is not as important as the mission they are intended to do, but nonetheless some possible designs are readily apparent. In general, most policing craft should be relatively inexpensive to produce, because significant numbers will be required to disperse along the most vital celestial lines of communication. Some of these systems will need to perform escorting functions to protect the most strategically important space-based assets, including satellites used for position, navigation, and timing, space stations, and critical commercial satellites. Inexpensive microsatellites could be used for this escort mission and could defend high-value space assets from hostile attack by terrestrial or space-based weapons. When a potential threat is identified – like an inbound anti-satellite weapon – these policing craft could move into a position that blocks line-of-sight weapons from hitting their intended target. In fact, the use of microsatellites has grown more prevalent in recent years, as indicated by the United Kingdom's University of Surrey Space Centre building dozens of microsatellites to perform a wide range of scientific and surveillance missions.[17] These inexpensive and small systems have been marketed to countries around the world, and some have already stated that such systems serve as a potential means of interfering with another's use and access of space.[18]

Some policing systems will need to rapidly traverse large regions of space. This type of spacecraft may be used to deny the enemy's ability to access and use his physical communications in space. For instance a small, inexpensive, and expendable satellite could be used to ram an enemy's space-based system. This kind of craft will need to "sprint" to the enemy's location, thus forcing the enemy to either expend limited quantities of onboard fuel to avoid impact or submit to the inevitable collision and potential destruction of his space system.

In a somewhat more technologically complicated application of this strategic concept, policing craft may be dispersed in location, while concentrating their effects where and when needed. Therefore, when employing non-physical methods against the enemy, a widely distributed policing constellation could be built which allows one to selectively direct offensive effects against the adversary's positions. Whereas these directed effects might cause minor harm when employed by a single policing craft, they might on the other hand be designed to cause devastating effects when the entire constellation simultaneously concentrates its effects against a single target. For example, a single policing satellite could direct a low-power blocking transmission that interferes with an adversary's communications signal in a limited manner, but several policing satellites working in cooperation could block the enemy's lines of communication within a wider region of space. This idea also has meaning for information operations, in that the number of space-based systems used in exploiting data and information for one's gain determines the severity and range of effects against a foe. It also follows that, since effects may originate from various locations, some of these policing systems may be terrestrially based, while delivering their effects into space. Consequently, land, sea, or air systems can be distributed and employed to protect and defend many near-earth celestial lines of communication. Such "earth-bound" policing systems may be mass-produced without incurring the expense associated with launching spacecraft into orbit.

Albeit a policing strategy entails protecting those critical systems that communicate from, into, and through space, in the end it is ultimately more important to ensure the viability of space communications even after one is attacked. Therefore, some policing systems should be specifically designed to have a redundant capability to emulate those satellites they protect. Such craft might provide a redundant mission capability through the deployment of several distributed satellites with similar capabilities, thereby assuring space communications even after the primary transmission node becomes inoperative.

The concept of dispersal and concentration should not be considered a panacea for the "friction" and "uncertainty" that are present during all wars.[19] History has shown that ambiguity, miscalculations, incompetence, and chance are all ingredients during hostilities and conflicts. It should not be expected that war in space will be any different in this regard. It has been touted by some that technology can eliminate the need for those defensive approaches meant to handle friction and uncertainty.[20] Despite the advantages of technology, technological sophistication – even onboard today's space-based systems – will not eliminate friction and uncertainty, but may at times merely reduce it. For, with the technological advancement of one belligerent, the other belligerent is likely in time to counter any such advancement. This is the natural order of warfare. Any belief that the technological sophistication required for space warfare will obviate the role of chance and uncertainty fails to accurately acknowledge the lessons of history and is a misguided and foolhardy belief.

Additionally, the unified idea of dispersal and concentration should not be construed as an endorsement of what has become known as "network-centric warfare."[21] Based on the persistent need for effective command and control, which is commensurate with the general principle of unity of effort, the employment of all military assets should work toward a common objective. Therefore, the dispersal and concentration of forces and effects must act collectively toward this military end as well. This observation, however, says nothing about a centralized hub of decision making and execution or warfare that is centered around a network.[22] As long as all forces, assets, and systems share the same unity of effort through proper command and control, there is no need to limit the execution of dispersal and concentration whatsoever. An overly networked approach to warfighting would in all likelihood limit the advantages of dispersal and concentration, since it will constrain autonomy of action. Autonomy of action – while adhering to the mission objectives and command guidance – is a necessary element of effective and unencumbered warfare.

Space warfare should not attempt to become something it is not. It is merely a subset of general warfare, just as land, sea, and air warfare are. As such, it will follow many of the time-honored lessons and observations concerning the nature of warfare. It should never be assumed that, since warfare in space is a relatively new concept, the rules and lessons of the past do not apply. That said, warfare in space will involve non-military actions as well as military ones, for both are means of achieving success. The strategic similarities between maritime and space activities have shown the proper relationship of space warfare to that of warfare as a whole, while hinting at a suitable lexicon and context for discussing its strategic concepts. Based on the lessons of history, both "victory" and "defeat" will be used to describe the results of future actions in space.

Chapter 13

Actions by lesser powers

As borne out by the discussions on command of space, command is normally in dispute, and those with less influence and command may choose to improve their relative standing. Lesser space powers are those that do not exercise command to the extent that those more powerful and influential in space do. The descriptor "lesser" is not meant pejoratively but is only meant to indicate the relative standing of those exercising command of space. Although it is often useful to discuss command of space, along with those that contest it, from the perspective of nation states, the various interests related to space communications and space-based activities pertain not just to state actors but to non-state actors as well. Therefore, many organizations and groups also have a stake in accessing and using space. In deciding to contest the command of another, a less capable space power must weigh the potential risks and rewards, and from that deliberation three possible conclusions may be reached: decide to become stronger, keep the status quo, or become weaker. The decision made is based on which outcome is most in the power's vital interests.[1]

The first case is most readily understandable, since those with less power and influence in space activities may want to improve their situation. Such an improvement can be achieved through a variety of military or non-military activities. To improve one's standing as a space power and consequently increase the degree of command that can be exercised, one could undertake an aggressive space militarization buildup. This could include the procurement of systems meant to deny another's access to lines of communication in space, like anti-satellite weapons. Non-military methods of improving one's standing may include advocating changes to international regulations that favor one's interest. Yet even after one expends the time, effort, resources, or lives required to improve one's standing as a space power, there is no guarantee of eventual success. Therefore, all prior sacrifices may be for naught.

The second case is when it is in one's interest to maintain the status quo. While it might be presumed that every lesser power should always want to improve their standing among space powers, this is not always true. The reason for this is that there may be some advantage to being a lesser space power, as when one is in a cooperative relationship with another who has primacy in space or is able to exercise general and persistent command. Because of the benefits gained in such a cooperative relationship, it may in fact be best to maintain one's standing as a lesser space power without contesting the command exercised by a superior power. A lesser power can take advantage of the superior's technological developments in launch systems or satellites, without laying out large research and development costs itself. Furthermore, a less capable space power can maintain minimal space related training and education infrastructure, while still having considerable access to space by "piggy backing" on the efforts of others. The monetary savings enjoyed in such a cooperative relationship can then be used for those non-space activities that are considered more critical. So a cooperative relationship of this kind enables a lesser space power to achieve many of the same benefits as a superior power, without taking the same risks or expending the same amount of resources.

Likewise, in a cooperative, almost symbiotic relationship with a lesser space power, the superior power can gain from the arrangement too. While the superior may exercise general and persistent command of space, a cooperative relationship may provide advantages and benefits in non-space related activities. For example, having a cooperative security arrangement – where one's superior space forces are pledged to be used for the security and defense of a lesser power – may result in diplomatic, economic, or information benefits, which would not exist without the relationship. For example, the United States has been the dominant military member of those signing the North Atlantic Treaty of 1949, which mutually engaged several countries along with the United States into a cooperative security agreement. While the military capabilities of these other nations might not match that of the United States, the United States has garnered more diplomatic and economic support than it would have otherwise without such a security arrangement.

The third case is when a lesser power would want its influence in space further diminished. While such instances are few, they do exist. These cases may occur when domestic or world economic conditions require cutting costs in space activities. When a temporary economic downturn is expected and more pressing security problems exist, a scaling back in space activities may be warranted. Such a short-term scaling back can be pursued, knowing that an increase in space activities is planned once economic conditions rebound. Moreover, another instance when a diminished role in space is warranted is when one desires to lessen the utilization of celestial lines of communication. A state, for instance, that has historically relied on space-based telecommunication systems for the transfer of news, data, and information might decide to increase their use of fiber optic cable or wireless cellular phone systems to perform similar communication functions.

In such a case, one's reliance on space-based communications is lessened, while a proportional increase in non-space based communication offsets the difference. A move like this, which intentionally reduces one's involvement in space activities, may be seen as a suitable method of reducing one's vulnerability to future space-based attack. Therefore, actions that at first appear to make oneself weaker in fact make oneself stronger.

Non-military actions

Although a lesser space power may have limited military capability when it comes to presence, coercion, or force, the lesser power can still achieve positive results, and these results may be achieved through non-military means. To many warfighters, the application of military might is more readily understood as a means of contesting another's superior command of space, but non-military methods can be equally effective in achieving political goals. The use of non-military methods is nothing new in war, as exemplified by Sun Tzu's timeless advice that it is best to win without fighting.[2] Even though the general subject here is space warfare, it is still useful to look at non-military methods that affect and are affected by a nation's strategy, specifically related diplomatic, economic, and information instruments of power. It is reasonable to presume that lesser space powers will attempt to use the most effective instruments at their disposal, effectively "leading with their best suit," which may frequently included non-military means. In doing so, a lesser power will attempt to bolster its power and influence, while diminishing the instruments of power of a superior adversary.

As with diplomacy used to gain or exercise command of space, diplomacy can also be used to contest it. Lesser space powers can gain diplomatic influence by establishing a notable presence in space and then subsequently proposing international treaties or laws that advance their interests on relevant issues. Although it is not an absolute prerequisite, those with the most presence in outer space and space-based activities will have the greatest chance of shaping international laws and regulations. By getting a seat at the "space table," lesser powers can begin the protracted process of gaining the respect and deference of others, and eventually they can advance issues regarding their own access and use of space communications. Once established as a legitimate member of the space community, a lesser space power can move closer to the head of the table by continuing to increase its presence in space and through the successful passage of diplomatic initiatives. Similarly, a less influential state can improve its diplomatic leverage by forming a coalition of lesser powers to push cooperative agreements, thus gaining recognition as a body with international influence. A loose coalition of lesser powers can be formed in this way to counter and dispute the preeminence of superior space powers. However, the coalition's effectiveness is predicated on its combined relative strength and capability. This idea is illustrated by the Plenipotentiary

Conference of the International Telecommunication Union in Nairobi, Kenya, in 1982. In this conference, Third World countries objected to the "first come, first served" method of allocating scarce space resources.[3] Despite their objection, nothing of real substance ever resulted from their collective action, because their presence in space was quite minimal.

Even though diplomacy is a distinct and separate method of influencing others, diplomatic changes can send shockwaves that affect other areas, like economic and military activities. A less capable power that is able to significantly increase its presence in space – such as by obtaining more geostationary orbital slots or associated bandwidth for its telecommunication satellites – can attempt to diminish the military influence of a superior power, by proposing United Nations resolutions that restrict the presence of military assets in space or by restricting what frequencies may be used in military applications.

Economic measures can also be used to contest command and gain greater influence. A lesser power that provides a unique commercial or business service can threaten to withhold its space-based service in order to negotiate better terms on some contentious issue. Moreover, a lesser state can prohibit those who provide space-based services from doing so within the lesser state's sovereign territory. The last two scenarios illustrate what would effectively be an embargo and a boycott of space-based commercial services. Through such economic coercive methods, a lesser space power can attempt to influence the future decisions of a superior power. One of the best methods, however, to gain greater economic influence is by increasing the presence of space-based commerce, trade, and business. This is because economic presence of this kind will give one more influence in the writing and shaping of future international regulations on economic activities. Therefore, being a major stakeholder in the process can further advance one's economic interests in space.

In the last of the non-military methods, information actions can be used to achieve positive results similar to those achieved by diplomatic and economic measures. Even though less capable space powers can use the advantage of cooperative action and increased economic presence to increase their power and influence, information methods are frequently the simplest method to contest a superior space power. Information services include the transfer of data, information, news, and intelligence; because of this, the information provided by a lesser power can be used to influence the perceptions of others. Minor achievements in space or other significant activities can be touted through media outlets and, if international media outlets also report the story favorably, these seemingly insignificant events can reach a worldwide audience. By conducting a sustained campaign to promote news that advances one's long-term strategy, a lesser power can over time change what is perceived or considered as fact by others. Within the military, this is commonly referred to as an information operations campaign. Depending on the desired strategy, information methods can cause a lesser power's status to be advanced or the superior power's status to be diminished, or a combination of both. So, for those states, organizations, or groups with less capability, space-based communications are a viable method of promoting news, achievements, culture, and social values. Other specific actions that lesser powers may take include gaining greater access to communication bandwidth, getting the best orbital positions for satellites, and procuring the most effective space-based communication systems.

The launch of *Sputnik I* by the Soviet Union illustrates the impact of information. Although the launch of the man-made satellite into orbit was a notable first and milestone, more strategic meaning was assigned to it than warranted.[4] The successful launch was used by some as a vindication of communism, while also being used to highlight the failings of the United States. Because of the domestic and international perceptions resulting from the Soviet space achievement, the Eisenhower administration was forced to react and modify national policy. The subsequent Soviet success of placing the first man into orbit further underscored these perceptions. More recently, the Chinese manned space program has received favorable press, and some have used the latest Chinese achievements to proclaim that United States dominance in space is threatened and that the Chinese have imperialistic goals in space. History, therefore, does support the notion that success in space can be used to promote a variety of views and agendas.

Military actions

Although non-military methods are available to contest the command of another, at times military measures may need to be employed by lesser space powers. A less capable space force is unlikely to win a decisive space engagement against a superior one; yet the lesser can still contest the command of space of a superior and consequently achieve limited political objectives. A strategy that disputes a superior power must fully recognize what is meant by command of space, and by understanding that concept, the methods of contesting another's power and influence are more easily determined. Because a lesser force is by definition less capable relative to a superior force, the lesser will need to gain local or temporary command in areas where the stronger force is not, thereby contesting the command exercised by a superior force. By attacking where or when the other is not strong, command can be gained and exercised for limited diplomatic, economic, information, or military purposes. For example, a less capable space force should attack the enemy's rearward lines of support or supply, thereby avoiding a direct engagement where the preponderance of the enemy's forces and assets are located. By concentrating its limited forces within a region for a specific period of time, a lesser power can gain a relative advantage. This idea is in keeping with maritime principles of local and temporary command.

Since military actions by lesser forces may be considered a mere nuisance to a superior force, they will by themselves be unable to decide the outcome of a war or conflict. Nonetheless, they can still achieve modest results. Minor actions can prevent the superior power from increasing its command of space and cause it to expend more resources and personnel to counter the threat of attack. If it is perceived that the minor attack has been a success, a lesser power's domestic morale may improve. Moreover, minor actions can delay one's defeat, until such time as allies or other forces can join the fight against the superior force. Depending on how the lesser's actions are perceived by others within the international community, other nation states, organizations, or groups may join the lesser's cause in contesting the command and influence of a superior space power.

Since it is paramount for lesser forces to avoid defeat so they can sustain a campaign that contests a superior power's command, the best strategy perhaps is to contest another's command without a foe knowing it. Through non-overt methods, the influence and effectiveness of the superior adversary can be diminished and, as long as the actions are not verifiable or suspected as being one's own, there is little reason to anticipate a counter-attack for such actions. While it is difficult to guarantee that non-overt methods will remain undetected, such actions hold the promise of being an effective means of contesting command. Methods may include the intentional interference of non-physical communications from, into, and through space. Tactical applications may include low-power jamming, degrading, or deceiving within the vicinity of the superior force's communications hubs. As long as such actions are not traceable back to oneself, non-overt interference techniques have the potential for success without incurring the wrath of one's adversary.

By understanding the measures of effectiveness of physical and non-physical communications, a lesser power can cause an adversary the most harm given any specific action. From earlier discussions, it was discerned that the effectiveness of physical communications is related to the path taken when the activities are commercial in nature, or whether the path was taken at all when the activities are more prestigious and diplomatic in nature. In contrast, it was discerned that the efficiency of non-physical communications is related to the transfer rate of communications. If a lesser power can successfully cause a superior adversary to use less effective physical and non-physical communications, the adversary will probably have to expend more manpower, time, and expense to accomplish any given task. During a protracted war, a lower effectiveness may be detrimental to the adversary's long-term sustainment capability. So, whereas a lesser power is unlikely to decisively defeat a superior space force in a single engagement, reducing the effectiveness of the enemy's space communications can weaken him over time. Examples employing this strategy include causing the superior power to use non-equatorial launch positions; forcing him to deviate from the optimal flight trajectory; causing the mission failure of a spacecraft that is associated with national prestige; reducing or minimizing a space-based communication's available bandwith; degrading the rate of data and information transfer; and minimizing the rate of energy that an enemy's space weapons can deliver to its intended target.

Force in being

Another effective method of contesting command is the "force in being" concept, which is a derivative of the naval "fleet in being" concept. Since naval and space operations are distinctly different, some critics may question whether a naval fleet in being concept is directly applicable to space warfare. This concern can be resolved, however, by understanding the strategic difference between naval and space operations. Whereas sea lines of communication were originally used extensively to transport communications, they have been in more recent times used to transport goods, supplies, personnel, and equipment. So predominantly physical communications are moved along sea lines of communications today. Lines of communication in space, on the other hand, move physical elements, but they are also used extensively to move non-physical elements as well, such as data and information. Consequently, the space equivalent to "fleet in being" should recognize this fundamental difference.

As with naval strategy, lesser space forces should be kept "in being" through active utilization and operations until the situation develops in their favor. Furthermore, by avoiding large-scale engagements with a superior space force, a lesser force can conduct minor attacks against a superior one's space communications or space-related activities, thus preventing the stronger power from gaining general and persistent command of space. In a tactical example relevant to the United States, weaponized microsatellites could be placed in the vicinity of space-based strategic assets, such as GPS or reconnaissance satellites. Consequently, this force in being of microsatellites could contest United States command in space, while also making a powerful political statement. By using a force in being strategy and employing low-cost, expendable satellites in the process, a lesser space power can mitigate the downside should these microsatellites be detected and subsequently destroyed.

At this point, however, naval and space strategies diverge on the subject. Because a less capable space power must impact non-physical communications, the force used to achieve this can be a "transparent force." Whereas the naval fleet in being strategy uses ships to dispute command of the sea, a space strategy employing a force in being may use physical assets as well as non-physical means. Physical assets are easily exemplified, such as microsatellites engaging an enemy satellite to limit its effectiveness. Non-physical force, while possibly having physically damaging effects against the enemy, can interfere, distort, or jam communication signals used for uplinks, downlinks, or crosslinks. Some critics may say that there is no difference between the naval fleet in being and the space force in being concepts, since physical systems will most likely be required to employ any non-physical effects in space, and therefore any distinction between the physical and non-physical is unnecessary. Yet there are distinct differences between the two concepts. One primary difference between the naval and space concepts is that a non-physical transparent force in the context of space warfare can more readily affect forces on land, at sea, and in the air, while the naval fleet in being concept mostly affects ships at sea or in port. This is because space activities are more fully integrated into different environments than are purely naval activities. Another primary difference is that non-physical effects in space can in some cases be achieved by non-physical means. This is exemplified by enemy space systems being forced to operate within regions with excessive amounts of interference to space communications, such as within Van Allen radiation belts or within these belts after the detonation of a nuclear warhead in orbit.

Commerce raiding

Drawn from centuries of maritime experience is the idea of commerce raiding, also referred to as *guerre de course*. The French navy employed this strategy when attacking along the British coastline and intercepting shipping along trade routes. This maritime strategy has applicability to space warfare, since many states use celestial lines of communication for trade and commerce and so, like the centuries old maritime practice of commerce raiding, lesser powers can negatively impact the economic interests of the more powerful. The intent of such action is meant to disturb the enemy's plans, while strengthening a lesser nation's power. If a small disposal force is used, then few repercussions come about if a superior force engages and destroys the lesser one. As with the force in being concept, a lesser power can use commerce raiding in space by employing non-physical methods of attack to degrade, diminish, or deny another's ability to use celestial lines of communication for economic gain. Methods of achieving this include using inexpensive satellites to deceive or block space-based telecommunication transmissions. Another method includes using non-physical effects, like the jamming or blocking of telecommunications signals, to degrade or prevent some commercial space-based communications.[5] Even though a physical asset is used in this method, the electromagnetic frequency blocking is still considered non-physical in effect.

Insurgencies

Space, as a medium of warfare, is a potential region for insurgent activity. Insurgents are defined as those that seek some political goal – which commonly includes autonomous self-governance – using a protracted guerrilla strategy.[6] To be successful, insurgencies must eventually garner public support, whether in times of peace or conflict. Although outer space and celestial lines of communications are not typically thought of as targets of attack by unconventional forces, any location or asset associated with diplomatic, economic, information, or military interests presents a viable target for others to exploit through hostile action. Maritime strategies, including the writings of Mahan and Corbett, however fail to provide much insight into a guerrilla strategy in space; nevertheless, the writings of Clausewitz and Mao Tse-tung give a suitable strategic framework for considering insurgencies. As a result, land warfare theory will be used to consider the strategy of insurgents in space.

According the theory of land warfare, insurgencies are usually initially smaller than a more powerful, traditional army, and therefore a single decisive battle against the larger enemy force should not be sought.[7] According to Clausewitz, an insurgency strategy is "like smoldering embers," which needs time to be effective.[8] Guerrilla attacks should be concentrated around exterior lines and should attempt to "nibble . . . around the edges" of the enemy's operating area.[9] These guerrilla attacks, according to Mao, allow insurgents to "hold the enemy in pincers."[10] Based on the lessons of land warfare, it is expected that insurgents attacking against space systems will also predominantly conduct small-scale attacks along exterior celestial lines of communication, and the most easily accessible locations along these communication routes will be targeted. Presently, this means that terrestrial facilities used for uplinks or as central distribution hubs for space-based information are likely targets for attack. Additionally, space agency headquarters and manufacturing facilities, as well as launch facilities that support space operations will be potential targets for insurgents. Guerilla attacks may be conducted along another's periphery of operations, such as against satellites in orbit, but, because of the technological sophistication required for such operations, these types of attacks currently prove more difficult to implement and accomplish.

Actions of terrorists

Differing from insurgents, terrorists do not seek a purely political objective or autonomous governance, and they include individuals wanting anarchy, chaos, or a state's disestablishment. Although the actions of many insurgents may be called "terrorism," insurgents and terrorists are considered separately, since the motives and methods of attack will commonly be quite different. Albeit terrorists may cite political reasons for their actions, their primary motivation is frequently to cause fear in others. Because of these motives, terrorists will prefer attacking easily accessible locations that cause the most sensational reactions by the local populace. To this end, terrorist actions will include inflicting large numbers of casualties, damaging major infrastructure, and targeting symbolic locations.[11]

Based on the intent and preferred methods of terrorist groups, it is possible to predict those assets and locations most likely to be targeted. Those corporate headquarters involved in the development or use of space systems are included on this list, because of their extensive economic involvement and sizable infrastructure. Manned spacecraft readying for launch may also be targeted, since destroying them will cause sensational reactions and gain media attention. Less sensational targets, but equally plausible, include those ground-based relay stations scattered around the globe that support space-based commerce and trade, because they are numerous and often not well protected. Perhaps those targets least likely to be attacked by terrorists are systems in orbit, such as manned space stations. This view is held since the technological challenges with getting something into space that can detect, locate, and engage its intended quarry are quite formidable. Nevertheless, a space-based system – especially a manned one – will be the most sought-after kind of target by terrorists, since its destruction can achieve the casualties, damage to space infrastructure, and sensationalism desired. Considering current and projected technological trends, one plausible scenario in the future includes a terrorist group launching an undetected small satellite aboard a third-party launch vehicle that is destined for a low-earth orbit. The satellite would then detach from the host when near a space station and ram itself into the station's environmental control system, while detonating its onboard incendiary munition. If the blast mixes with enough of the station's onboard oxygen, the results could be catastrophic.

Trading strategic advantage for time

In the case of insurgencies, they are fought from a point of initial weakness compared to the state supported army. Because of this, guerrilla warfare calls for attacking a foe and then retreating before any substantial counterattack by the stronger enemy takes place. Mao's philosophy on guerrilla warfare is exemplified in his famous statement, "the enemy advances, we retreat; the enemy camps, we harass; the enemy tires, we attack; the enemy retreats, we pursue."[12] Clausewitz thought that, because insurgents usually operate within the interior of their territory, a guerrilla strategy "calls for avoiding defeat by yielding the contested ground in time."[13]

It might at first seem uncertain whether this thought translates into space warfare, although a direct application of this thought includes terrorists attacking terrestrially-based systems used for space communications and then quickly dispersing or retreating to avoid detection and destruction. To determine the strategic equivalent of Mao and Clausewitz's thoughts for space warfare, a broader interpretation of these classical strategists must be taken. For those insurgents involved in contesting the dominance of a superior army, taking and controlling territory is a critical element of their strategy. Any of the hard-earned territory that is taken by the insurgents is considered of value and represents an advantage gained. In a sense, contested ground becomes akin to strategic advantage, since those that control the most ground are more apt to achieve victory. Therefore, a more general paraphrase of the previous thoughts – and of Clausewitz in particular – regarding the weaker insurgent would be that "to avoid defeat, some strategic advantage must be traded to buy more time."

This interpretation does prove applicable for insurgent activity in the context of space warfare, since strategic advantage in space warfare is often manifested by commanding space and holding certain positions. If insurgents hold local or temporary command in space or hold a certain strategic position, these can be "traded" to gain more time and further protract the conflict. An example of this idea would be for insurgent forces to use an offensive weapon from orbit (representing a strategic position used to exercise local command), while knowing full well that such hostile action will lead to weapon's detection and subsequent destruction. Yet the sacrifice of the strategic position is seen as a military achievement that will protract the conflict long enough for more forces to be brought to bear. Moreover, command and positions are not the only strategic advantages that insurgents may trade. Since the effectiveness of insurgents – and to a lesser extent terrorists – is often predicated on the popular support of the locals, the insurgents could give up some of their popular support in order to protract the conflict and buy time for their future efforts. Such a strategy could entail attacking civilian leadership who are involved in space activities, even though it is known in advance that a decline in popular sentiment will result from of such an attack. Giving up any strategic advantage is done at great cost. Nevertheless, if the purpose of such a sacrifice is to gain more time and prolong the conflict to await the support of allies, the demise of the stronger power, or an increase in popular support, then long-term gains may in fact be worth the short-term sacrifices.

Chapter 14

Comparisons

At this point, it is worth reiterating that a historically based maritime model served to inspire the development of the space strategy. Since a historical framework was used in this effort, it is necessary to compare the developed concepts against current expert observations and space literature to determine the strategy's potential utility. For this comparison, three different perspectives will be used: the 2001 Report of the Commission to Assess United States National Security Space Management and Organization – also known as the *Space Commission Report* – United States joint military doctrine, and the four contemporary "schools of thought" regarding space.[1]

The *Space Commission Report* was chosen over the Clinton administration's 1996 National Space Policy, National Security Presidential Directive (NSPD-15), even though the latter is the last official United States document on space policy. This decision was made because the *Space Commission Report* is more recent, besides being inclusive of and complementary to many of the ideas in the 1996 National Space Policy.[2] The United States Air Force's space doctrine was not used for direct comparison, since joint doctrine takes precedence over the service doctrine, and the joint publications address many of the same ideas as the Air Force's publications. Finally, the contemporary "schools of thought" are used for comparison since these viewpoints are still widely referred to when describing the various ideas concerning space operations and weaponization. By comparing the space strategy against these different perspectives, it will be determined whether a maritime-inspired space strategy appears relevant or not, while also noting the implications of any differences.

Space Commission Report

The *Space Commission Report* covers a broad range of issues pertaining to United States activities in space. The report lists current national interests regarding space operations including promoting the peaceful use of space; using the nation's potential in space to support its domestic, economic, diplomatic and national security objectives; assured access to space and on-orbit operations; space situational awareness; surveillance from space; global command, control, and communications in space; defense in space; homeland defense; and power projection in, from, and through space.[3]

Indeed, the overall ideas in the *Space Commission Report* are comparable to the maritime-inspired space strategy. The report notes that the United States' reliance on its space activities has made protecting these activities an issue of national security. Explicitly noting this thought, the report states, "Therefore, it is in the U.S. national interest to . . . use the nation's potential in space to support its domestic, economic, diplomatic and national security objectives."[4] Furthermore, the report even notes that other states will probably attempt to restrict or lessen the United States' influence in space.[5] In describing the methods for denying the enemy's access to outer space, the report includes restricting or denying freedom of access to and through space, attacking associated ground stations (whether physical attack or computer network intrusions), exploiting sensitive information about a satellite's orbital and system characteristics, and jamming ground-based communications equipment.[6] These thoughts are in keeping with the developed methods of denying access to and use of celestial lines of communications. While the *Space Commission Report* does not explicitly state the need for offensive weapons in space, it does imply this view by noting, "[W]e know from history that every medium – air, land, and sea – has seen conflict. Reality indicates that space will be no different."[7] Given this virtual certainty of future combat operations, the report maintains, the United States must develop the means to "deter and to defend" against hostile acts in and from space.[8] Although the word "deter" is used, the method of achieving this is compatible with the previously developed offensive strategy in space. In fact, most of the report's major ideas are compatible with the described space strategy, even though the terms and tactical examples used are different.

Despite the many similarities between the *Space Commission Report* and the maritime-inspired space strategy, there are three apparent differences. The *Space Commission Report* describes the need to promote the peaceful use of space among the international community; to reorganize and streamline the different United States' space-related agencies; and for the United States to invest its resources – both people and financial – to ensure the United States remains the world's leading spacefaring nation.[9] Although notable, these differences are explainable. The report's emphasis on promoting the peaceful use of space is understandable once the context of "peaceful" is recognized. It amplifies its use of "peaceful" as meaning "non-aggressive," or agreeing with the customary interpretation of the United States, which allows for "routine military activities in space."[10] As a result, applying force in and through space to support individual, collective, or "anticipatory" self-defense is implicit in the word "peaceful."[11] The bureaucratic reorganization and streamlining recommendations are because the report gives policy guidance to governmental agencies, and therefore it addresses topics outside the direct purview of military strategy. Lastly, the report's statement on needing to invest in space operations is not explicitly mentioned in the derived space strategy; yet the idea is implied, since space operations and activities are tied to a state's interests and thus need to be fiscally supported.

Joint Doctrine

Joint Publication 3-14, *Joint Doctrine for Space Operations*, primarily deals with establishing doctrine for space operations at the operational level of warfare.[12] Although "doctrine" is frequently used interchangeably with the term "strategy," the two are not considered synonymous here. "Doctrine" is taken to mean "what warriors believe and act on," and admittedly this definition does overlap somewhat with the role of strategy.[13] Yet by looking at what is included within the doctrine of *Joint Doctrine for Space Operations*, it is seen that much of the publication is concerned with assigning organizational responsibilities to individuals and commands. Of the 30 pages within the main body of the publication, only 14 deal with the issues related to military strategy.[14] Despite the paucity of actual strategy, the publication does address a few strategic issues that can be compared with the developed space strategy.

Like the *Space Commission Report*, *Joint Doctrine for Space Operations* states the need to protect United States space assets, while denying an adversary the use of his space assets.[15] This thought is comparable to the idea of commanding space to protect one's use of celestial lines of communications, while denying the enemy's ability to use the same lines of communication. In describing the role of the military in space, the publication lists four primary mission areas: force enhancement, space support, force application, and space control. Force enhancement is said to include intelligence, monitoring, communications, and navigation functions, while space support activities include operations that launch, deploy, augment, maintain, sustain, replenish, de-orbit, and recover space forces. Force application operations are those consisting of attacks against terrestrial-based targets carried out by military operations in or through space. These three mission areas contained within the joint publication are similar to the maritime-inspired space strategy, since both reference a variety of space-based activities, the importance of operations in and through space, and the use of military actions.

It is perhaps in defining *space control* that the most striking similarities between joint doctrine and the derived space strategy are apparent. In defining the mission area, the joint publication states:

> Space control operations provide freedom of action in space for friendly forces while, when directed, denying it to an adversary, and include the broad aspect of protection of U.S. and U.S. allied space

systems and negation of enemy adversary space systems. Space control operations encompass all elements of the space defense mission and include offensive and defensive operations by friendly forces to gain and maintain space superiority and situational awareness if events impact space operations.[16]

It is particularly noteworthy that the joint publication states that both offensive and defensive operations are needed, which is consistent with the derived space theory.

Other similarities exist as well. The publication notes that military, civil, and commercial sectors are increasingly dependent on space activities, and consequently the United States must protect its space interests. *Joint Doctrine for Space Operations* implicitly acknowledges that the prevalent use of orbits around the earth has resulted in extensively used lines of operations and communication in space. Finally, the publication notes the interdependence of space warfare with the land, sea, and air operations, by stating that space-based capabilities and operations must be integrated into the total warfighting effort.[17]

Besides the obvious administrative and organizational recommendations, the joint publication and the developed space strategy have differences. Some of these include semantic differences, such as the use of "freedom of action," "space superiority," and "situational awareness," which the maritime-inspired space strategy does not include. Such differences, however, are considered minor when comparing the strategic context of each. Other differences include the joint doctrine's being more narrowly focused on orbital space activities and not providing a more encompassing military strategy for space warfare. When attempting to discuss the strategic principles of space warfare, *Joint Doctrine for Space Operations* briefly discusses the application of the nine general principles of war: objective, offensive, mass, economy of force, maneuver, unity of command, security, surprise, and simplicity.[18] This in itself is not a failing, since space warfare must work under the overall military strategy and associated principles of war, but it nonetheless results in the joint publication presenting a "grab bag" of ideas and thoughts that fail to fully enlighten the warfighter on the strategy of space warfare. Space warfare deserves a lexicon and context all its own to describe its complexities and interactions, within a coherent strategic framework.

The four contemporary "schools of thought"

As described earlier, there are four contemporary viewpoints regarding space operations and the weaponization of space. During debates about the military's role in space, these different "schools of thought" are often used to conceptualize ideas and propose recommendations. Albeit each of these viewpoints does not constitute a sufficiently broad and in depth strategy for space warfare, their prevalence in the weaponization debate is reason enough for comparison. Whereas some of the underlying arguments from the sanctuary, survivability, high-ground, and control schools of thought are addressed by the derived space strategy, the conclusions regarding the role and utility of weapons are distinctly different.

Sanctuary

The sanctuary viewpoint notes the inherent benefits coming from operating in outer space, and concludes that these benefits should be preserved by keeping weapons out of the medium of outer space. Except for the final conclusion about keeping space a weapons-free medium, the other underlying assumptions are compatible with the derived space strategy, and it is noteworthy that the sanctuary school recognizes a similar interpretation of the "strategic positions" concept. Most of the divergences with the sanctuary school are due to its emphasis on debating the role of weapons on space, rather than developing a coherent strategic framework for space warfare.

Indeed, much of the current debate regarding space power and military strategy in space deals with – to the exclusion of almost everything else – the role of weapons in space. Such a narrow focus on just one part of strategy is a myopic approach to a subject deserving a broader scope of consideration. As a result, the often overstated arguments regarding whether weapons should be "allowed" in space or not have led to an underdeveloped understanding of the proper role of space strategy, along with its subordinate role within grand strategy.[19]

Survivability

Advocates of the survivability viewpoint say it is foolhardy to put national assets in space where they cannot be protected, since any space-based system is vulnerable to attack.[20] Moreover, space systems are seen as inherently less survivable than terrestrial assets and forces, being predicated on three assumptions: space systems are vulnerable to long-range weapons; space assets cannot effectively use maneuverability or terrestrial barriers to protect themselves; and states will not retaliate over the destruction of any space system due to its lack of political importance.[21] According to the maritime-inspired space strategy, the first two assumptions would be true if one just waited to be attacked without assuming a position of advantage or taking other defensive measures. Yet by understanding what a true defensive strategy entails – awaiting the blow from a position of advantage – it can be seen that these two assumptions are not warranted. Since space systems can be designed and positioned in a manner that minimizes the risk from long-range attack, space can be made a "barrier" that gives defensive protection. The last assumption regarding states not fighting over space-based systems would only be true if a state's interests did not lie in space. But, as has been described, some states, organizations, and groups already have interests in space, and these interests will need to be protected. For instance if the United States GPS constellation were threatened by hostile action, the American leadership would most likely view these satellites as worth defending because of their strategic importance for economic and military activities. Consequently, offensive or defensive actions may be employed to thwart an adversary's aggressive intentions.

High ground

As with the sanctuary school of thought, the high-ground school also accounts for strategic positions in space by recognizing the advantage of operating high above the earth, thereby taking advantage of the earth's "gravity well" and extensive field-of-view. This high ground gives one the ability to more effectively employ weapons and conduct surveillance against the enemy below. Even *Joint Doctrine for Space Operations* pays homage to this idea by stating, "Space is the ultimate high ground."[22] The failings of the high-ground school come from its obsession with near-earth operations and activities, along with the conclusion that offensive weapons should have a dominant role in military space applications. Although its basic idea of taking advantage of gravity well effects and extensive field-of-view when conducting offensive operations against earth-based targets is sound, space warfare is ultimately concerned with much more that just near-earth operations and offensive space-to-ground actions. Because of its inordinate focus on near-earth effects, the high-ground school does not fully recognize the importance of celestial lines of communication, except those going from near-earth orbit to the earth. As demonstrated previously, the strategy of space warfare must also be concerned with space-to-space effects and the implications on broad national issues, such as commerce and trade.

Control

The control school of thought draws upon the concept of control contained within air power and sea power theories. As in air power theory, which states that controlling the air allows for exerting control over the land and sea beneath, space control is viewed in a similar manner; as in sea control strategy, which says that sea lines of communication must be controlled to win wars at sea, so too must space lines of communication be controlled in space warfare. Since the developed space strategy contained within this work was inspired by maritime theory, which includes a variation of the concept of control, many similarities exist between the control school and the maritime-inspired space strategy. Despite the similarities, the space control approach provides a too narrowly focused theoretical lens for considering the breadth of space interests and activities, and consequently it fails to deliver the principles and concepts needed to understand the complexities of space warfare. For instance, the control school approach does not address ideas such as interdependence with other operations, the need to disperse space forces, and the possible actions of lesser powers. As a result, the control school viewpoint is not really a strategy at all, but more like a supposition.

"So what?"

A critic could well ask this question. A maritime-inspired space strategy seems to have merely substantiated the preponderance of what was already known or written about. Indeed, much of the derived space strategy is consistent with the *Space Commission Report*, joint doctrine, and the "control school" of thought. Therefore, one could argue that nothing of real value has been added by developing a historically based space strategy. This view, however, is not correct.

Despite the many similarities with popular space literature or contemporary viewpoints, there are three ideas from the developed strategic space theory that are neither explicitly nor implicitly mentioned elsewhere. These ideas are using policing systems to ensure one's access to celestial lines of communication, the dispersal and concentration of forces as a general practice, and making space a "barrier" to protect oneself from attack. These differences could mean one of two things: these particular points are baseless and consequently should be discounted; or they are pertinent, but contemporary literature and viewpoints have not adequately addressed them as yet. Since a maritime-inspired theory is relevant as a strategic framework for understanding space strategy, and the majority of resulting principles and concepts are validated by contemporary thought, it is therefore concluded the remaining three ideas remain relevant also. Even though at first these three ideas may appear unrelated, they each deal with the methods of protecting and defending one's celestial lines of communication.

This is a significant result. By using a maritime-inspired strategic framework, a preferred method of defending space assets and ensuring access to celestial lines of communications has been discerned. Through the use of policing systems, one can protect those critical space communications routes pertaining to the movement of trade, materiel, supplies, personnel, military effects, data, and information. Since the environment of space is vast and one's available fiscal resources necessitate balancing the number of desired space-based capabilities against the number of systems that can be procured, these policing systems should be relatively inexpensive to allow for the production of significant numbers. Once produced in significant numbers, these space systems should then be dispersed to protect and defend the far flung regions where celestial lines of communication are located, while maintaining the capability to concentrate firepower or other effects against the enemy when and where needed. In allocating and utilizing space systems in this manner, the highest level of command of space possible can be achieved. In doing so, one can effectively make space a "barrier" against one's adversaries, thereby precluding the most devastating methods of attack from, into, or through space. The end result is that the vast majority of one's security interests in space are protected against major attacks, while any minor attacks can be dealt with rapidly and decisively.

Part III

Implications and recommendations

Chapter 15

Space policy

A space strategy with historical underpinnings provides an encompassing context for investigating the nuances of military operations in space. Consequently, the intricate relationship between offensive versus defensive strategies, the methods used to contest another's superior space capability, and the importance of strategic positions can all be readily understood. Moreover, since a maritime-inspired space strategy is inclusive of many contemporary thoughts and proves applicable as a strategic framework for space warfare, its underlying value is that it can be used to predict concerns and develop ideas that have not yet been discerned. This applicability is critical, especially when considering governmental guidance in the form of policy.

The term "policy" is often used to describe many things. In some circles, "policy" is used interchangeably with "strategy." For instance, some say policy provides the guidance that establishes the vision, objectives, procedures, and implementing measures for a given course of action.[1] This definition of policy does indeed seem to overlap with the purpose of strategy. Yet policy is usually thought of within a context of explicitly stated capabilities that are needed to achieve some political goal. As such, policy commonly provides guidance for governmental departments and agencies, while delineating resources to make political goals a reality. Although policy includes some "strategy-like" elements, policy is not strategy. Policy most often refers to official governmental positions, commonly in the form of documents or speeches. These policy documents or speeches provide the necessary guidance to reconcile competing requirements in order to balance one's "ends" with one's limited "means."[2]

Why should the warfighter care about policy? Policy appears to be the realm of governmental officials and state leaders, and therefore it seems of little consequence to those concerned about offensive or defensive operations from, into, and through space. Moreover, it could be said that a maritime-inspired space strategy should "stay in its lane" and thus not try to comment on areas outside its purview. As the Prussian master of strategy suggested, however, warfare is a continuation of policy.[3] Consequently, policy is often used to "shape" military strategy. But policy and strategy are not isolated from each other, as either one can affect the other.

Some strategists and critics may take exception to the previous statement, viewing policy as influencing strategy in a classical Clausewitzian manner. Accordingly, some believe that this relationship in not reversible: that is strategy cannot influence policy.[4] In a conventional interpretation of warfare, such a view seems reasonable. For strategy balances one's ends with one's means, and policy provides the political guidance to make strategy work. Yet warfare is a dynamic creature, with chance and uncertainty. Therefore, the results of combat may affect one's available means. Such a condition is typically seen after a major defeat, when one belligerent's forces are decimated. With a significant reduction in one's fighting ability following such a defeat, strategy necessitates that one should change or adjust one's ends. Consequently, a change in one's desired ends most often necessitates a change in political objectives and official policy. Not to belabor the discussion, or to delve into a too theoretical or academic discussion, it is simply meant that policy and strategy have a complexity and interplay where changes in one can affect the other.

So a reciprocal relationship exists: military strategy at times can shape policy. For the warfighter, this means that a sufficiently broad and sound space strategy can be used to propose policy recommendations, especially if current policy guidance proves wanting.

Past and present policy

The lessons of the past have indeed revealed that policy has shaped military strategy in space, along with our perceptions on how space is to be used. Although these international and domestic policies have historically covered a broad range of concerns and issues, the primary scope of this work is space warfare and, as a result, that remains the primary lens through which relevant space policy recommendations will be viewed. The areas of space policy that have shaped military strategy and operations can be divided into three general areas: international security and cooperation; protecting one's interests; and the role of weapons in and through space.

International cooperation and security

International treaty law and customary international law have long guided what is considered appropriate and acceptable behavior between nation states. Although the use of force is perfectly acceptable when defending oneself, it is not deemed acceptable when one is unprovoked or when used for purely aggressive aims. Much of what is considered in the modern view as a "just war" is based on these ideas. Presently, the United Nations Charter serves as a common framework for considering the appropriate actions between states. Although the charter serves as a framework, other treaties, resolutions, and regulations also serve to amplify and expand upon what are considered legitimate actions between states. This is especially true in the case of activities in space.

Many state and government leaders during the 1950s and 1960s were concerned about whether space was to become another arena where Cold War tensions would play out. Because of the fear of a single state gaining supremacy in space, international agreements were reached that limited and more clearly defined those space-based activities considered acceptable and non-threatening. One of the outcomes of this fear was the declaration that space was to be used for "peaceful purposes." This declaration was agreed to by many in the international community as a way to minimize the militarization of space and keep permanently based weapons out of space.[5] During the Eisenhower administration, it was declared, "[I]t is the policy of the United States that activities in space should be devoted to peaceful purposes for the benefit of all mankind."[6] This policy of "space for peace" was intended to limit the Cold War's escalation, while recognizing that using space for peaceful purposes was in the benefit of all nations.

As with Eisenhower's policy, the Outer Space Treaty of 1967 included the idea that outer space should be used for peaceful purposes and cannot be claimed as sovereign territory.[7] Furthermore, it emphasized that space is open to exploration and use by the entire international community. Along a similar line, the Moon Treaty of 1979, more formally known as the Treaty Governing the Activities of States on the Moon and Other Celestial Bodies, was also an attempt to underscore that space is a domain that concerns all nations.[8] Although the Moon Treaty failed to ultimately achieve international legitimacy, since only nine states successfully ratified it, the endorsement of the treaty by several countries illustrated the prevalent perception that all of mankind must decide how space is used, and not just the most influential space powers.[9] Countries opposing the Moon Treaty, which included the United States, took exception to one of the phrases included in it. Unlike the Outer Space Treaty, which used the "province of all mankind," the Moon Treaty used the "common heritage of mankind" instead. Some interpreted this latter phrase to mean that space powers must share in the economic profits gained through the use and exploitation of outer space.[10]

Also exemplifying the idea that space is a medium where the international community as a whole should decide upon critical issues was the formation of the International Telecommunications Union. This international organization was formed to oversee the allocation of operating frequencies used by satellites.[11] The entire frequency spectrum used by communication satellites was seen as a finite resource, and therefore this finite resource must be doled out through an international organization to ensure equitable access and use of space by all countries. The creation of the International Telecommunications Satellite Consortium, moreover, served as the legal mechanism to establish the first global commercial telecommunications satellite system. These previous examples illustrate that to many having access to outer space is seen as a right of every sovereign country, and therefore international cooperation is required.

Protection of national interests

Although space is recognized as a medium where international cooperation is at times essential, many state leaders have understood that space activities and their country's national security are closely interconnected. In 1958, United States policy noted that the Soviet Union had captured the imagination and admiration of the world through its successes in space and, if Soviet superiority in space continued, United States prestige and security could be undermined. As a result, official United States policy stated, "reconnaissance satellites are of critical importance to U.S. national security" as a hedge against Soviet superiority and as a means of deterrence.[12] Additionally, the National Aeronautics and Space Act of 1958 had in its preamble that "the general welfare and security" of the United States requires adequate provisions for aeronautical and astronautical activities.[13]

In a 1978 policy document, President Jimmy Carter reemphasized that outer space is open to use by all nations, while interfering with a state's space systems would be viewed as an infringement upon sovereign rights. Moreover, it was the official position of the United States that it would pursue space activities that uphold the inherent rights of self-defense, strengthen national security, deter attack from another, and support arms control agreements.[14] The Clinton administration's 1996 National Space Policy of the United States noted that space defense and intelligence activities contribute to national security by upholding the inherent right of self-defense and the defense of allies; deterring, warning, and defending against attack; ensuring access to space; and denying access to our enemy when required.[15] Whereas the policy of the United States throughout the years may have had different tones and diplomatic motivations, these various policies have been in consistent agreement that there are national interests in space, and these interests should be protected.

Space weapons

The desire for international cooperation and the need to protect national interests are not necessarily in competition with each other. In most circumstances, the goals and objectives of the global community are compatible with those of individual states. Yet when discord between states exists, military force may result. For this reason, the role of weapons in space has been and will be a subject of debate. In the language of the Outer Space Treaty, "peaceful purposes" is a key phrase, and a number of states have taken the position that "peaceful purposes" excludes military activities. The consistent interpretation of the policy of the United States, however, has been that "peaceful purposes" means non-aggressive purposes.[16] Therefore, weapons in space are allowed if they are used to protect national interests and defend against attack.

Although some have interpreted the Outer Space Treaty and other international agreements as granting weapons a legitimate role in space, there are precedents for certain restrictions on their use and employment. In October 1963, the Soviet Union and the United States jointly agreed not to place nuclear weapons in orbit as part of the Limited Test Ban Treaty.[17] The 1967 Outer Space Treaty further reiterated restrictions on some weapons and military activity, by including a ban on deploying nuclear weapons or other weapons of mass destruction from space and stating that military bases, installations, and fortifications may not be erected, nor may weapons tests be undertaken on natural celestial bodies.

There is a wide variety of viewpoints on the employment and basing of weapons in space. While some have taken the position that the weaponization of space is a legitimate need, others believe adamantly that outer space should be weapons-free. Still others take the middle ground between these two views, believing that weapons should not be excluded from space but questioning the timing of such weaponization and even which regions are eventually weaponized. Policy advocates taking the middle ground frequently imply that the weaponization of space is inevitable but nonetheless the permanent basing of weapons in space should be delayed as long as possible.[18] According to one argument, since the United States is currently perceived as enjoying superiority in space, if it were to escalate the militarization and weaponization of space, other countries would be encouraged to contest such superiority. Consequently, escalation by the United States results in others doing likewise, thereby leading to a destabilizing effect in the global community. Furthermore, some have advocated for a space policy restricting certain types of weapons – like those creating excessive space debris in the most congested near-earth orbits, since residual debris from these weapons could foul orbits around the earth for years and make them unusable for many space-based systems.

Touching on the intangibles

Before delving into the arena of future space policy, one needs to fully comprehend the nature of warfare in space. It has been argued here that there are a wide variety of interests in space, and these interests will be protected through the diplomatic, economic, information, and military instruments of national power. Moreover, space is a medium – just as land, sea, and air are – where the use of force is a legitimate option.[19] Cognitively, these are rational arguments, but it is perhaps more important to determine how space is perceived. For, although the United Nations Charter and the legal regime established by prior international treaties and regulations have shaped our ideas, one needs to take a step back and determine not only how people *think* about space activities but how they *feel* about them also.

For millennia, mankind has looked to the heavens for portents to predict the future, inspiration from the "gods," and guidance for passage across the seas and oceans of the world. The celestial heavens are part of the human psyche, holding special meaning for many and symbolizing the hope for a better way of life. Any future space policy regarding the promotion of national interest and the basing of weapons in space needs to address these perceptions. Some critics could well argue that both the sea and air were perceived differently in the past – like the seas being the home of serpents and mermaids and the air medium not being the realm of man, since he was born without wings – but a more modern understanding about the utility of the sea and air has made these previous perceptions outdated. Current perceptions about space, it could be argued, are likely to change too, so why be concerned with perceptions? This is a fair argument. Yet current perceptions must be considered, along with the potential repercussions resulting from policy changes. Radical policy departures that are counter to the perceptions of the majority are unlikely to be supported by the international community, and therefore such a new policy would be considered as lacking legitimacy. So, whereas maritime and international law are well suited for considering future space policy, policy changes must take into account the fact that many in the international community still consider outer space a place where nations do not wage war but act in the common interest of the human race.

Policies and recommendations for the future

With a fundamental understanding of what space warfare is and what the strategic principles entail, one can contemplate those policies and recommendations that are most relevant to military space operations. Albeit policy should be guided by rational thought, a dose of the irrational – such as perceptions surrounding the debate – must at least be considered, even if the policy eventually runs counter to them. As when considering past space policies, future considerations pertain to international security and cooperation, protecting one's interests, and the role of weapons in space. Because the focus of this work is on space warfare, also included are those considerations specifically relevant to the military's organization and training. Even though the presented policy considerations are general enough to be pertinent to most space powers, some of the recommendations and suggestions are specifically meant to address United States space policy issues.

Uphold the current legal regime

The framework provided by customary international law and the Charter of the United Nations serves as precedent for appropriate and legitimate actions between states during peace and war. Because it serves as precedent, any policy should be compatible with this historical legal regime. Additionally, policy that is related to the procurement of military space systems and their employment should observe the provisions contained within the Law of Armed Conflict, especially the right of self-defense. The prevalent interpretation within the United States regarding "peaceful purposes" does this, since this interpretation recognizes that national interests must be protected and defended, even in space. The present policy position of the United States, therefore, takes into account the legal regime as delineated by both historical precedent and international law.

Some critics have called the Outer Space Treaty of 1967 a "tragedy" since it is said to have drained away the "impetus, determination, and desire" that the remaining twenty years of the Cold War could have held for space exploration.[20] Specifically, it is claimed the treaty's call for collective action among the international community eliminated the competition for space-based assets and commodities, thus seriously curtailing the development and pursuit of nationalistic space activities.[21] Because of this, states had little incentive to spend significant amounts of fiscal resources or incur substantial risk to advance their national interests in space, with the result that some states chose not to take such risks. Since the Outer Space Treaty has proved a failure, it is argued, the United States should withdrawal from it.

Despite such calls for withdrawal from the Outer Space Treaty, such a move by the United States is neither recommended nor needed from a purely military perspective. There is nothing contained within the Outer Space Treaty that specifically hinders protecting or defending a state's interests in space. The Outer Space Treaty declares the need to use space in accordance with the Charter of the United Nations, along with the need to maintain international peace and security.[22] Even with the restrictions regarding military activities and permanent bases on celestial bodies, the treaty's non-specific language allows for a broad enough interpretation to protect national interests. The treaty as written does not limit the legitimate use of force, just the manner in which it is delivered.[23] Since neither the Outer Space Treaty nor its contemporary interpretation by the United States precludes any of the time-honored actions included within customary international law, along with the Charter of the United Nations, the treaty's provisions should still be observed.

Nevertheless, it has been adeptly argued that the Outer Space Treaty fails to endorse the idea of rewarding those willing to take risks with economic or territorial gain.[24] While these shortfalls are related to economic incentives and territorial claims – which are beyond the intended scope of the space theory and strategic principles present here – these issues may still be addressed indirectly through the strategic framework previously provided. Under the Outer Space Treaty, spacecraft, stations, and facilities in space are considered sovereign territory, although their "footprint" on a celestial body is not.[25]

Since some of the locally obtained materials and surrounding terrain may be required to support the operation of these space systems and facilities, such material and territory can be considered vital and essential. So, instead of confronting the issue of declaring sovereign territory in space head-on, a more "diplomatic" solution is achieved by designating territory or necessary materials as "mission essential" and therefore necessary to protect and defend when required. Such a designation uses language similar to that used by the United States military in their Supplemental Rules of Engagement, thereby allowing for the protection of interests, without actually laying claim to regions in space or territory on celestial bodies.

Admittedly, this solution fails to address concerns regarding the exploitation of celestial bodies for commercial gain and profit. Since states and businesses may want to reap rewards from their risky and expensive space ventures, it is likely that some economic gain will be sought. Such an expectation is not a bad thing, because the resulting rewards will spur others to follow suit and allow for reinvesting into future activities. Despite this nod to capitalism, it is expected that international consensus will be needed to achieve a lasting solution to this problem of deciding upon the equitable distribution of materials and profits coming from commercial space activities. In fact, economic disputes like these where there is no sole claim of ownership have a historical precedent of being settled through negotiation and agreement, and therefore a similar solution should be expected regarding economic and commercial activities in space. Previous precedents include agreements on fishery rights in international waters and the deep-sea mining of the ocean floor.[26]

Weaponize at the right time and in the right place

As mentioned above, the weaponization of space is a topic of heated emotional debate. Instead of just stating a somewhat arbitrary position on the subject, one that is based on personal inclinations, it is best to contemplate the role of weapons under the strategic lens of the maritime-inspired space strategy and the concept of command of space in particular. Implicit in the idea of command of space is that those that exercise it would like to keep it, and those that do not would like to contest it. Although this is an oversimplification of the strategic concept, this idea often holds true and is therefore useful in considering the subject of weapons.

Many experts would agree that the United States currently leads other states in the economic, scientific, and military use of outer space. Thus, when compared to others, the United States has gained and currently exercises command of space. Albeit the United States does not subjugate others with the command it exercises, the power and influence of its space activities are dominating. Since the United States presently exercises command of space, it is in its national interests to maintain it. As a result, those possible policy options that recognize this idea include gaining an even greater commanding lead or just maintaining the lead.

If the governmental leadership of the United States were to implement a policy that strove to dramatically expand its dominance in space, such a policy could probably enjoy short-term success. Thanks to its extensive research and development infrastructure, along with expertise in designing technologically sophisticated weaponry, the United States could attempt and possibly succeed in further outdistancing any near-peer competitor. Such a strategy of primacy could include the fielding of weapons that are either space-based or launched responsively to attack an enemy's space assets when the need arises. Presently, it appears doubtful that other countries could adequately compete if the United State chose to increase its military capability in this manner.

Arms control advocates, on the other hand, have repeatedly argued against deploying weapons in space, fearing that the action would lead to an uncontrollable escalation in the weaponization of space by all spacefaring nations. Although such an escalation is indeed possible, there is nothing to suggest that this kind of outcome is predestined. History has illustrated that the deployment or use of any new weapon system may sometimes produce destabilizing effects but may also produce stabilizing ones. For example, the Industrial Revolution enabled the mass production of artillery and precision rifles, which led to increased levels of carnage during wars of the later half of the 1800s and early 1900s. On the other hand, the advent of the nuclear age led to a somewhat stabilizing effect between the United States and the Soviet Union through the mutual assured destruction policy. It is therefore difficult to definitively determine whether placing weapons in space will increase the likelihood of conflict or not. Because of this, it is better to ask whether the weaponization of space is in the best interests of the United States, and the answer to this question is that it depends on the manner in which weapons are deployed.

If the United States were to aggressively pursue a space weaponization policy, whether for offensive or defensive purposes, such a policy would very likely succeed in protecting national security interests. Nevertheless, the natural tendency is for those with less power and influence to dispute those perceived as having the most. This means that, if the United States is perceived as becoming more powerful too quickly, others might collectively attempt to contest this space hegemony through diplomatic, economic, information, and perhaps even military endeavors. Less capable space powers would be more inclined to limit and restrict the United States' ability to operate in outer space, if the intentions of the United States seem overly aggressive. Consequently, a weaponization program that attempts to accelerate one's dominance in space increases the probability that others will counter such a program with a space weaponization program of their own. For this reason, it is recognized that a substantial space weaponization effort is likely to incur significant costs, and after the completion of any expensive multi-year weapons program there is no guarantee that national security and the ability to command space will be improved in the end.

There are exceptions to the tenet that those with less power contest those with more. Most notably, those states with less power and influence in space are less likely to dispute a weaponization of space policy if such a policy is in their own security interests. Therefore, if the United States were to enter into a cooperative security alliance with other states – one that promises to use the space-based weapons to defend the interest of the others – support for a weaponization policy is more probable.

In light of this natural resistance against those who are considered more powerful and influential – except as noted above – the best option for the United States is to maintain its relative level of command of space and not attempt to dramatically increase its power and influence in space. Despite this observation, doing nothing is not a suitable course of action. This is because a "do nothing" space policy relies to an inordinate degree on the actions of others. The leaders of free and democratic states are ultimately responsible for protecting the interests and security of those who put them in office, and so these leaders must be proactive in dealing with ever-changing global security challenges. Since the United States should not want to be perceived as overly aggressive, but also cannot handover national security to happenstance, programs to develop and field space-based weapons should be pursued *very slowly*, to an extent that the pursuit appears nonexistent. Instead of an "arms race" in space, more of an "arms walk" approach should be taken. This kind of unhurried approach is less likely to cause others to contest one's command of space or increased military capability.

When considering the implications coming from the concept of command of space, some policy makers could surmise that an even better solution would be for an international organization, perhaps under the auspices of the United Nations, to control when and how anyone's space-based weapons are used. This kind of arms control agreement – one that gives control to an international body – could be seen by some as a suitable method of curtailing the proliferation of weapons in space. In general, international arms control agreements have enjoyed successes, especially in regard to limiting the proliferation of nuclear, chemical, and biological weapons. Therefore international arms control agreements in space, it could be said, would make it even more unlikely that space-based weapons would be employed for purely aggressive intentions. Despite this view, it seems doubtful that the United States – or any sovereign state – would spend the resources to build advanced and expensive weapon systems only to "turn over the keys" to an international organization. The relinquishing of control of one's military capability is seldom in the interests of any state power, including the United States. The exception to this observation is when the international community, or coalition of states, jointly expends the manpower and fiscal resources to build space weapons that support the collective security and interests of the entire group. So if the United States, Russia, China, and the European Union were to collaborate to build and field space weapons, then the authority for their potential employment would reside within that group of countries. This would be in keeping with cooperative alliances of the past and, based on the Charter of the United Nations, those being part of such alliances may come to the aid of others when attacked, which could include using newly developed space-based weapons and technology. Such a cooperative arrangement could employ these jointly owned and space-based technologies in a manner that helps keep the world's most dangerous weapons out of the hands of the most dangerous rogue nations.[27]

Future employment of any space-based weapons must take into account the Law of Armed Conflict. As contained within the Law of Armed Conflict, the principle of military necessity calls for using only that degree and kind of force required for the partial or complete submission of the enemy, while considering the minimum expenditure of time, life, and physical resources.[28] So military planners must consider under what conditions the use of space-based weapons is an appropriate and proportional response in times of conflict. It should be determined ahead of time whether the employment of space-to-ground and space-to-space weapon systems is an excessive level of response and whether such an action will be interpreted as an escalation in hostilities. For instance, the use of a space-based laser against a small number of insurgents holed up in a village would be considered by many as a disproportionate level of response and therefore against the principle of military necessity. These types of deliberations are always called for prior to the application of force in support of lawful military purposes.

Furthermore, it is reasonable to expect some restrictions on where weapons are based in space. The precedent of international treaties, such as the Antarctica Treaty, show that some areas and regions in any medium of warfare can be declared weapons-free.[29] A similar application of this thought would be a multinational declaration that some regions in space be declared free from the permanent basing of weapons. From the lessons of history, it seems improbable that weapons will be successfully prohibited from the entire outer space medium, but history also suggests that at times it will be in the common interest of the international community to pass and enforce some arms control measures in space to restrict the use of certain types of weapons or the location where they are based and employed. This means that clearly defined regions could be declared off limits for the permanent basing of weapons or certain types of munitions could be restricted. Examples of this thought might include declaring the earth's geostationary orbit a "weapons-free sanctuary" or prohibiting the basing of offensive and defensive weapons on the moon, as is already included in some people's interpretations of the Outer Space Treaty.[30] Additionally, some types of fragmentation warheads or weapons that produce electromagnetic pulses could be prohibited in specified areas. Even so, if a belligerent attacks another's assets in space, it is the duty of the leaders of the transgressed state to protect and defend their interests. Since those attacked have the right to defend themselves, the restrictions imposed by international arms control agreements may, under certain conditions, have to be overridden by national security concerns and the right of self-defense. Consequently, at times a country may require "temporary passage" of weapon systems through those prohibited regions of space to thwart an aggressor.

Incorporate more defensive strategies

Despite the best efforts of joint doctrine to educate and provide guidance, an inordinate amount of thinking about military strategy in space deals with offensive weapons and strategy. This is in part due to the fascination that many people have with the latest cutting-edge technology, including lasers, particle beams, and anti-satellite weapons. Another reason is because of the lasting influence of Mahan, Douhet, and Mitchell on the development of space strategy. All three of these strategists put an emphasis on offensive military actions and almost totally discounted the advantages of the defense. Unfortunately, their influence has led to an underdeveloped appreciation of defensive strategies in general, which has resulted in a prevalent misunderstanding of the role of the defense in space warfare.

The advantages of the defense should not be "oversold" either. Indeed, the offense is often necessary to deny the enemy's use of his lines of communication and to bring a conflict to a conclusion. The defense merely has its proper role in military thought. The object of space warfare is to ensure one's access to and use of celestial lines of communication, while denying or degrading the enemy's ability to do likewise. This declaration says nothing about the object of space warfare being to destroy assets through offensive means. So to understand the role of the defense is to recognize that the defense enables ensuring one's own access and use of space. Despite the necessity of the defense within the strategy of space warfare, little attention currently seems to be paid to it.

To remedy this current shortcoming in the perceptions of space warfare theory, more emphasis needs to be put on defensive strategies, especially among policy makers and military professionals. The defense ought to be universally recognized as the "stronger" form of warfare, as Clausewitz and Corbett have advocated. Such recognition will help enable the implementation of techniques and technologies that more fully embrace defensive strategy. Moreover, recognizing the advantages of the defense will enable putting other viewpoints regarding space warfare – like sanctuary, survivability, high-ground, and control schools of thought – in proper perspective, all within a broad space strategic framework.

From a policy that acknowledges the stronger form of warfare, specific programs and recommendations can be proposed. Since self-defense is an inherent right of all, any system that protects a population from attack is an appropriate course of action. Consequently, defensive systems that protect sovereign countries from ballistic missile attack should be more actively pursued. Moreover, since defensive measures are advantageous, space-based systems should incorporate more defensive technologies. For instance, satellites and systems in space should be hardened against laser, particle beams, and general electromagnetic attack. Also, more systems that perform defensive missions should be placed in orbit to ensure one's access to and use of space. These can include systems that provide redundancy in case the primary satellite fails or is destroyed. A strategy that ensures access to and use of space is useful in times of peace just as in times of war, since space systems that provide critical services may fail or become inoperative in the absence of hostile action.

Also relevant to the idea of placing more emphasis on defensive strategies is the need to take advantage of positions that improve one's overall defensive capability. When deciding where to place systems in orbit around the earth or in space in general, the most easily defendable positions should be considered first. Understandably, often mission requirements dictate where a satellite is to be located, as in the case of many communication satellites. Nevertheless, adequate forethought must be given when deciding where to locate assets. In some cases, merely placing a satellite in orbit above the earth provides the advantage of "high ground." Yet, in other cases, positions should be chosen that make it more difficult for a potential foe to directly attack the satellite or block its communications. Such a potential position includes collocating one's own satellite with the enemy's, since an enemy may be reluctant to attack if his space operations may be degraded as a result. Similarly, a "position of advantage" can apply to non-physical communications, such as radio frequency transmissions. Consequently, one may choose to overlay one's frequency spectrum with that of the enemy's, thereby causing him to duly consider the consequences before attempting to block electromagnetic communications. Yet another possibility that takes advantage of positions is placing operational satellites in unconventional locations, such as in satellite "graveyard" orbits or where there are high concentrations of orbital debris. These kinds of locations may provide a defensive advantage, since assets located there may be more difficult to locate or their intended purpose more difficult to discern.[31]

In many instances, a sufficient level of defensive capability allows one to enjoy the same level of command that is traditionally thought of as enjoyed through offensive means. A defensive posture, when properly attained, will ensure a significant level of access to and use of celestial lines of communications. Moreover, such a defensive capability allows for a measure of self-defense against a surprise attack, control over the escalation of a conflict, and can minimize the most devastating enemy counterattacks.

So under certain conditions, including times of relative peace, a defensive strategy enables a level of command in space to be achieved, without having to field or employ purely offensive weapons.

Emphasize dispersal as a general practice

Before such a time as one attacks another through hostile action, dispersing forces and assets is the best practice. The reason is that one is better able to conceal the location and disposition of forces and assets. Additionally, dispersal allows the hiding of one's true intentions that an attack is pending. Thanks in part to the current debate concerning the role of space-based weapons, concentration of forces and effects is readily understood, but not dispersal. The corrective action, therefore, is to implement strategies and programs that take advantage of dispersal.

There are several methods of implementing such a dispersal strategy. One option is to produce large quantities of relatively inexpensive systems. If one of the systems fails or is destroyed, then there are ample numbers to take up the duties of the inoperative system. Included in this thought is distributing the functions performed by any one satellite to as many different systems as possible. A distributed arrangement like this improves the likelihood of maintaining the ability to perform a desired mission, regardless of minor hostile actions. A dispersed and distributed arrangement allows for a "collective will" to perform required missions and functions in concert with one another. This does not imply in any way that autonomy of individual action is absent in this scheme. Nor is a centralized or hub-and-spoke network of decision making needed. A dispersed and distributed arrangement provides the greatest advantages when hostile action is absent, while allowing one to concentrate firepower or other effects in the most effective and expeditious manner when needed.

Create a separate space service . . . eventually

Another issue of current debate among the professional military community is whether a separate space service is needed or not. In the United States, oversight of space operations and operational requirements is given to the Air Force, since it acts as Executive Agent regarding space issues within the Department of Defense.[32] Unfortunately, whether a separate service is needed or not is not a topic that strategy is meant to solve. Organizational structure is more the realm of doctrine, as well as defense department policy. Nevertheless, it is worthwhile to see if history has any salient lessons. To do this, one needs to look at how the different armed services have organized their forces to operate within the same medium, as well as how they organize to operate within different media. The lessons of the history of the United States offer conflicting results. Both the Navy and Marine Corps are employed for operations within the maritime environment. Air operations are provided by four separate services – the Army, Navy, Marine Corps, and Air Force. Yet the Navy also performs operations in the air, at sea, and under the sea, and the Army also has ships, aircraft, and soldiers. Thus, there are examples where two or more services support operations in the same medium, and examples where a single service supports operations in multiple environments. Based on the United States' military currently being without equal, such a seemingly arbitrary organizational service structure appears to work, even though it may not appear logical.

Consequently, the answer is apparent to whether a separate military space service question is needed: it shouldn't really matter. The mission of the military is to fight and win wars, and preferably quickly too. So as long as a service's organizational structure does not impede this mission, the overall military effectiveness should be the same in either case. However, this is not the whole story either. Pragmatic and realistic considerations must be acknowledged, since humans are imperfect creatures. Therefore, just because it *shouldn't* make a difference, does not mean it actually *doesn't*. The present military strategy of most countries is to use space systems to support operations on land, at sea, and in the air. The current trend indicates that interests in space will continue to increase with time and, as a result, it is expected that the need for dedicated military assets to protect these interests will increase with time as well. For these reasons, military professionals will need to devote more manpower and fiscal resources to space activities in the future. At some point, the need for the most efficient and effective combat operations will probably tip the scales in favor of a dedicated and separate space service. Such an action is not needed presently, but such a move is considered an eventuality nonetheless.

Establish a space war college

Considering that establishing a separate space service is still years away, if a prospect at all, military culture and strategy needs to acknowledge that space is a relevant medium of warfare. The warfighter is obligated to fight and win in the most effective and efficient manner possible. Since space is a separate and distinct medium of warfare, military operations and strategy in space should be considered a distinct warfare area, even though organizationally it falls under the purview of the Air Force. Only by changing the mindset of the professional warfighter can space be acknowledged as a distinct and equal medium of warfare – like land, naval, and air warfare – and the nation's interests be best served.

To this end, a Space War College should be established. An action like this would indicate to the professional military community that space warfare is a subject that deserves separate and dedicated strategic study, since there are vital interests in space that need to be defended and protected. Additionally, such a move would foster a conducive environment where more fully developed strategies for space warfare can be contemplated. Although it might prove difficult to establish a Space War College without a separate space service advocating its establishment and providing the needed resources, it is believed that establishing such a war college is the only method – short of establishing a separate service – by which warfighters and policy makers will recognize that more thought and effort should be expended to protect our nation's interests and security in space.

Critics opposing the establishment of a Space War College may argue that such an action sends conflicting signals to the general public and other countries. For whereas the United States does not want to give the impression that it is moving aggressively toward weaponizing space, establishing such an institution of warfare could be construed as having belligerent intent. Using the phrase "War College" in the institution for higher learning's name could admittedly be construed inappropriately, as is frequently already done by the general public regarding what goes on at the other military services' war colleges. Yet the subjects taught at the new institution would be the historical study of strategy and policy, resource allocation, and coalition and joint operations. Such academic topics, when properly understood by the scrutinizing critic, should alleviate any perceptions regarding belligerent intent. Also, some critics may argue against the establishment of an additional academic institution due to the projected expense, while also stating that the United States has done quite well without one so far. Although the United State military can get by for some time without a separate space service, the longer it waits to establish a separate school where space strategy can be studied, developed, and debated, the worse off in the long run the United States will be. The theory, strategic principles, and doctrine of space warfare need to be well understood at all levels within the military – from the most junior recruit to the most senior flag officer – before they are actually needed. For when they are needed, it will be too late to ensure such understanding. Whereas establishing a separate and dedicated school of this kind will likely incur modest startup and operating costs, the expected cost would definitely be much lower than the additional expense of creating a separate space service. Proportional to how much trade and commerce is currently reliant upon space-based technology, any cost incurred should be considered a bargain.

Moreover. . .

The previous policy recommendations are indeed relevant for several reasons. State and non-state actors have interests in space, and leaders have an obligation to protect the interests of those they govern, wherever they lie. Since there are presently a variety of interests regarding the access and use of space, these interests will need to be protected as well. The aforementioned policies and recommendations all serve this end. Although the focus of discussion here has been with respect to warfare, such as focus should not be thought of as implying that the use of force is one's first and only course of action to protect interests or resolve conflicts in space. Military means are but one of four instruments used to resolve disputes between nations and protecting one's interests. Yet, the application of military force in space is a legitimate course of action, when conditions warrant it.

Furthermore, a nation's interests and activities in space are relevant to operations on land, at sea, and in the air. For this reason, space warfare is a concern of all warfare specialties. So those in the Army, Navy, Marine Corps, and Air Force are to some extent already players in the realm of space warfare. Such an observation highlights the need for both military professionals and government policy makers to become more cognizant of the proper role of space warfare in supporting military strategy and the broader national grand strategy.

Chapter 16

Summary and conclusions

Of all the historically based strategies, maritime strategy comes closest to representing the many diverse concerns and breadth of issues regarding warfare in space. Both air and naval frameworks are too militarily focused and do not sufficiently take into account the importance of non-military actions. Yet by expanding the purview of naval activities to include those pertaining to maritime activities – which include the interaction of the land and sea – the best historical and strategic framework for thinking about space warfare is determined.

Admittedly, space operations at first glance appear most analogous to air operations, since the technology, tactics, and doctrine of these two environments of warfare seem similar. Paradoxically, while space operations are more similar to air operations at the tactical level of warfare, space operations are more similar to maritime operations at the strategic level. This realization may explain why strategists have grappled with discerning a strategic framework for space warfare all these years. Nevertheless, any strategic theory of space warfare – if it is in fact a strategic theory – should remain timeless in its applicability. So, as technology changes, along with the tactics that employ new technologies, a truly meaningful space strategy must endure.

Space is not the sea. This is indeed true, but, since maritime and space activities share similar interests, they will share similar strategic principles as well. Despite the similarities between maritime and space operations at the strategic level, technological and employment differences necessitate that a space warfare strategy has a context and lexicon all its own. So, although the preeminent work of Sir Julian Corbett can be used to think about military operations in space, maritime and space strategies must in the end diverge. As Clausewitz warned, a theoretical and strategic framework for warfare is not intended to prescribe specific actions. So the maritime-inspired space strategy is merely meant to serve as a framework that provides a common language and understanding for thinking about military operations from, into, and through space.

By using maritime strategy as a guide in thinking about space warfare, it has been possible to discern specific strategic concepts and principles. The following summarizes the most significant of these concepts and principles.[1]

Space is tied to national power

Space operations and activities have national power implications during peace and war. Not being an absolute, national power only has meaning relative to others and is directly related to one's national security. Because of the breadth of issues and concerns pertaining to the use of space, actions in space can have repercussions that affect the diplomatic, economic, information, and military instruments of national power. These instruments of national power are interrelated, and changes in any one of them can affect the dynamic of the others. For this reason, military actions in space – including minor ones – can affect the balance of wealth, power, and influence between nations. Furthermore, since international diplomacy is influenced by domestic politics, those that influence domestic politics – including nation states, organizations, and groups – can affect this dynamic as well.

Space operations are interdependent with others

Operations in space are interdependent with those on land, at sea, and in the air. A nation's overarching goals are contained in its grand strategy and, if its efforts are properly marshaled, all sub-strategies – such as land, naval, air, and space – should work toward those goals. As such, space strategy should work within the overall military strategy, and space forces must operate in concert with other military forces, since space warfare is just a subset of general warfare. Additionally, military space actions can directly impact the adversary's long-term warfighting capability, since space actions can affect those revenues realized through space-reliant commerce and trade that are used to fund military operations. Despite the apparent effectiveness of space warfare, space operations can only in the rarest exceptions determine a war's outcome alone; to be ultimately successful, most wars will require the combined and effective use of land, sea, air, and space forces.

Celestial lines of communications

The inherent value of space is the utility and access it provides, and this utility and access is enabled through celestial lines of communication. Generally stated, celestial lines of communications are those lines of communications from, into, and through space used for the movement of trade, materiel, supplies, personnel, spacecraft, military effects, and electromagnetic transmissions. By ensuring access to one's "lines of passage and communication" in space, a nation can protect its diplomatic, economic, information, and military interests.[2] Because lines of communications in space are often vitally important, the primary objective of space warfare is to protect and defend one's own lines of communications, while limiting the enemy's ability to use his. As with maritime communications, lines of communication in space often run parallel to the enemy's and may even be shared with him, and, because of this, an enemy's space communications frequently cannot be attacked without affecting one's own.

Also important to the discussion of space warfare is space communications, which refers to the overall activity of communicating through space. In order to properly develop the theory and strategic principles of space warfare, it is further necessary to differentiate the types of communications possible, whether physical or non-physical. Physical communications refer to the movement of tangible assets, such as materiel, supplies, personnel, and spacecraft. Non-physical communications refer to the movement of things not directly tangible to humans, including electromagnetic frequency transmissions and subatomic particles discharged by particle beam weapons.

Command of space

Command of space entails the ability to ensure one's access to and use of celestial lines of communications when needed to support the instruments of national power, whether diplomatic, economic, information, or military in nature. It also includes the ability to prevent or deny the enemy's access to and use of his celestial lines of communications space, or at least minimize the most severe consequences that an adversary can deliver along them. Since space assets and the fiscal resources that enable command of space are finite, efforts to gain some degree of command in space require choosing between using presence, coercion, and force to gain command within specific areas and regions. The various types of command can be differentiated as general and local or as persistent and temporary. Yet, even if the highest level of command of space is achieved (one that is both general and persistent), one's enemy is not impotent, and as a result the normal state of affairs will be for command of space to be in dispute.

The inherent value of space is what it allows you to do. Space serves as a conduit for terrestrial- and celestial-based movement and transfer of communications, and, because of its value, those with interests in space will attempt to preserve and promote their continued access to and use of space. Due to the range of interests involved, achieving command of space is relevant for nation states, as well as organizations and groups. Since command of space connotes the ability to use space communications when and where needed, it is a measure relative to others.

Strategy of offense and defense

Offensive strategy in space is called for when political objectives necessitate wresting or acquiring something from the adversary. Such operations are frequently needed to protect one's interests in space and ensure access to celestial lines of communication. The offensive is the more "effective" form of warfare, and offensive operations in space should usually be attempted by the stronger space power. However, an offensive force looking for a decisive victory will probably not find it, since the enemy will usually move to or be stationed at positions of relative safety. Furthermore, caution must be used when deciding in favor of offensive operations, otherwise space assets may be thrown away on ill-considered offensives.[3]

Defensive strategy, on the other hand, is called for when political objectives necessitate preventing the enemy from achieving or gaining something. By their inherent nature, defensive operations are the "stronger" form of warfare and should be used extensively by less capable space forces until the offensive can be assumed. A truly defensive posture is one that "awaits the blow" and does so from a position of advantage. Although it is easiest to discuss offensive or defensive strategies separately, they are each mutually dependent on each other and so intertwined that in actuality, one is not ultimately successful without the other. For instance, planning for successful offensive operations using space-based assets necessitates defending the very lines of communication that enable such operations.

Strategic positions

Strategic positions are locations or regions that impart some relative advantage or hold value due to the importance of the activities performed there. Since the inherent value of space is as a means of communication, strategic positions are often located where it is better to have communication routes. For example, strategic positions include those locations that enable more efficient or effective use of celestial lines of communication, such as preferred launch locations or highly desirable satellite orbits. They also include hubs of activity, like launch facilities, space bases or stations, and focal areas where space communications tend to converge. Although not conventionally thought of in terms of "positions," the most desirable and important frequency spectrums for space communications are also included in this concept. Through the exploiting of strategic positions, a space force can restrict the movement of the enemy's forces or information, thus improving the conditions for military operations. Since it often proves difficult to force an adversary into a decisive engagement, it is better to control his strategic positions and threaten his commerce and operations, thereby forcing him to battle on favorable terms. By exploiting strategic positions through the occupation of the enemy's lines of communication and closing his points of distribution, one impacts the enemy's "national life" in space.[4]

Blocking

Blocking is preventing one's adversary from using his celestial lines of communication, thus denying the movement of spacecraft, equipment, materiel, supplies, personnel, military effects, data, or information. Methods of achieving this may include using weapons or systems that cause either permanent or temporary effects. Moreover, blocking can be categorized into close and distant blocking and blocking either physical or non-physical communications. Close blocking equates to preventing the deployment, launch, or movement of space systems near hubs of activity. It also pertains to interfering with communications in the vicinity of up-, down-, and crosslinks. Suppressing operations at these hubs and distribution points obliges the adversary to submit or fight. In contrast, a quite capable space power can employ distant blocking to force an adversary into action, by occupying or interfering with the distant and common celestial lines of communications. Whether employing close or distant blocking, the methods may include using either physical assets or interference effects against the enemy's space communications.

Space as a "barrier"

Through a comprehension of the previous concepts, it is understood that command of space enables one's access to and use of celestial lines of communications, yet space becomes a "barrier" to those not having such access and use. One's ability to access and use lines of communications in space is paramount, and only by doing so can the advantages of operating in space be realized. If such access and use are not possible – whether one is being denied access to lines of communication in space or one's technological capability is insufficient to launch space vehicles into orbit – then space effectively becomes an obstacle or barrier. The concept of using space as a barrier has implications for the conduct of space warfare. This is because there are three motives or intents for using space as a barrier: the intent can be purely defensive, thus providing protection against a surprise attack; the intent can be to initiate a war with limited aims and prevent the enemy's ability to escalate the conflict in space; or the intent can be for unlimited aims, where one seeks the total defeat of one's adversary and desires to prevent his unlimited counterattack. Best summarizing the various reasons and applications for using space as a barrier is a paraphrase of Corbett's observation, "He that commands space is at great liberty and may take as much or as little space warfare as he will."

Dispersal and concentration

Space forces and systems should, in general, be dispersed to cover the widest possible area, and yet they should retain the ability to rapidly concentrate force and effects. By dispersing forces and assets, one can protect a variety of interests, while facilitating defensive operations along many celestial lines of communication. When firepower must be employed to defend against or neutralize a significant threat, space forces and systems should concentrate firepower or other desired effects to rapidly defeat the adversary. This concept of dispersal and concentration pertains to both physical assets and non-physical effects. Employing this strategy of dispersal and concentration will preserve the flexibility of protecting one's space communications, while allowing an adversary's "central mass" to be engaged when and where needed.[5]

The primary object of space warfare is to ensure one's ability to use space communications, which will require the application of dispersal and concentration. Consequently, a means of ensuring this is required. As a result, a "cruiser" conceptual equivalent – like policing systems – is needed to protect and defend one's interests in space. These systems will need to have effect where space communications tend to congregate, like chokepoints, but also disperse along the vast regions occupied by celestial lines of communication. Due to the primacy of the policing system's mission, space systems that perform purely offensive operations – those with negligible influence on celestial lines of communications – are of secondary importance. The ultimate form and design that this strategic concept takes is dependent upon whether the specific mission is blocking line-of-sight weapons, escorting high-value assets, denying the enemy his lines of communication, or providing a redundant capability in the event that the services of the primary provider are lost.

Actions by lesser powers

Although a less capable space force is unlikely to win a major and decisive space engagement, lesser forces can still contest a more capable power's command of space, and in doing so achieve limited political objectives. Methods to contest the command of another include both non-military and military actions. Regarding the use of non-military actions, it is reasonable to presume that a less capable space power will attempt to use the most effective instruments at its disposal, which may include non-military means such as diplomacy, economic, and information instruments of power. When employing military actions, a lesser force should usually attempt to gain local or temporary command in areas where the stronger force is not. Additionally, lesser space forces can disrupt commercial or economic interests along space communications routes and perform minor interference against space-based systems. No matter which method is ultimately chosen – whether military or non-military in nature – a less capable adversary will most likely attempt to bolster his power and influence, while diminishing the instruments of power of the superior adversary.

Another effective method by which a lesser space force can contest command is the "force in being" concept. Since it is important for a relatively inferior space force to avoid decisive engagements against a stronger one, a less capable space force should be kept in being through active utilization and operation until the situation develops in its favor. Furthermore, by avoiding large-scale engagements with a superior space force, a lesser one can conduct minor attacks along celestial lines of communication or against space-related activities, thus preventing the stronger power from gaining command of space that is either general or persistent. The available options are applicable not only to nation states but equally to other less capable forces, such as insurgents and terrorists.

Policies, recommendations, and implications

Policy and warfare are not isolated from each other, as either one can affect the other. As has been well established previously by renowned strategists, policy influences warfare. Therefore, it is not a great departure to presume that warfare at times can likewise influence policy. For the policy maker and warfighter, this means that a sufficiently broad and sound space strategy can be used to propose policy recommendations, especially if current policy guidance proves wanting. The following summarizes those policies and recommendations resulting from a maritime-inspired space strategy.

Uphold the current legal regime

From a military and national security perspective, there is nothing contained within the current legal regime, which includes the Outer Space Treaty, that specifically hinders protecting or defending a state's interests in space. The Outer Space Treaty declares the need to use space in accordance with the Charter of the United Nations, along with the need to maintain international peace and security. Even with the restrictions regarding military activities and permanent bases on celestial bodies, the treaty's non-specific language allows for a broad enough interpretation to protect national interests and does not limit the legitimate use of force, just the manner in which it is delivered. Since neither the Outer Space Treaty nor its contemporary interpretation by the United States precludes any of the time-honored actions included within customary international law, the treaty's provisions should still be observed. For those contentious issues outside the realm of military affairs, such as the exploitation of celestial bodies for commercial gain and profit, history suggests that international agreements can be used to achieve a lasting solution in such areas.

Weaponize at the right time and in the right place

The historical precedents coming from customary international law and the Law of Armed Conflict show that nation states have the right to protect their interests, wherever they lie. Furthermore, the guiding principles of military necessity and proportionality during war also support the notion that the application of force into, from, or through space is under certain conditions a legitimate course of action. Therefore, when the need arises to protect one's security – particularly when in self-defense – the employment of space weapons may be a reasonable, legitimate, and appropriate response.

Whereas weaponizing space is a legitimate option for any state, how it is done must be thoughtfully considered. If the United States is perceived as becoming more powerful, too quickly, other countries will be more inclined to collectively attempt to contest this space supremacy through diplomatic, economic, information, and perhaps even military endeavors. The best option for the United States, therefore, is to maintain its relative level of command of space and not attempt to dramatically increase its power and influence in space. Nevertheless, doing nothing is not in its interests either, since national security cannot be left to happenstance and the actions of others. Because of this, programs to develop and field space-based weapons should be pursued *very slowly*, to the point at which they almost appear non-existent. Moreover, the deployment of weapons in space should take into account historical precedent and customary law. It should be expected that at times it will be in the interests of the United States and the international community to establish clearly defined regions that prohibit the permanent basing of weapons or restrict certain types of munitions. Examples of this thought might include declaring the earth's geostationary orbit as a "weapons-free sanctuary" or prohibiting the use of electromagnetic pulse generating weapons from regions that would unduly affect neutral parties.

Incorporate more defensive strategies

An inordinate amount of thinking about military strategy in space deals with offensive weapons and strategy. This is in part due the lasting influence of Mahan, Douhet, and Mitchell on the development of general military strategy. Unfortunately, their influence has led to an underdeveloped appreciation of defensive strategies in space, thereby resulting in a misunderstanding of the proper role of the defense in space warfare. To remedy this current shortcoming in the perceptions of space warfare theory, more emphasis needs to be put on defensive strategies, especially among policy makers and military professionals. This includes greater employment of defensive systems that protect sovereign countries from ballistic missiles and also includes hardening space systems against laser, particle beams, and general electromagnetic attack. Additionally, it must be recognized that some positions have more defensive advantage over other positions. When deciding where to place systems in orbit around the earth or in space in general, the most easily defendable positions should be considered first. The idea of "positions" also pertains to non-physical communications, and consequently some parts of electromagnetic frequency spectrum are more desirable and advantageous than others, and should be acknowledged in defensive strategy.

Emphasize dispersal as a general practice

Current military strategy and doctrine are inadequate in describing the combined concept of dispersal and concentration. The latter part, concentration, is readily understood, thanks to the overemphasis on offensive strategies. Yet, before offensive actions are warranted, dispersal is called for first. Unfortunately, the general practice of dispersal is not recognized within the context of space warfare, and this must be remedied. The corrective action is to implement strategies and programs that take advantage of dispersal. Such recommended strategies include producing greater quantities of relatively inexpensive space systems, along with distributing the functions performed by any one satellite to as many different systems as possible. Therefore, if one systems fails or is destroyed, then there are ample numbers to take up the lost duties and responsibilities. Some of these dispersed systems must also protect celestial lines of communication, as that is the primary concern of space warfare. By using a dispersed arrangement that is spread throughout those regions where celestial lines of communication are most critical or prevalent, dispersal may be subsequently combined with the concept of concentration to achieve dramatic results where and when needed. In such a combination of dispersal and concentration, one's interests can be protected and defended, while employing assets in the most effective and decisive manner possible.

Create a separate space service . . . eventually

Based on the example of the United States military, a separate space service is not currently required. The mission of the military is to fight and win, and there is no indication that a separate service would improve the overall warfighting effectiveness of the United States. Even though vital interests currently lie in space, military space systems are primarily used to support operations on land, at sea, and in the air. It is expected that the need for dedicated military assets that protect the ever-growing interests in space will increase with time. At some point, the need for the most efficient and effective combat operations will probably tip the scales in favor of a dedicated and separate space service, but such a move is not presently needed.

Establish a space war college

Although a separate space service is not currently needed, a Space War College should be established. Only by changing the mindset of the professional warfighter can space be acknowledged as a distinct and co-equal medium of warfare – like land, naval, and air warfare. To do this, a separate war college should be established. This would indicate that space warfare is also a category of warfare in which vital interests must be defended and protected. The establishment of a Space War College is the only method, short of establishing a separate space service, by which warfighters and policy makers will recognize that more thought and effort should be expended to protect our nation's interests and security in space. Granted that there will be startup and operational costs associated with the establishment of such a school, such a cost is quite small in comparison with how much space-reliant commerce and trade currently takes place domestically and abroad.

Final thoughts

It is somewhat remarkable that a historically based and maritime-inspired strategy has so many similarities to current thought regarding space strategy. Although the context provided by the derived theory and strategy of space warfare is distinctly different, many ideas and concepts are also strikingly similar to those contained within joint doctrine, the *Space Commission Report*, and today's literature on the subject. So it could be argued that we have had an encompassing space strategy all along, but never recognized it. Even though this observation may not be very satisfying to those involved with the development and study of military strategy, it is remarkable nonetheless.

The maritime-inspired theory of space warfare has also highlighted the major shortcomings of current space strategy and thought. Current thinking by many regarding warfare in space is more in line with the thoughts of Mahan, Douhet, and Mitchell. Thus, the strategy of space warfare is incorrectly presented in the context "space power." Such a context places an overemphasis on offensive strategy and operations, while tending to minimize defensive strategies and non-military methods. The maritime-inspired space strategy, however, has allowed for correctly discerning the proper interrelationship of offensive and defensive strategies, along with determining when each is the strategy of choice. Additionally, since a historical and maritime-based strategic framework for space warfare proves relevant, balanced, and appropriate, it can be used to consider future governmental policy and suggest the most appropriate recommendations regarding military endeavors in space.

One such policy recommendation presented here concerns the application of weapons in space. Military action has been and always will be an appropriate response under certain situations, including self-defense. The acknowledgment of the legitimate application of military force in space is not meant to discount the role of arms control initiatives regarding space-based weapons. Arms control agreements have played a crucial part in promoting stability among the international community. The major shortfall of many of today's arms control policy recommendations is that they espouse policy that disconnects peacetime and wartime strategies. A truly sound policy should be just as applicable during peace as it is in war. Therefore, any proposed policy that limits space-based weapons or prohibits their use within a specified region must hold meaning before and after hostilities have commenced. Arms control advocates should recognize that weapons in space may be employed legitimately to protect one's interests. Nonetheless, space weaponization advocates must also recognize that arms control initiatives, including treaties and international regulations, have their place as well, as they may be used to enhance national security and promote international stability. From the examples of land, sea, and air warfare, it should be expected that certain types of weapons may be prohibited or their placement precluded in some regions of space. Those regions of space most extensively used by states and commercial activities would top the list as potential areas to limit weapons. Sound arms control policy regarding the role of weapons in space can establish a more lasting peace and may on occasion even deter wanton aggression.

Since a maritime-inspired space strategy proves applicable in addressing the issues and concerns of space warfare, other naval and maritime theorists of the past can be "rediscovered" to determine if they have salient lessons regarding the strategy of space warfare. For instance, the literary works of Charles E. Callwell (*Military Operations and Maritime Preponderance*, 1905), Wolfgang Wegener (*The Naval Strategy of the World War*, 1929), Raoul Castex (*Strategic Theories*, 1931–9), and James Cable (*Gunboat Diplomacy*, 1971) can also be used to glean insight into the development and application of the strategic thought of space warfare.[6] The theory and strategy of space warfare can consequently leverage hundreds of years of maritime experience to think about military operations in space.

Space is presently a medium that supports the actions of the other military services. To a significant extent soldiers, marines, sailors, and airmen are already involved with many issues regarding space warfare. We effectively already have, therefore, "space warriors." So the time when the strategic principles of space warfare become relevant is not some obscure and distant moment in the future: it has already arrived. It is up to us to realize it.

Notes

Preface

1   US Commission to Assess United States National Security Space Management and Organization, *Space Commission Report*, viii, xxx. The report refers to "a trained cadre of military and civilian space professionals" within the Department of Defense and the intelligence community, and throughout the government more generally.

I Where we are and where we're going

1   Some theorists have used the term "space power" theory, whereas others have used "space control." To present a more objective argument and avoid the pitfalls of preconceived ideas, the terms "space strategy" and "strategy of space warfare" will be used instead.
2   Gray, "The Influence of Space Power upon History," 293. "Despite its growing importance, no comprehensive theory of space power has been formulated."
3   Handel, *Masters of War*, 19.
4   General Carl von Clausewitz is renowned for his unfinished work *Vom Kriege* [*On War*].
5   Clausewitz, *On War*, 578. Clausewitz also warns against blindly following theory by stating, "Theory cannot equip the mind with formulas for solving problems, nor can it mark the narrow path on which the sole solution is supposed to lie by planting a hedge of principles on either side." Ibid.
6   Hattendorf, "The Uses of Maritime History in and for the Navy," 20. "[H]istorical understanding and knowledge of past events is not the object but rather one of several means to improve the ability of professionals to solve problems more wisely than arbitrary choice, pure chance, and blind intuition would allow."
7   Not intending to quibble over definitions, "principles," "concepts," or "tenets" could equally as well be used in place of each other. Reference to such terms is simply meant to express those things that should be considered by war planners.
8   Strategy and Force Planning Faculty, *Strategy and Force Planning*, 20. For another description of strategy, see Collins, *Grand Strategy*, 14.
9   A separate term, astrostrategy, has even been coined in an attempt to relate military strategy to space. It is defined as "the identification of critical terrestrial and outer space locations, the control of which can provide military and political

dominance of outer space, or at a minimum can insure against the same dominance by a potential opponent state." Dolman, *Astropolitik*, 15.

10   Other divisions of warfare exist. Sokolovskii, *Soviet Military Strategy*, 88. "The
theory of military art, as applied to military operations of various scope, is divided into strategy, operational art, and tactics."

11   Baron Antoine-Henri de Jomini shared a similar view. He stated, "principles
are unchanging, independent of the kind of weapons, of historical time and
of place." Earle, *Makers of Modern Strategy*, 84. Originally cited in *Traité des
grandes operations militaires*, Vol. 3, 333. Similar thoughts are in Jomini, *The
Art of War*, 17, 347.

12   It is acknowledged that some use the word "doctrine" in place of "strategy,"
but the author considers the scope of doctrine to be less than that of strategy. When the discerning strategist actually looks at what is contained within
military doctrine publications, a large portion of them goes into describing the
organizational structure and job responsibilities, which are not directly related
to the realm of strategy.

13   US Joint Forces Command, "Joint Forces Command Glossary." Diplomatic, Information, Military and Economic (DIME) are areas of national power that are
used in "effects-based" operations.

14   Wu, *Economic Warfare*. This reference gives an overview on the methods of using economic influence against others.

15   Wu, *Economic Warfare*, 1; Collins, *Grand Strategy*, 5; Hill, *Maritime Strategy
for Medium Powers*, 8; Klein, "Corbett in Orbit," 60.

16   US Joint Forces Command, "Joint Forces Command Glossary."

17   Vego, *Operational Warfare*, 643, 647. The strategic level of warfare deals with
the situation within a given theater and with the war as a whole. The operational level of warfare deals with the situation within a given theater of operations.

18   Hyatt *et al.*, *Space Power 2010*, 93. Original citation is attributed to Carol Lay-
mance, "Science of Space," in *Space and Missile Orientation Course* (Vandenberg AFB, CA 30th Operations Support Squadron, 1993), 1–3.

19   US Joint Chiefs of Staff, *Joint Doctrine for Space Operations*, GL-5.

20   Thomas & Duncan, *International Law Studies, Vol. 73: Annotated Supplement
to the Commander's Handbook on the Law of Naval Operations*, 149. "Although there is no legally defined boundary between the upper limit of national airspace and the lower limit of outer space, international law recognizes
freedom of transit by man-made space objects at earth orbiting altitude and
beyond." This is commensurate with the lowest perigee definition, which is
dependent on the vehicle's orbital velocity. See also Goldman, *American Space
Law*, 105–6.

21   Those looking within this text for an extensive discussion of orbital mechanics
and astrophysics will probably be disappointed by the cursory treatment of the
subject, but are encouraged to feed their curiosity on the subject nonetheless.
Good places to start are Muolo, *Space Handbook* and Damon, *Introduction to
Space* (see bibliography).

22   US Commission to Assess United States National Security Space Management
and Organization, *Space Commission Report*, 18.

23   Ibid., xi.

24   Hays *et al.*, *Spacepower for a New Millennium*, 2–3. Some have also included
the "international sector" in the list. Johnson, *Space: Emerging Options for National Power*, 18.

25   "Telecommunications" has been defined as comprising "fixed voice and video-
broadcast services offered by international and private communications net-

works, cable television programming, telemedicine, and tele-education." Lambakis, *On the Edge of the Earth*, 26.
26 Hays *et al.*, *Spacepower for a New Millennium*, 2.
27 Low-earth orbits are typically said to begin around 60 miles above the surface, are nearly circular, and often have a period of 90 minutes. The geosynchronous orbit is located 22,400 miles above the surface of the earth, is over the equator, and has a period of 23 hours, 56 minutes. Another orbit sometimes used is the Molniya-type orbit, which is a hybrid of low- and high-earth orbits. It is a semisynchronous 12-hour, highly elliptical orbit, and it is typically used to provide detailed surveillance when the satellite is at its closest point of approach, or perigee.
28 The International Telecommunications Union regulates frequency spectrum assignments as well.
29 Goldman, *American Space Law*, 106. This refers to the Bogotá Declaration.
30 Damon, *Introduction to Space*, 70.
31 It has been estimated that there are 8,000 to 9,000 objects in near-earth orbit that are large enough to be tracked by monitoring equipment, or those with a diameter of four inches or more. Fewer than 1,000 of these objects are working satellites, with the rest being non-functioning satellites or the remnants of vehicle launch systems, such as rocket boosters. If considering debris the size of a marble or larger, the estimated amount of debris is over 100,000 objects. For more data, see O'Hanlon, *Neither Star Wars nor Sanctuary*, 35, 42.
32 Damon, *Introduction to Space*, 52. These are also called Lagrange Liberation Points and are named for the eighteenth century French mathematician who first predicted their existence.
33 Ibid., 52.
34 Ibid., 53.
35 Dolman, *Astropolitik*, 77–8. The reference gives the velocity advantage as 1,670 kilometers per hour.
36 Ibid.
37 Sadiku, *Elements of Electromagnetics*, 3; Stutzman and Thiele, Antenna Theory and Design, 1. "Electromagnetics" pertains to the relations between electric current and magnetism, and it refers to the propagation of many types of waves and signals, including radio, radar, microwaves, lasers, and electromagnetic pulse generation. Visible light and radio waves make up just a small part of the electromagnetic frequency spectrum.
38 US Congress, *Space Law*, 86–7.
39 Ibid., 176.
40 The Outer Space Treaty is considered the most definitive on the subject, but it owes much of its content to the 1963 Declaration of Legal Principles Governing the Activities of States in the Exploration and Use of Outer Space. Goldman, *American Space Law*, 68.
41 Goldman, *American Space Law*. See the reference's appendixes 1, 2, 3, and 4.
42 Dolman, *Astropolitik*, 88; O'Hanlon, *Neither Star Wars nor Sanctuary*, 3, 15. Although the administration of George W. Bush formally announced in December 2001 the withdrawal of the United States from the Anti-Ballistic Missile Treaty, and officially withdrew in June 2002, the treaty still served to shape current perceptions on the uses of space.
43 Dolman, *Astropolitik*, 88–9.
44 US Congress, *Space Law*, 23. The Outer Space Treaty was ratified by the President of the United States on 24 May 1967 yet entered into force on 10 October 1967.
45 Thomas and Duncan, *International Law Studies*, 149.

46 Ibid., 150.
47 US Air Force, *Space Operations*, 35.
48 The banning of nuclear weapons testing in outer space owes its lineage to the 1963 Treaty Banning Nuclear Tests in the Atmosphere, in Outer Space and Under Water. US Congress, *Space Law*, 9–11.
49 US Congress, "Statement by Ambassador Arthur J. Goldberg," 9–10. The interpretation by United States officials at the time was that the treaty's language did not give a "free ride" to other countries that failed to expend fiscal resources on space activities.

2 Contemporary space strategies

1 Gray, *The Navy in the Post-Cold War World*, 126.
2 Thomas and Duncan, *International Law Studies*, 150.
3 Gray, *The Navy in the Post-Cold War World*, 133.
4 Gray, "The Influence of Space Power upon History," 305.
5 Bruce M. DeBlois, "Ascendant Realms: Characteristics of Airpower and Space Power," in Meilinger, *The Paths of Heaven*, 571n5. "One should note, however, that despite the publication of a variety of airpower theories, there is no comprehensive theory of airpower on par with the land power theory of Clausewitz or the sea power theory of Mahan."
6 Douhet, *The Command of the Air*, 15–29.
7 Ibid., 15.
8 Ibid.
9 Ibid., 20.
10 Ibid., 4.
11 Ibid., 5.
12 Ibid., 29.
13 Mitchell, *Winged Defense*, 4.
14 Mark A. Clodfelter, "Molding Airpower Convictions: Development and Legacy of William Mitchell's Strategic Thought," in Meilinger, *The Paths of Heaven*, 79.
15 Mitchell, *Our Air Force*, xix.
16 Fadok, David S. "John Boyd and John Warden: Airpower's Quest for Strategic Paralysis," in Meilinger, *The Paths of Heaven*, 371.
17 Meilinger, *The Paths of Heaven*, xxiv.
18 White, "Air and Space are Indivisible," 40–1.
19 Lupton, *On Space Warfare*, 10, 16. Lupton notes that the primary difference between the 1955 AFM-1-2 and its 1959 successor was the replacement of the word "air" with "aerospace."
20 White, "Air and Space are Indivisible," 40–1.
21 Ibid. 41.
22 Smith, *Ten Propositions Regarding Spacepower*, 109. The term "aerospace integrationists" refers to those sharing General White's view that air and space are indivisible.
23 Ibid. "Aerospace integrationists frequently argue that spacepower is in no way different from airpower because it delivers similar products to users, as if aircraft can do what spacecraft can do. This is simply not the case."
24 US Air Force, *The Aerospace Force*, i.
25 Lupton, *On Space Warfare*, 65.
26 Hattendorf, "The Uses of Maritime History in and for the Navy," 20.
27 Ibid.

28 Potter and Nimitz, *Sea Power*, 19.
29 Ibid.
30 Turner, "Missions of the U.S. Navy," 3–4.
31 Mueller, "Totem and Taboo," 18. Admittedly, many of these critics realize that, as our interests in space expand beyond near-earth orbits, the parallels between sea and space power may become more relevant. Ibid., 27n39.
32 Potter and Nimitz, *Sea Power*, 134.
33 Lupton, *On Space Warfare*, 19–21.
34 In the highly regarded work *On Space Warfare: A Space Power Doctrine*, David Lupton categorizes the various perceptions regarding the value of space, along with the associated role of military space power in each approach. His work is frequently referenced and noted in United States Air Force publications, academic theses, and literature on space strategy. Although other strategists have provided modifications or amplifications to Lupton's four categories, his categories remain the most widely recognized.
35 Lupton, *On Space Warfare*, 20. The sanctuary school of thought holds that any future treaties would hold little promise without the space system's ability to provide treaty verification through uninhibited surveillance and monitoring.
36 Ibid., 26n5. This model is a result of the "Open Skies" strategy used during the Eisenhower administration. This strategy was meant to ease tensions between the United States and the Soviet Union during the transition to the Missile Age. Eisenhower was prepared to turn over the locations of military bases and installations to permit regular and frequent inspection flights over US territory in return for the same privilege over the Soviet Union. See McDougall, . . . *the Heavens and the Earth*, 127.
37 Lupton says the "vulnerability school" may be a more accurate label.
38 Lupton, *On Space Warfare*, 21.
39 Ibid.
40 Futrell, *Ideas, Concepts, Doctrine: A History of Basic Thinking in the United States Air Force, 1907–1964*, Vol. 1, 500. The sentiment is attributed to Wernher von Braun.
41 Lupton, *On Space Warfare*, 21. He notes that of all the four schools of thought, the control approach declines to place an exact value on space forces, but only hints at their value through air power and sea power analogies.
42 General Thomas A. White, from an address to the National Press Club, 29 November 1957. General White is considered by many to be the founder of the control school. Reference cited in Futrell, *Ideas, Concepts, Doctrine: A History of Basic Thinking in the United States Air Force, 1907– 1964*, Vol. 1, 506.
43 Lupton, *On Space Warfare*, 21. Lupton notes that the control school doctrine is the dominant view among the United States military community, especially regarding the value of space and the role of space weapons. Furthermore, of the four schools of thought, he personally assesses the space control approach as being the best for the employment of space assets and forces. Ibid., 71.
44 Hattendorf, "The Uses of Maritime History in and for the Navy," 19.
45 Hattendorf, "Introduction" in Mahan, *Mahan on Naval Strategy*, ix.
46 Mahan, *Mahan on Naval Strategy*, 130.
47 Hattendorf, "The Uses of Maritime History in and for the Navy," 27.
48 Eric J. Grove, "Introduction" in Corbett, *Some Principles of Maritime Strategy*, xxxvi. Comments attributed to the London *Times*.
49 Ibid., xiv, xxii.
50 Ibid., xxxvii. Comment attributed to Lieutenant Alfred Dewar in *Pall Mall Gazette*, 22 December 1911.
51 Ibid, xxxviii, as attributed to the *New York Evening Post*.

3 Maritime strategic principles

1 Colin S. Gray and John B. Sheldon, "Spacepower and the Revolution in Military Affairs," in Peter Hays *et al.*, *Spacepower for a New Millennium*, 239. It is said to be useful and forward-looking to consider what convoys, chokepoints, and blockades might mean for space warfare. However, it is warned, "What is needed most urgently today is not so much some grand vision of spacepower, or even some vision of America's future in space, *useful though those would be* [authors' emphasis]. Instead, what we need is a relatively mundane understanding of the space environment as yet another environment for conflict." Ibid., 247.

2 Corbett's "Green Pamphlet" appears as an appendix in the edition of *Some Principles of Maritime Strategy* previously referenced.

3 Corbett, *Some Principles of Maritime Strategy*, 5, 8.

4 Ibid., 10.

5 Ibid., 4.

6 Ibid., 26.

7 "Military" here is used in the context of any armed service, and not in the historical context that referred to land armies.

8 Corbett, *Some Principles of Maritime Strategy*, 307. This is quite similar to Clausewitz's sentiment that "war is not a mere act of policy but a true political instrument, a continuation of political activity by other means." Clausewitz, *On War*, 86–7.

9 Corbett, *Some Principles of Maritime Strategy*, 308. "It must be taken as a general rule that no question of grand strategy can be decided apart from diplomacy." Corbett's use of diplomacy implies both the domestic and international arenas. Clausewitz expresses this same sentiment in stating that "policy . . . will permeate all military operations, and, in so far as their violent nature will admit, it will have a continuous influence on them. . . ." Clausewitz, *On War*, 86–7.

10 Corbett, *Some Principles of Maritime Strategy*, 102.

11 Ibid.

12 Ibid., 99.

13 Ibid., 101. "Whereas on land, economic pressure usually begins after decisive victory, but at sea economic pressure starts at the first."

14 Ibid., 117.

15 Ibid., 60. In referring to "minor actions," Corbett alluded to Clausewitz's concept of war with limited aims as described in Chapter 7 of Book 8 of *On War*.

16 Corbett, *Some Principles of Maritime Strategy*, 61.

17 Ibid., 16. Similarly Corbett states, "Naval strategy does not exist as a separate branch of knowledge. It is only a section of a division of the art of war . . . The true method of procedure then is to get hold of a general theory of war and so ascertain the exact relations of Naval Strategy to the whole." Ibid., 307.

18 Ibid., 15.

19 Ibid., 16.

20 Ibid., 11, 16.

21 Ibid., 100 and 93. Corbett uses the term "military communications," meaning what is today called land-based lines of operation and supply.

22 Ibid., 315–16.

23 Ibid., 95.

24 Ibid., 323.

25 Ibid., 100, 322.

26 Ibid., 100.

27 Ibid., 316. Naval strategy should be preoccupied with communications, so in effect naval strategy can be distilled in terms of "passage and communication." Ibid.
28 Ibid., 91.
29 Ibid., 94.
30 Ibid., 320.
31 Corbett does note his exclusion of fishing activities and fishery rights in his statement.
32 Corbett, *Some Principles of Maritime Strategy*, 317.
33 It is unclear why he states this, since he does explicitly and implicitly state that maritime strategy applies in both peace and war.
34 Corbett, *Some Principles of Maritime Strategy*, 318.
35 Ibid.
36 Ibid., 319.
37 Ibid., 104.
38 Ibid., 105.
39 Ibid., 321.
40 Ibid., 91.
41 Ibid., 31, 310. Corbett notes that the advantages of the offense are readily apparent, yet lists the disadvantages of offensive strategy: it grows weaker as it advances by lengthening its lines of communications; it tends to operate on unfamiliar ground; it continually increases the difficulty of retreat.
42 Ibid., 34.
43 Ibid., 167.
44 Ibid., 323–4.
45 Ibid., 35, 310.
46 Eric J. Grove, "Introduction," in *Some Principles of Maritime Strategy*, xxviii. Original citation comes from a bound lecture volume, as part of the Corbett Papers collection, p. 22/137.
47 Corbett, *Some Principles of Maritime Strategy*, 158.
48 Ibid., 324–5.
49 Ibid., 32.
50 Ibid., 33.
51 Ibid., 32, 310–11.
52 Ibid., 310–11. These thoughts are like those of Clausewitz.
53 Ibid., 32. He bolsters his case by noting that the "counter attack" is the same as Clausewitz's idea of the "surprise advantage of defense." Ibid., 311.
54 Ibid., 311.
55 Ibid., 32.
56 Eric J. Grove, "Introduction," in Corbett, *Some Principles of Maritime Strategy*, xxviii note 46. Citation attributed to Corbett's private papers.
57 Corbett, *Some Principles of Maritime Strategy*, 313.
58 Ibid., 28.
59 Ibid., 59.
60 Ibid., 57, 59.
61 Ibid., 58. Attributed to Francis Bacon (1561–1626), who was a prominent Elizabethan and Jacobean politician, lawyer, philosopher, and writer. Original reference comes from *Essays* 29, "Of the True Greatness of Kingdoms."
62 Corbett, *Some Principles of Maritime Strategy*, 165.
63 Ibid., 210.
64 Ibid., 261–2.
65 Ibid., 61.

66 Ibid., 166. Here, Corbett counters the "seek out and destroy" school of thought.
67 Ibid., 211.
68 Ibid., 214. The first execution of the "fleet in being" concept is attributed to Arthur Herbert, Earl of Torrington (1647–1716).
69 Corbett, *Some Principles of Maritime Strategy*, 224.
70 Ibid., 106. Corbett listed examples of focal areas as "Finisterre, Gibraltar, Suez, the Cape, Singapore, and many others."
71 Ibid., 72.
72 Ibid., 262.
73 Ibid., 185.
74 Ibid., 183.
75 Ibid., 185.
76 Ibid., 203.
77 Ibid., 205.
78 Ibid., 183.
79 Ibid., 158.
80 Ibid., 206.
81 Ibid., 187, 208.
82 Ibid., 117. "The object of naval warfare is to control maritime communications."
83 Ibid., 183.
84 Ibid., 113. Vice Admiral Horatio, first Viscount Nelson (1758–1805), was at the time and still is regarded by many as Great Britain's greatest naval officer.
85 Ibid., 116–17.
86 Corbett calls support ships "auxiliaries."
87 Corbett, *Some Principles of Maritime Strategy*, 114.
88 Ibid., 112, 114.
89 Ibid., 132.
90 Ibid.
91 Ibid., 133.
92 Ibid.
93 Ibid., 130.
94 Ibid., 128.
95 Ibid., 131.
96 Ibid., 152.
97 Hill, *Maritime Strategy for Medium Powers*, 35.

4 Space is tied to national power

1 Clausewitz, *On War*, 87. "We see, therefore, that war is not merely an act of policy but a true political instrument, a continuation of political intercourse, carried on with other means."
2 Clausewitz, *On War*, 605. Similarly, Sun Tzu noted, "War is a matter of vital importance to the State," Sun Tzu, *The Art of War*, 62.
3 A similar view is illustrated by the statement, "Indeed, in the United States space has always been a subfield of other areas – foreign, national security, economic, and science policy being the most prominent." Johnson-Freese, "China's Manned Space Program," 53.
4 Sun Tzu, *The Art of War*, 77. "To subdue the enemy without fighting is the acme of skill." For a brief biography of Sun Tzu, see Samuel B. Griffith, "Preface," in Sun Tzu, *The Art of War*.

5 Johnson-Freese, "China's Manned Space Program," 53.

6 Braunschvig, Garwin, and Marwell, "Space Diplomacy," 159.

7 Johnson-Freese, "China's Manned Space Program," 57.

8 Information Office of the State Council, *China's Space Activities*.

9 Johnson-Freese, "China's Manned Space Program," 63.

10 Johnson-Freese, *The Chinese Space Program*, 98.

11 "Congratulations, China," *The Economist*, 11; Johnson-Freese, "Space Wei Qi," 133.

12 Johnson-Freese, "China's Manned Space Program," 54.

13 Ibid., 60–1.

14 Hays *et al.*, *Spacepower for a New Millennium*, 11.

15 It seems doubtful that orbital locations or frequency assignments are truly "limited" resources. It is just current technology that limits the number of satellites that can operate within a certain orbit or determines the increments for frequency bandwidth assignments.

16 US Joint Forces Command, "Joint Forces Command Glossary."

17 Ordway and Sharpe, *The Rocket Team*, 376. "*It would be a blow to U.S. prestige if we do not do it first.*" Italics are in the referenced material and the remark is attributed to Wernher von Braun.

18 McDougall, . . . *the Heavens and the Earth*, 119.

19 Ibid., 246. An independent newspaper in Manila is reported to have noted the importance of the Soviets getting the first man in space, in writing of "its effect on the people of the uncommitted countries, who see in all this the supposed superiority of the Communist way of life, economic system, and materialistic philosophy."

20 McDougall, . . . *the Heavens and the Earth*, 145. In a *Life* magazine article, it was lamented, "Let us not pretend that Sputnik is anything but a defeat for the United States." McDougall observes, however, that the negativity was not as pronounced as many would be led to believe.

21 Johnson-Freese, "China's Manned Space Program," 52.

22 "China in Space: Ground Control to Colonel Yang," *The Economist*, 78. "China's possession of its own manned space programme will also increase pressure on Americans to allow China to participate in the allegedly 'International' Space Station."

23 Sun Tzu, *The Art of War*, 88.

24 Damon, *Introduction to Space*, 2.

25 US Congress, *Space Handbook: Astronautics and its Applications*, 7–8. "Some of the unique opportunities that seem to lie in astronautics that are of obvious importance include . . . [delivering] nuclear weapons from remote regions of space."

26 Stares, *The Militarization of Space*, 80. Early anti-satellite programs of the United States include SAINT and Thor.

27 Logsdon, *The Decision to Go to the Moon*, 47–8; Ritchie, *Spacewar*, 56–83.

28 Simon P. Worden, "Space Control for the 21st Century: A Space 'Navy' Protecting the Commercial Basis of America's Wealth," in Hays *et al.*, *Spacepower for a New Millennium*, 235; Stares, *The Militarization of Space*, 225.

29 Stares, *The Militarization of Space*, 99; Durch, *National Interests and the Military Use of Space*, 77.

30 Johnson-Freese, "China's Manned Space Program," 52n7.

31 Ibid., "China's Manned Space Program," 66. A comment attributed to a 2000 Chinese newspaper suggests that many countries may view themselves as unable to compete militarily against the United States with conventional warfare, such

as tanks and airplanes, so attacking the space systems of the United States may be an "irresistible choice."

32 Johnson-Freese, "China's Manned Space Program," 66.

33 This same argument can be made by noting the reactions after the launch of *Sputnik I*, which was a non-military action during the Cold War. The event had great domestic and political effects in the United States, and therefore it is presumed that major or minor military actions in the future could also have such a dramatic effect.

5 Space operations are interdependent with others

1 Clausewitz, *On War*, 89. "The first . . . mainly concerns the people; the second the commander and his army; the third the government."

2 Strassler, *The Landmark Thucydides*.

3 Potter and Nimitz, *Sea Power*, 184–5.

4 This view that naval forces need to work with other forces, such as the army, goes back at least one hundred years, as reflected within the writings of Charles E. Callwell in *Military Operations and Maritime Preponderance*.

5 Meilinger, *Airpower: Myths and Facts*, 1.

6 Mitchell, *Winged Defense*; Douhet, *The Command of the Air*; Mark A. Clodfelter, "Molding Airpower Convictions: Development and Legacy of William Mitchell's Strategic Thought" in Meilinger, *The Paths of Heaven*, 79, 95.

7 Meilinger, *Airpower: Myths and Facts*, 15.

8 Ibid., 16. Original citation from United States Strategic Bombing Survey (USSBS), "Over-all Report (European War)," 95–6.

9 Meilinger, *Airpower: Myths and Facts*, 16. Original citation from USSBS, "The Effects of Strategic Bombing on Japan's Urban Economy," March 1947, 25.

10 Daalder and O'Hanlon, *Winning Ugly*, 4–5.

11 Ibid.

12 This is based on Clausewitz's thought that war deals with the people, the commander and his army, and the government. Clausewitz, *On War*, 89.

13 This is contrary to the position that "Who controls low-Earth orbit controls near-Earth space. Who controls near-Earth space dominates Terra. Who dominates Terra determines the destiny of humankind." Dolman, *Astropolitik*, 8.

14 McDougall, . . .*the Heavens and the Earth*, 166.

15 Ibid., 154.

6 Celestial lines of communication

1 The phrase "lines of passage and communications" was chosen by Corbett to more fully describe his idea of maritime communications.

2 Others have also noted the value of lines of communication in and through space. For example, it has previously been written that access to and utilization of space are a vital national interest because space activities are critical to national security and economic well-being. US Department of Defense, *Directive 3100.10: Space Policy*, 2.

3 Credit for the acronym "CLOC" is given to Colonel Peter Zwack, US Army, having defined the term while conducting his research as a Mahan Scholar at the Naval War College in 2003. In this context, "celestial" is commensurate with the meaning "the visible sky and heavens."

4 This definition of "space communication" is a departure from maritime strategic thought since, for Corbett, maritime communications were equivalent to the sea

lines of communication. As used in this work, the term "space communications" refers to the lines of communication, along with the means of using them.

5 Admittedly, the term "space communications" is similar to the term "space-based communications," which pertains to transmissions that relay data and information coming from satellites in orbit. Despite the potential confusion with the term's usage, its context is in keeping with the time-honored usage of the word "communications."

6 "Intangible" is not meant to imply that electromagnetic transmission – such as lasers, data, and information – cannot be detected and monitored, but only that they lack sufficient mass and volume to be readily felt by humans.

7 Clausewitz uses the term "physical" when referring to strategic elements that affect war. In his usage, physical applies to the size of the armed forces, their composition, and armament. Clausewitz, On War, 183.

8 This is similar to how sea lines of communication may remain fixed or move, depending on the specific need or activity.

9 Stutzman and Thiele, Antenna Theory and Design; Sadiku, Elements of Electromagnetics.

10 Of course, a longer distance may equate to a longer amount of time, but this is not a necessary condition.

11 McDougall, . . .the Heavens and the Earth, 154.

12 Ibid., 242–4.

13 Whitman, "Keeping Our Bearing: The Coming War Over the Global Position System." The Russian company Aviaconversia marketed a 4-watt GPS jammer, weighing about 19 pounds, which was capable of denying GPS reception for about 125 miles. Often, such jamming systems can be effectively countered through "home-on-jam" weapons or using other means to rebroadcast the GPS signal.

7 Command of space

1 Many space strategists have defined "space control" – along with the need to think about space – in similar ways to sea control. The control school of thought, as described by Lupton, was an outcome of this view. Lupton, On Space Warfare, 21.

2 The idea that command of space is applicable during peacetime is contrary to maritime strategy as defined by Corbett, as he thought command of the sea existed only during times of war. He thought that claims of having command during peacetime only meant that a nation had sufficient positions or number of ships to obtain command during war. Corbett, Some Principles of Maritime Strategy, 318.

3 Goldman, American Space Law, 106–7.

4 Braunschvig, Garwin, and Marwell, "Space Diplomacy," 159.

5 Ibid., 161.

6 O'Hanlon, Neither Star Wars nor Sanctuary, 36–7. See reference for complete list of countries with satellites in orbit.

7 Wu, Economic Warfare, 9, 367. "Economic warfare" has been defined as "when a country tries to increase the current supply of goods to itself and reduce that to its adversary." The use of boycotts is excluded in this definition. Economic warfare is meant to deny the enemy the use of his outside resources – thereby reducing his economic power and influence – and to also interfere with the effective use of his own internal resources.

8   This is in agreement with Clausewitz's thought of compelling the enemy to do one's will, by affecting the people, the military, and the governmental leaders. Clausewitz, *On War*, 75, 89.
9   This concept is also sometimes referred to as "information operations," "information warfare," or "psychological warfare." US Joint Forces Command, "Joint Forces Command Glossary."
10 Although the Soviet Union and the United States did not directly confront each other in general warfare, they did use third party countries to battle over their values and ideals. These confrontations included actions in Korea, Cuba, Vietnam, and Afghanistan.
11 Curtis, "Unforeseen Results of Reform," *Russia: A Country Study*.
12 This is a derivation of Corbett's maritime strategy. Corbett, *Some Principles of Maritime Strategy*, 91.
13 Ibid., 104–5. "Persistent" was chosen over Corbett's choice of "permanent," since the former connotes some degree of opposition, which will be likely during times of war, and does not imply an absolute, as the latter term does. Other analysts of command of the sea and sea control support this sentiment of command not being an absolute. Hill, *Maritime Strategy for Medium Powers*, 81.

8   Strategy of offense and defense

1   Clausewitz, *On War*, 236. Clausewitz writes, "The destruction of the enemy forces is admittedly the purpose of all engagements."
2   US Joint Chiefs of Staff, *Department of Defense Dictionary of Military and Associated Terms*, 215.
3   Article 51 states, "Nothing in this present Charter shall impair the inherent right of individual or collective self-defense if an armed attack occurs against a Member of the United Nations, until the Security Council has taken measures necessary to maintain international peace and security." United Nations, *Charter of the United Nations*.
4   US Department of the Navy, *The Commander's Handbook*, 6-5.
5   Ibid. This concept is also sometimes referred to as the principle of proportionality.
6   Ibid., 8-1.
7   Ibid. From paragraph 8.1.1, "Military objectives are combatants and those objects which, by their nature, location, purpose, or use, effectively contribute to the enemy's war-fighting or war-sustaining capability and whose total or partial destruction, capture, or neutralization would constitute a definite military advantage to the attacker under the circumstance at the time of the attack." From paragraph 8.1.2, it is stated, "Civilian objects consist of all civilian property and activities other than those used to support or sustain the enemy's war-fighting capabilities. Attacks on installations such as dikes and dams are prohibited if their breach or destruction would result in the loss of civilian lives disproportionate to the military advantage to be gained. Similarly, the intentional destruction of food, crops, livestock, drinking water, and other objects indispensable to the survival of the civilian population, for the specific purpose of denying the civilian population of their use, is prohibited."
8   "Nothing in the present Charter shall impair the inherent right of individual or collective self-defense if an armed attack occurs against a Member of the United Nations, until the Security Council has taken measures necessary to maintain international peace and security." United Nations, *Charter of the United Nations*, Article 51.

9 Chairman of the US Joint Chiefs of Staff, *Standing Rules of Engagement for US Forces*, 1.
10 Ibid., Enclosure A (Unclassified Appendix), A-4.
11 Dolman, *Astropolitik*, 121; United Nations, *Antarctica Treaty*.
12 Dolman, *Astropolitik*, 121.
13 United Nations, *Antarctica Treaty*, Preamble. The twelve original participating governments are Argentina, Australia, Belgium, Chile, the French Republic, Japan, New Zealand, Norway, the Union of South Africa, the Union of Soviet Socialist Republics, the United Kingdom of Great Britain and North Ireland, and the United States of America.
14 Ibid., Article 1, paragraph 1.
15 Ibid., Article 1, paragraph 2.
16 Dolman, *Astropolitik*, 149–50.
17 Gray, "The Influence of Space Power upon History," 302.
18 Logsdon, *The Decision to Go to the Moon*, 47–8; Ritchie, *Spacewar*, 56–83; Durch, *National Interests and the Military Use of Space*, 77; Stares, *The Militarization of Space*, 80, 99; Preston *et al.*, *Space Weapons: Earth Wars*, 11–14.
19 Clausewitz, *On War*, 236. The quotation is a paraphrase of Corbett. Corbett, *Some Principles of Maritime Strategy*, xxviii. Original citation from a bound lecture volume, from the Corbett Papers collection, p. 22/137.
20 Clausewitz, *On War*, 358. Italics are his emphasis.
21 Ibid.
22 Gray, "The Influence of Space Power upon History," 305.
23 Clausewitz, *On War*, 357–8.
24 Corbett, *Some Principles of Maritime Strategy*, 35.
25 Clausewitz, *On War*, 363.

9 Strategic positions

1 Oberg, *Space Power Theory*, 6. "Spaceflight today operates through an extremely narrow series of 'choke points,' ranging from the handful of operational launch sites to the limitations on communications paths and ground stations."
2 Stares, *Space and National Security*, 14; O'Hanlon, *Neither Star Wars nor Sanctuary*, 55.
3 Gray, "The Influence of Space Power upon History," 308n21.
4 Oberg, *Space Power Theory*, 70.
5 O'Hanlon, *Neither Star Wars nor Sanctuary*, 38.
6 Gray, "The Influence of Space Power upon History," 308n21. Low-earth orbits are typically said to range from 60 to 300 miles above the earth, and the geostationary orbit is 22,300 miles above the earth. In addition to military advantage, it is possible to realize diplomatic, economic, and information advantage as well.
7 Lindström, "The Galileo Satellite System and its Security Implications," 10, 12, and 18. The Global Position System comprises 24 NAVSTAR satellites with one or more orbital spares. A complete GLONASS system consists of 24 satellites, but the constellation is currently only partially operational. The Galileo system is projected to have 27 satellites, with 3 orbital spares.
8 Goldman, *American Space Law*, 106.
9 Damon, *Introduction to Space*, 52–3.
10 Again, the "sanctuary" and "high ground" schools of thought correspond to the categories as described by Lupton. Lupton, *On Space Warfare*, 20–1.

11 High-value positions, on the other hand, do not necessarily denote a position of inherent advantage but a position where there is a great concentration of space activity and communication; nevertheless, these high-value systems often will be located at positions with inherent advantage.

12 At times, the counterattack also incorporates these traits.

13 Corbett, *Some Principles of Maritime Strategy*, 95. Taken from Corbett's thought that by exploiting strategic position through occupation of the enemy's maritime communications and closing his points of distribution "we destroy [the enemy's] national life afloat."

14 Johnson-Freese, "China's Manned Space Program," 65.

10 Blocking

1 CLOCs is the acronym for celestial lines of communication.

2 Both Clausewitz and Corbett believed that offensive strategy is the "more effective" form of warfare, and defensive strategy is the "stronger" form. Clausewitz, *On War*, 97, 380; Corbett, *Some Principles of Maritime Strategy*, 310.

3 Similar thoughts are contained in Simon P. Worden, "Space Control for the 21st Century," in Hays *et al.*, *Spacepower for a New Millennium*, 236.

4 The choice of these terms is in keeping with Corbett's maritime strategy usage, although he does use the term "open" for "distant" on some occasions.

5 Klotz, "Space, Commerce, and National Security," 42; Simon P. Worden, "Space Control for the 21st Century," in Hays *et al.*, *Spacepower for a New Millennium*, 227. Officials of Tongasat, the national satellite company of the South Pacific island nation of Tonga, accused Indonesia of deliberately interfering with its satellite's communications signals. The alleged motive of the jamming was an Indonesian demand that one of their own satellites be allowed to operate in the same geosynchronous slot that was assigned by the International Telecommunications Union.

6 Whitman, "Keeping Our Bearing: The coming war over the Global Position System."

7 It is, of course, permissible to block communications between the transmitting and receiving stations, but that is considered distant blocking.

8 It has also been written that satellites could be used to shade another's solar panels to cause power deficit shut-downs. Simon P. Worden, "Space Control for the 21st Century," in Hays *et al.*, *Spacepower for a New Millennium*, 236. Also, a reflective "parasol" has been suggested to block the harmful effects of laser weapons. Ritchie, *Spacewar*, 118.

9 Technical considerations include knowing what signal-to-noise ratio the enemy's system can detect, along with what kind of onboard processing capability his system has to counter the effects of jamming.

10 Corbett, *Some Principles of Maritime Strategy*, 203. The inherent weakness of the close blockade, Corbett believed, is its arrested offensive posture, and therefore the close blockade has a defensive attitude.

11 Simon P. Worden, "Space Control for the 21st Century," in Hays *et al.*, *Spacepower for a New Millennium*, 234.

12 Corbett, *Some Principles of Maritime Strategy*, 187, 208. Corbett believed that the method chosen, whether the close or distant blockade, depends upon one's objectives, along with determining which method is more economical and efficient.

13 This is in keeping with Sun Tzu's idea of employing deception. Sun Tzu, *The Art of War*, 53.

11 Space as a barrier

1 Corbett, *Some Principles of Maritime Strategy*, 94.
2 Stares, *The Militarization of Space*, 225; Simon P. Worden, "Space Control for the 21st Century" in Hays *et al.*, *Spacepower for a New Millennium*, 235.
3 Martel, *The Technological Arsenal*, 55; O'Hanlon, *Neither Star Wars nor Sanctuary*, 61–90.
4 Clausewitz, *On War*, 89.
5 Corbett, *Some Principles of Maritime Strategy*, 58.
6 "Maneuver space" is a term used among many military professionals, which denotes a region in which maneuver warfare can be conducted. US Joint Chiefs of Staff, *Joint Doctrine Encyclopedia*, 481.
7 US Secretary of Defense, "Department of Defense Space Policy," 6.

12 Dispersal and concentration

1 Strategy and Force Planning Faculty, *Strategy and Force Planning*, 20.
2 US Joint Chiefs of Staff, *Doctrine for Joint Operations*, A-1.
3 Mao, *Selected Military Writings of Mao Tse-tung*, 97.
4 Clausewitz, *On War*, 195. Although Clausewitz believed in concentration of forces, he did not believe in the principle of economy of force.
5 Mao, *Selected Military Writings of Mao Tse-tung*, 134.
6 Ibid., 132.
7 From an understanding of the Law of Armed Conflict, it is realized that the amount of force that is "practical" involves taking into consideration the principles of military necessity and proportionality.
8 Corbett, *Some Principles of Maritime Strategy*, 138.
9 Ibid., 132.
10 Ibid., 131.
11 Ibid., 132.
12 Ibid., 131. The term comes from Corbett's paraphrasing of Mahan.
13 Clausewitz, as with most interpretations of the principle of concentration, addresses the need to concentrate forces or "mass" and does not explicitly address the need to concentrate military effects. Clausewitz writes, "[T]here is no higher and simpler law of strategy than that of *keeping one's forces concentrated.*" Clausewitz, *On War*, 204. Italic emphasis is Clausewitz's own. Even in United States joint doctrine, the principle of mass is defined in a similar manner to Clausewitz. US Joint Chiefs of Staff, *Doctrine for Joint Operations*, A-1.
14 Although considered secondary, these other functions that are performed may in fact be essential to eventually winning the war.
15 For a short discussion on the use of "escorts," see Simon P. Worden, "Space Control for the 21st Century," in Hays *et al.*, *Spacepower for a New Millennium*, 235–6.
16 These needed mission areas could be performed by some terrestrial-based systems also.
17 O'Hanlon, *Neither Star Wars nor Sanctuary*, 87. It is reported that in June 2000 the University of Surrey launched a five-kilogram microsatellite onboard a Russian booster, and the microsatellite was built for less than $1 million. Once in orbit, the microsatellite then detached and maneuvered to photograph two Russian and Chinese satellites that had also been placed in orbit by the same booster.

18 Johnson-Freese, "China's Manned Space Program," 64. "China has warned that it might consider using microsats to deny US use of space in a crisis or conflict."
19 Clausewitz, *On War*, 101, 119. "Friction" and "uncertainty" are the words chosen by Clausewitz.
20 Alberts, Garstka, and Stein, *Network Centric Warfare*, 159.
21 Ibid., 5–13.
22 "Network-centric warfare" has many different meanings to many different people. But words have meaning and, if network-centric warfare does not denote warfare that is centered around a network, then the term serves no substantive purpose and should be discarded.

13 Actions by lesser powers

1 Hill, *Maritime Strategy for Medium Powers*, 21.
2 Sun Tzu, *The Art of War*, 77.
3 Goldman, *American Space Law*, 107.
4 McDougall, . . .*the Heavens and the Earth*, 144–5.
5 A July 1962 high-altitude nuclear device test, named "Starfish Prime," affected both the inner and outer Van Allen radiation belts. The test involved a 1.4 megaton nuclear weapon and eliminated the low-radiation slot separating the two belts for a period of time, and radiation within both belts increased. The effects are said to have damaged three satellites in orbit. Stares, *The Militarization of Space*, 108; Muolo, *Space Handbook: An Analyst's Guide*, 14; Lambakis, *On the Edge of the Earth*, 123.
6 See Clausewitz, "The People in Arms," in *On War*, 479–83 for a general discussion on insurgencies and the strategy of guerrilla warfare.
7 Ibid., 480; Mao, *Selected Military Writings of Mao Tse-tung*, 208–9.
8 Clausewitz, *On War*, 480.
9 Ibid., 480–1.
10 Mao, *Selected Military Writings of Mao Tse-tung*, 220.
11 Symbolic locations can hold cultural, religious, or political significance.
12 Mao, *Selected Military Writings of Mao Tse-tung*, 111. This is somewhat similar in style to Sun Tzu's comment, "When the enemy is at ease, be able to weary him; when well fed, to starve him; when at rest, to make him move." Sun Tzu, *The Art of War*, 96.
13 Clausewitz, *On War*, 469.

14 Comparisons

1 The "schools of thought" are presented using the terminology in Lupton, *On Space Warfare*, 20–1.
2 Demonstrating that the *Space Commission Report* is meant to amplify and complement the 1996 Clinton administration National Space Policy is the statement, "The Commission believes the U.S. Government should vigorously pursue the capabilities called for in the [1996] National Space Policy. . .." US Commission to Assess United States National Security Space Management and Organization, *Space Commission Report*, xii.
3 Ibid., xvi.
4 Ibid., vii.
5 Ibid., 16. "The U.S. will be tested over time by competing programs or attempts to restrict U.S. space activities through international regulations." This thought

is akin to the concept of lesser space powers attempting to dispute another's command of space.

6 Ibid., 19.
7 Ibid., x.
8 Ibid.
9 Ibid., vii–x. The maritime-inspired space strategy does not explicitly state the need to promote the peaceful use of space, but it does emphasize non-military uses of space instead.
10 Ibid., 36.
11 Ibid., 37. "Anticipatory" is interpreted to mean "preemptive."
12 US Joint Chiefs of Staff, *Joint Doctrine for Space Operations*.
13 US Joint Chiefs of Staff, *Joint Doctrine Encyclopedia*, 253. The definition of "doctrine" is attributed to Captain Wayne P. Hughes, Jr., USN. Similarly, doctrine has been defined as "the officially approved systems of concepts on the basic, fundamental problems of war." Sokolovskii, *Soviet Military Strategy*, 130.
14 Even when considering US Air Force doctrine, such as *Space Operations: Air Force Doctrine Document 2-2*, only 16 out of 54 pages deal with the strategy of space warfare, with the remainder dealing primarily with organizational responsibilities, background, and command and control issues.
15 US Joint Chiefs of Staff, *Joint Doctrine for Space Operations*, vii.
16 Ibid., x. Many strategists have developed similar definitions, usually using the terms "space control" or "space power."
17 Ibid., I-1
18 Ibid., IV-2–5.
19 To some extent, the survivability, sanctuary, and high-ground schools all suffer from being too narrowly focused on the role and impact of weapons in space.
20 Lupton, *On Space Warfare*, 20.
21 Ibid., 21.
22 US Joint Chiefs of Staff, *Joint Doctrine for Space Operations*, I-3.

15 Space policy

1 Marc J. Berkowitz, "National Space Policy and National Defense," in Hays *et al.*, *Spacepower for a New Millennium*, 37. "The purpose of policy guidance is to establish the vision, objectives, procedures, and implementing measures for a course of action."
2 "Strategy" has been defined as balancing one's ends and means. Strategy and Force Planning Faculty, *Strategy and Force Planning*, 20.
3 Clausewitz, *On War*, 69. "*[W]ar is nothing by the continuation of policy with other means.*" Italics are Clausewitz's own.
4 Sokolovskii, *Soviet Military Strategy*, 98. "The acceptance of war as a tool of politics determines the relationship of military strategy to politics and makes the former completely dependent on the latter."
5 In this work, "militarization" and "weaponization" are defined differently. "Militarization" refers to activities and systems in space used to support military operations. "Weaponization" refers to the placement or basing of weapons in space, whether for offensive or defensive purposes.
6 National Aeronautics and Space Act of 1958 (as amended). "The Congress hereby declares that it is the policy of the United States that activities in space should be devoted to peaceful purposes for the benefit of all mankind." As cited in US Congress, *Space Law*, 499.

7 While outer space cannot be claimed as sovereign territory, the systems and spacecraft operating there are considered sovereign territory, as indicated by Article VIII of the Outer Space Treaty.

8 Goldman, *American Space Law*, 26, 262–71.

9 Ibid., 26. This reference gives the number of countries who have ratified the Moon Treaty as eight, but since its publication the number is now nine.

10 Ibid., 93. What this sharing exactly entails, however, was not elaborated upon. US Congress, "Statement by Ambassador Arthur J. Goldberg," 8.

11 Goldman, *American Space Law*, 28–9.

12 NSC 5814/1, "Preliminary U.S. Policy on Outer Space," was approved in August 1958. "The USSR has . . . captured the imagination and admiration of the world." If it maintained superiority in space, it could undermine the prestige and security of the United States. As cited in McDougall, *. . .the Heavens and the Earth*, 180.

13 US Congress, *Space Law*, 499.

14 Ibid., 559. From a White House press release dated 20 June 1978 describing the Presidential Directive on National Space Policy.

15 The White House, "Fact Sheet: National Space Policy," 14.

16 Thomas and Duncan, *International Law Studies*, 149n114.

17 The Limited Test Ban Treaty is more formally known as the Treaty Banning Nuclear Weapons Test in the Atmosphere, In Outer Space and Under Water. Reprinted in US Congress, *Space Law*, 9–14.

18 O'Hanlon, *Neither Star Wars nor Sanctuary*, 105–42.

19 US Secretary of Defense, "Department of Defense Space Policy," 6.

20 Dolman, *Astropolitik*, 138.

21 Ibid.

22 US Congress, *Space Law*, 26.

23 Force is a legitimate recourse in some circumstance, although the use of nuclear weapons or other weapons of mass destruction would not be considered appropriate under the provisions of the Outer Space Treaty.

24 Dolman, *Astropolitik*, 138–9.

25 Outer Space Treaty, Article VIII. "A State Party to the Treaty on whose registry an object launched into outer space is carried shall retain jurisdiction and control over such object, and over any personnel thereof, while in outer space or on a celestial body. Ownership of objects launched into outer space, including objects landed or constructed on a celestial body, and of their component parts, is not affected by their presence in outer space or on a celestial body or by their return to Earth." As reprinted in Goldman, *American Space Law*, 236.

26 The United Nations Convention on the Law of the Sea, which the Clinton Administration has signed but the US Senate has not ratified, addressed some concerns regarding the exploitation of the oceans and deep-sea mining.

27 George W. Bush, "State of the Union," 20 January 2004.

28 US Department of the Navy, *The Commander's Handbook*, 6-5.

29 McDougall, *. . .the Heavens and the Earth*, 181.

30 Article IV of the 1967 Outer Space Treaty, as reprinted in Goldman, *American Space Law*, 235. "The establishment of military bases, installations, and fortifications, the testing of any type of weapons and the conduct of military maneuvers on celestial bodies shall be forbidden."

31 It has also been stated that placing satellites in very high orbits may make them more difficult to detect and track, thereby providing some degree of "stealth" and concealment. Lambakis, *On the Edge of the Earth*, 130.

32 US Commission to Assess United States National Security Space Management and Organization, *Space Commission Report*, xxxiv, 89. Designating the US

Air Force as Executive Agent within the Department of Defense was a recommendation coming out of the report. The role of the US Air Force as Executive Agent includes the responsibility to organize, train, and equip for prompt and sustained offensive and defensive air and space operations.

16 Summary and conclusions

1 Klein, "Corbett in Orbit: A Maritime Model for Strategic Space Theory," 58–74. The summary of the strategic concepts is a modification of the referenced article.
2 The phrase "lines of passage and communication" is used by Corbett to more fully describe lines of communications at sea.
3 This is a direct application of Corbett's thoughts.
4 "National life" is the phrase used by Corbett.
5 "Central mass" is the phrase used by both Clausewitz and Corbett.
6 See bibliography for full references.

Bibliography

Alberts, David S., John J. Garstka, and Fredrick P. Stein. *Network Centric Warfare: Developing and Leveraging Information Superiority*. 2nd edn. Washington, DC: Command and Control Research Program, 2002.

Braunschvig, David, Richard L. Garwin, and Jeremy C. Marwell. "Space Diplomacy," *Foreign Affairs* 82, no. 4 (July/August 2003): 156–64.

Bush, George W. President of the United States. "State of the Union Address," 20 January 2004. http://www.whitehouse.gov/news/releases/2004/01/20040120-7.html (accessed 15 March 2004).

Cable, James. *Gunboat Diplomacy: Political Applications of Limited Naval Force*. New York: Praeger, for the Institute of Strategic Studies, 1971.

Callwell, Charles E. *Military Operations and Maritime Preponderance*. 1905. Reprinted and edited by Colin Gray. Annapolis, MD: Naval Institute Press, 1996.

Castex, Raoul. *Strategic Theories*. 1931–9. Reprinted and edited by Eugenia Kiesling. Annapolis, MD: Naval Institute Press, 1994.

Chairman, US Joint Chiefs of Staff. *Standing Rules of Engagement for US Forces*. CJCSI 3121.01A Instruction. Washington, DC: 15 January 2000.

"China in Space: Ground Control to Colonel Yang." *The Economist*, 18–24 October 2003, 78–9.

Clausewitz, Carl von, *On War*. Edited and translated by Michael Howard and Peter Paret. Princeton, NJ: Princeton University Press, 1989.

Collins, John M. *Grand Strategy: Principles and Practices*. Annapolis, MD: Naval Institute Press, 1973.

"Congratulations, China." *The Economist*. 18–24 October 2003, 11–12.

Corbett, Julian S. *Some Principles of Maritime Strategy*. London: Longmans, Green and Co., 1911. Reprinted with introduction and notes by Eric J. Grove. Annapolis, MD: Naval Institute Press, 1988.

Curtis, Glenn E., ed. *Russia: A Country Study*. Washington, DC: Federal Research Division, Library of Congress, July 1996. http://www.russiansabroad.com/russian_history_190.html (accessed 6 June 2004).

Daalder, Ivo H. and Michael E. O'Hanlon. *Winning Ugly: NATO's War to Save Kosovo*. Washington, DC: Brookings, 2000.

Damon, Thomas D. *Introduction to Space: The Science of Spaceflight*. 3rd edn. Malabar, FL: Krieger, 2001.

DeBlois, Bruce M. "The Advent of Space Weapons," *Astropolitics* 1, no. 1 (Summer 2003): 29–53.

Dolman, Everett C. *Astropolitik: Classical Geopolitics in the Space Age*. London: Frank Cass, 2002.

Douhet, Giulio, *The Command of the Air*. Translated by Dino Ferrari. New York: Coward-McCann, 1942. Reprint, Washington, DC: Air Force Museums and History Program, 1983.

Durch, William J., ed. *National Interests and the Military Use of Space*. Cambridge, MA: Ballinger, 1984.

Earle, Edward Mead, ed. *Makers of Modern Strategy: Military Thought from Machiavelli to Hitler*. Princeton, NJ: Princeton University Press, 1971.

Fabian, Robert A. "Space Economic Development in the Province of all Mankind: If No One Goes, We All Lose," *Astropolitics* 1, no. 1 (Summer 2003): 89–98.

Futrell, Robert F. *Ideas, Concepts, Doctrine: A History of Basic Thinking in the United States Air Force, 1907–1964*. Vols 1 and 2. Maxwell AFB, AL: Air University, 1971.

Goldman, Nathan C. *American Space Law: International and Domestic*. 2nd edn. Ames, IA: Iowa State University Press, 1996.

Gray, Colin S. *Modern Strategy*. London: Oxford University Press, 2000.

——. "The Influence of Space Power upon History," *Comparative Strategy* 15, no. 4 (October–December 1996): 293–308.

——. *The Navy in the Post-Cold War World: The Uses and Value of Strategic Sea Power*. University Park, PA: Pennsylvania State University Press, 1994.

Handel, Michael I. *Masters of War: Classical Strategic Thought*. 3rd edn. London: Frank Cass, 2001.

Hays, Peter L., James M. Smith, Alan R. Van Tassel and Guy M. Walsh. *Spacepower for a New Millennium: Space and National Security*. New York: McGraw-Hill, 2000.

Hill, J. R. *Maritime Strategy for Medium Powers*. Annapolis: Naval Institute Press, 1986.

Hyatt, James L. III, Paul L. Laugesen, Michael A. Rampino, Ronald R. Ricchi and Joseph H. Schwarz. *Space Power 2010*. Maxwell Air Force Base, AL: Air Command and Staff College, May 1995.

Information Office of the State Council. China. *China's Space Activities*, 22 November 2000. White Paper. http://www.spaceref.com/china/china.white.paper.nov.22.2000.html (accessed 13 February 2004).

Johnson, Dana J., Scott Pace, and C. Bryan Gabbard. *Space: Emerging Options for National Power*. Santa Monica, CA: RAND, 1988

Johnson-Freese, Joan. "China's Manned Space Program: Sun Tzu or Apollo Redux?" *Naval War College Review* 56, no. 3 (Summer 2003): 51–71.

——. "Space Wei Qi: The Launch of Shenzhou V," *Naval War College Review* 57, no. 2 (Spring 2004): 121–145.

——. *The Chinese Space Program: A Mystery within a Maze*. Malabar, FL: Krieger, 1998.

Jomini, Antoine Henri de. *The Art of War*. Reprint, London: Greenhill Books, 1992.

Klein, John J. "Corbett in Orbit: A Maritime Model for Strategic Space Theory," *Naval War College Review* 57, no. 1 (Winter 2004): 58–74.

Klotz, Frank G. "Space, Commerce, and National Security." A Council on Foreign Relations Paper, 1998.

Lambakis, Steven. *On the Edge of the Earth: The Future of American Space Power*. Lexington, KY: University Press of Kentucky, 2001.

Liddell Hart, B. H. *Strategy*. 2nd revised ed. New York: Meridian, 1991.Hattendorf, John B. "The Uses of Maritime History in and for the Navy," *Naval War College Review* 56, no. 2 (Spring 2003): 13–38.

Lindström, Gustav. "The Galileo Satellite System and its Security Implications." European Union Institute for Security Studies Occasional Papers, No 44. April 2003.

Logsdon, John M. *The Decision to Go to the Moon: Project Apollo and the National Interest*. Cambridge, MA: Massachusetts Institute of Technology, 1970.

Lupton, David E. *On Space Warfare: A Space Power Doctrine*. Maxwell Air Force Base, AL: Air University Press, June 1988. http://www.maxwell.af.mil/au/aul/aupress/Books/Lupton/lupton.pdf (accessed 20 April 2002).

Mahan, Alfred T. *Mahan on Naval Strategy: Selections from the Writings of Rear Admiral Alfred Thayer Mahan*. Introduction and edited by John B. Hattendorf. Annapolis, MD: Naval Institute Press, 1991.

Mao Tse-tung, *Selected Military Writings of Mao Tse-tung*. 2nd edn. Peking: Foreign Languages Press, 1966.

Martel, William C., ed. *The Technological Arsenal: Emerging Defense Capabilities*. Washington, DC: Smithsonian Institute Press, 2001.

McDougall, Walter. . . .*the Heavens and the Earth*. New York: Basic Books, 1985.

Meilinger, Phillip S. *Airpower: Myths and Facts*. Maxwell Air Force Base, AL: Air University Press, 2003.

——, ed. *The Paths of Heaven: The Evolution of Airpower Theory*. Maxwell Air Force Base, AL: Air University Press, 1997.

Mitchell, William. *Our Air Force: The Keystone of National Defense*. New York: Dutton, 1921.

——. *Winged Defense: The Development and Possibilities of Modern Air Power – Economic and Military*. Toronto: 1925. Reprint. Port Washington, NY: Kennikat Press, 1971.

Mueller, Karl P. "Totem and Taboo: Depolarizing the Space Weaponization Debate," *Astropolitics* 1, no. 1 (Summer 2004): 4–28.

Muolo, Michael J. *Space Handbook: An Analyst's Guide*, Vol. 2. Maxwell Air Force Base, AL: Air University Press, 1993.

Oberg, James E. *Space Power Theory*. Colorado Springs, CO: US Space Command, 2000. http://space.au.af.mil/books/oberg/ (accessed 23 October 2003).

O'Hanlon, Michael E. *Neither Star Wars nor Sanctuary: Constraining the Military Uses of Space*. Washington, DC: Brookings Institution Press, 2004.

Ordway, Fredrick I. and Mitchell R. Sharpe. *The Rocket Team*. New York: Thomas Y. Crowell, 1979.

Potter, E.B. and Chester W. Nimitz, eds. *Sea Power*. Englewood Cliffs, NJ: Prentice Hall, 1960.

Preston, Bob, Dana J. Johnson, Sean J. A. Edwards, Michael Miller, and Calvin Shipbaugh, *Space Weapons: Earth Wars*. Santa Monica, CA: RAND, 2002.

Ritchie, David. *Spacewar*. New York: Atheneum, 1982.

Sadiku, Matthew N. O. *Elements of Electromagnetics*. Fort Worth, TX: Saunders College Publishing, 1994.

Smith, M.V, *Ten Propositions Regarding Spacepower*, thesis paper, Maxwell Air Force Base, AL: Air University Press, June 2001.

Sokolovskii, V. D. *Soviet Military Strategy*. Translated by Herbert Dinerstein, Leon Gouré, and Thomas Wolfe. Englewood Cliffs, NJ: Prentice-Hall, 1963.

Stares, Paul B. *Space and National Security*. Washington, DC: Brookings, 1987.

——. *The Militarization of Space: U.S. Policy, 1945–1984*. Ithaca, NY: Cornell University Press, 1985.

Strassler, Robert B., ed. *The Landmark Thucydides: A Comprehensive Guide to the Peloponnesian War*. Translated by Richard Crawley. New York: Free Press, 1996.

Strategy and Force Planning Faculty, *Strategy and Force Planning*. 3rd edn. Newport, RI: Naval War College Press, 2000.

Stutzman, Warren L. and Gary A. Thiele. *Antenna Theory and Design*. New York: John Wiley & Sons, 1981.

Sun Tzu. *The Art of War*. Translated by Samuel B. Griffith. Oxford: Oxford University Press, 1971.

Thomas, A. R. and James C. Duncan. *International Law Studies, Volume 73: Annotated Supplement to the Commander's Handbook on the Law of Naval Operations*. Newport, RI: Naval War College, 1999.

Turner, Stansfield. "Missions of the U.S. Navy." *Naval War College Review* (March–April 1974): 2–17. http://www.nwc.navy.mil/press/Review/1998/winter/art10w98.htm (accessed 13 February 2004).

United Nations. *Charter of the United Nations* (26 June 1945). http://www.un.org/aboutun/charter/index.html (accessed 20 November 2003).

——. *Antarctica Treaty* (23 June 1961). http://www.antarctica.ac.uk/About_Antarctica/Treaty/treaty.html (accessed 13 February 2005).

US Air Force. *Space Operations: Air Force Doctrine Document 2-2*. Washington, DC: 27 November 2001.

——. *The Aerospace Force: Defending America in the 21st Century*. Washington DC, 2000. http://www.af.mil/library/posture/taf.pdf (accessed 01 March 2004).

US Commission to Assess United States National Security Space Management and Organization. Report of the Commission to Asses United States National Security Space Management and Organization. Washington, DC: 11 January 2001. Also referred to as the *Space Commission Report*.

US Congress. House. Committee on Commerce, Science, and Transportation. *Space Law: Selected Basic Documents*. 2nd edn. 95th Cong., 2nd sess. 1978.

——. Select Committee on Astronautics and Space Exploration. *Space Handbook: Astronautics and its Applications*. 85th Cong., 2nd sess. 1959. Staff Report.

US Congress. Senate. "Statement by Ambassador Arthur J. Goldberg," in Hearings Before the Committee on Foreign Relations. 90th Congress, 1st sess. 7 March 1967.

US Department of Defense. *Department of Defense Directive 3100.10: Space Policy*. Washington, DC: 9 July 1999.

US Department of the Navy. *The Commander's Handbook on the Law of Naval Operations*, NWP 1-14M. Washington, DC: October 1995.

US Joint Chiefs of Staff. *Department of Defense Dictionary of Military and Associated Terms*, Joint Publication 1-02. Washington, DC: 23 March 1994.

——. *Doctrine for Joint Operations*, Joint Publication 3-0. Washington, DC: 10 September 2001.

——. *Joint Doctrine Encyclopedia.* http://www.dtic.mil/doctrine/joint_doctrine_encyclopedia.htm (accessed 15 March 2004).

——. *Joint Doctrine for Space Operations*, Joint Publication 3-14. Washington, DC: 9 August 2002.

US Joint Forces Command. "Joint Forces Command Glossary," http://www.jfcom.mil/about/glossary/htm (accessed 2 September 2004).

US Secretary of Defense, "Department of Defense Space Policy," Memorandum, 9 July 1999.

Vego, Milan N. *Operational Warfare.* Newport, RI: Naval War College, 2000.

Wegener, Wolfgang. *The Naval Strategy of the World War*, 1929. Reprint, Annapolis, MD: Naval Institute Press, 1989.

White, Thomas D. "Air and Space are Indivisible," *Air Force* 4, no. 3 (March 1958): 40–1.

White House, The. National Science and Technology Council. "Fact Sheet: National Space Policy." Washington, DC, 19 September 1996. http://www.ostp.gov/NSTC/html/fs/fs-5.html (accessed 4 January 2004).

Whitman, David. "Keeping Our Bearing: The Coming War Over the Global Position System," *USNews.Com*, 25 March 2003. http://www.usnews.com/usnews/news/iraq/articles/gps030325.htm (accessed 3 May 2004).

Wu, Yuan-Li. *Economic Warfare.* New York: Prentice-Hall, 1952.

Index

Advanced Composition Explorer 9
aerospace, definition of 14–15
Aerospace Force, The 15
aerospace integrationists 15, 168n22
    and n23
aerospace power 15, 168n19
Age of Sail 16, 20
Agreement on the Rescue of Astronauts
    11
Air Force Doctrine Document 2-2 12,
    181n14
air forces: and ability to win wars alone
    14, 47–8; being the most important
    14; compared with space forces
    15, 17, 31, 154, 168n23; effect on
    civilian workforce 14, 47–8; needing
    other armed services 48; strategic
    bombing 47–8; *see also* air power
Air Force, US 150–1, 153, 182n32
air power: strategy and theory 3, 18,
    132; weaknesses of using for space
    strategy 3, 18
allies 23, 52, 78, 121, 126, 140
Antarctica Treaty 72–3, 147–8, 177n13
Anti-Ballistic Missile Treaty 11, 167n42
antipodal choke-point 83
anti-satellite systems and programs
    41–2, 73, 90, 173n26
Ariane rocket 10
armies: being needed to achieve victory
    45–6, 49; being supported by other
    armed services 20, 45; and winning
    wars alone 45–6
arms control agreements 7, 41, 86, 140,
    146–8, 164
Army Air Corps, US 47
Army, US 151, 153
astrostrategy 165n9

Athens 45
autonomy of action 114, 150

balance of power 22–3, 42
ballistic missiles and defense against x,
    17, 57, 149, 101–2, 161
barrier, space as a: for defensive intent
    101–2, 131, 158; for limited intent
    102–3, 158; for unlimited intent
    104–5, 158; reasons for making
    100–1, 105–6, 133–4, 158
Battle of the Nile 16, 46
Battle of Trafalgar 46
battleships 30
blockades, naval 21, 29–30, 91–2, 98,
    178n10 and n12
blocking: close 91, 94–5, 97, 158;
    compared with naval blockade 91,
    97–8; criticisms of 97–9; defined
    92, 158; distant 91, 94–7, 157;
    historical examples 58–9; methods
    92–5, 123, 149, 158–9; reasons for
    92–3, 95
Bogotá Declaration 62, 85, 167n29
Bonaparte, Napoleon *see* Napoleon
    Bonaparte
Braun, Wernher von 50, 169n40,
    173n17
Brazil 12
Brilliant Pebbles 41
"buying time" 78–9, 126

Cape Canaveral 10, 82
Carter administration 140
celestial lines of communication
    174ch6n3, 178ch10n1; defined 51,
    155; degrading and denying use 83,
    91, 100–1, 128; and need to defend

51, 59, 66, 73, 89, 110, 133, 155;
routes, predictable 52–3, 97; shared
between belligerents 51, 78, 90, 105,
155
chance and uncertainty 89, 114, 138
Chiang Kai-shek 108
China 147; as a space power 40;
economy 38; gaining respect 62,
173n22; goals in space 37–8;
manned space program 37, 62, 120,
173n22; national pride 38; prestige
37, 40
choke-points: in space 81–4, 90–1, 111,
157, 159, 170n1, 177n1; on earth
21, 83, 157
Clausewitz, Carl von 4, 14, 165n4;
Corbett influenced by 20–23,
27, 43, 109, 148, 171n52 and
n53, 178ch10n2, 183n5; on
concentration 108–9,179n4 and
n13; on guerrilla war 124–6,
180ch13n6; on defensive strategy
74–5, 148, 178n2; on friction
and uncertainty 114, 179n19; on
offensive strategy 69, 74, 89, 178n2;
on role of politics 36; on theory of
warfare 4, 44–5, 137–8, 154, 165n5,
170n8, 172n1; on trinitarian analysis
of war 45, 102, 174ch5n1 and n12,
175ch8n8; writings see On War
(Clausewitz)
Clinton administration 140, 180ch14n2
coalitions 48, 117–18, 147
coastal raiding see guerre de course
coercive communications 65–6
Cold War 7, 36–37, 39–41, 61, 139,
143, 145; see also United States, and
the space race
collateral damage 70
collective action and coalitions 46, 48,
64, 118–19, 143
command and control 83–4, 114
command of space 175n2; compared
with space control 60–1; contesting
67–8, 120–2, 145, 159; defined
60; general 66–7, 74, 97, 102, 104,
156; highest level possible 67, 156;
local 66–7, 103, 120, 126, 156,
159; normally in dispute 68, 156;
persistent 66–7, 74, 97, 102, 104,
156, 176n13; temporary 66–7,
103, 120, 126, 156, 159; through
coercion 63–6; through force 66–8;

through presence 61–3, 118–19;
United States 144–5
command of the sea: controlling the
escalation of war 27–8; defined
24; general 24–5; local 24–5,
29; normally in dispute 25, 28;
permanent 25; temporary 25, 29
commerce raiding see guerre de course
commercial space activities 7–9, 35,
37–9, 53, 55, 59, 132, 160
communications: directional 54, 95–7;
interference with see blocking; non-
physical 53–4, 56–8, 80–1, 94–8,
102, 110, 121, 149, 155, 162; omni-
directional 54, 57; physical 52–3,
55–8, 80, 82–4, 94–8, 110, 121–3,
155; predictable 52–3, 97
concentration, principle of 30–1, 108–
10, 179n13; problems with 109
concentric ring theory 14
control of the air see air power
Convention on the Prohibition of
Military or Any Other Hostile Use
of Environmental Modifications
Techniques 11
Conventions on Liability 11
Conventions on Registration 11
cooperative relationship 116–19,
146–7; see also collective action and
coalitions
Corbett, Sir Julian S. 3; compared
to Clausewitz 20–3, 27, 43, 109,
148, 171n52 and n53, 178ch10n2,
183n5; compared to Mahan 20, 23,
31, 124; compared to Nelson 30; on
maritime strategy (theory) 21–32; on
blockades (close and open) 21, 29–
30, 178n10 and n12; on command
of the sea 24–5, 27, 175n2; on
cruisers 30–31; on defensive
strategy 25–7, 148, 178ch10n2;
on dispersal and concentration
30–1, 109; on disputing command
28; on fleet in being 28, 171n68;
on interdependence of operations
22–3; on maritime communications
(sea lines of communication) 22–4,
170n27, 172n82, 174ch6n1 and
n4; on national power 22–3; on
offensive strategy 25–7, 171n41,
178ch10n2; on positions 28–9; on
power of isolation 27–8, 100; on
purpose of naval warfare 22, 24; on

purpose of the battle fleet 30; on the counterattack 26–7; on theory 21–2; weaknesses of his maritime strategy 31–2, 154; writings *see Some Principles of Maritime Strategy* and "Green Pamphlet"
cost savings 117
counterattack 177ch9n12; and defensive strategy 26–7, 74–5, 77, 149–50, 171n53
cruisers: in maritime context 29–31; in space strategy context 111–15, 133, 159
customary and international law 6, 10–12, 61, 71, 138, 143, 160

data and information 5, 10, 16, 38–41, 99, 122: and national security 40–1, 64; defined 39; *see also* intelligence
debris in space 9, 77–8, 88, 90, 96, 105, 141, 149, 167n31
decisive point 108–11
defensive strategy: being the "stronger" form of war 26, 74–5, 77–8, 148, 157, 178ch10n2; and the counterattack 26–7, 74–5, 77, 149–50, 171n53; and offensive strategy 25–27, 69, 74–5, 78, 93, 149–50, 157; and positions of advantage 75–6, 157, 162; and self-protection 76; and "strategic defense" 76; when called for 26, 74–5, 92, 157
definitions: aerospace 14–15; blocking 92, 158; celestial lines of communication 51, 155; command of space 60, 156; command of the sea 24–5; cruisers 30; customary law 11; diplomacy 36; diplomatic 5; doctrine 129, 181n13; economic warfare 175ch7n7; electromagnetics 167n37; grand strategy 4; *guerre de course* 23; information 5, 39; international law 11; Law of Armed Conflict 69–70; lesser powers 116; limited aims 102; maritime 19; militarization 181n5; national power 5, 35; naval 15–16, 19; non-physical communications 155; physical communications 156; policy 5, 137, 181n1; political 5; politics 36; principles 4; sea power 15–16; space (outer space) 6; space communications 51–2,

174ch6n4 and n5; strategic positions 157; strategy 4, 181n2; tactics 4; telecommunications 166n25; theory 4; unlimited aims 102; war 22, 172n1; weaponization 181n5
diplomacy 35–7
directed energy weapons 53, 57, 110
dispersal: and concentration as one 30–1, 109–11, 159, 162; different from the principle of concentration 31, 150, 162; and principle of economy 108
disposal force 23
distributed systems and networks 56, 81–2, 113–14, 150
doctrine 47, 129, 181n13 and n14; and strategy 129, 166n12
Douhet, Giulio 14, 47, 148, 161, 163
Dyna-Soar space plane 42, 73

economic gain 38, 123, 144
economic measures 5, 37–9, 119
economic warfare 166n14, 175ch7n7; at sea 22, 28–9, 170n13; in space 49, 64, 104
economy of force, principle of 108, 130, 179ch12n4
effects, military 104, 110, 112, 123, 132, 158, 179n13
Eisenhower administration 39–41, 120, 139, 169n36
"elastic cohesion" 30
electromagnetic pulse weapons 68, 77, 149, 161
electromagnetics *see* frequency spectrum
equatorial launch sites 10, 121–2
escalation 98–9, 141, 145, 147
European Space Agency 64
European Union 37, 40, 147

failure in space 39–40, 56, 58, 101, 122
Federal Aviation Administration 7
field of view 8, 86–7, 132
fleet in being, concept of 28, 171n68
force in being, concept of 122–3, 159
fouling orbits 77–8, 90, 96, 141; *see also* debris
fractional orbital bombardment systems (FOBS) 41, 73
France and its people 10, 16, 27, 46, 82, 123, 167n32
French Space Center 10, 82

frequency spectrum (electromagnetic) 10, 37, 53, 62, 82, 96, 98, 123, 139, 149, 157, 167n37, 173n15; *see also* celestial lines of communication
friction and uncertainty 114, 179n19

Galileo program 37, 40, 62, 68, 84, 177n7
Germany and its people 47–8
Global Orbiting Navigation Satellite System (GLONASS) 62, 68, 84, 177n7
Global Positioning System (GPS) x, 37, 59, 62, 68, 84, 132, 175n13, 177n7
Gorbachev, Mikhail 65
grand strategy 4–6, 15, 22, 36–7, 44, 69, 131, 155, 170n9
gravity well, earth's 86–7, 132
Great Britain and its people 20, 23, 27, 30, 45–6, 72, 100, 172n84
"Green Pamphlet" (Corbett) 21, 170n2
ground stations 8–9, 81, 96, 128, 177n1
guerre de course 23, 28, 123–4
guerrilla actions and warfare 108–9, 124–5, 180n13; *see also* Mao Tsetung
Gulf War (1991) 41

high ground *see* schools of thought, high-ground
history, application of 4, 13, 35, 48, 68, 115, 145, 147, 150, 164, 165n6
holistic scope 15, 18–20, 23

incidental injury 70
India 37
Indonesia 95, 178n5
Industrial Revolution 145
information operations or warfare x, 64, 111, 113, 119–20, 175ch7n9
insurgents 108, 124–6, 147, 160; compared with terrorists 124–5; *see also* guerrilla actions
intelligence 7, 16, 18, 39–41, 49, 56, 102, 105, 111, 140; in gaining surprise and initiative 41
intelligence, surveillance, and reconnaissance missions 7, 17, 39; in promoting international stability 41, 86; *see also* Open Skies policy
intercontinental ballistic missiles (ICBM) 7, 36, 41–2, 101, 104

international law *see* customary and international law
International Space Station 7, 40, 173n22
International Telecommunications Convention 10–11
International Telecommunications Satellite Consortium 139–40
International Telecommunications Satellite Organization Agreement 11
International Telecommunications Union 7–8, 88, 139, 167n28, 178n5
Iraq, War in (2003) 59, 95
Islamic nations 65–6

jamming communications 10, 59, 95–7, 105, 121, 123, 128, 175n13, 178n9; *see also* blocking
Japan and the Japanese 46–8, 177n13
Joint Doctrine for Space Operations (JP 3-14) 6, 127, 129–30, 132
Jomini, Baron Antoine-Henri de 166n11
"just" war 138

Khrushchev, Soviet Premier 58
kinetic weapons 68, 86, 111
Kosovo 48

Lagrange liberation points 9, 85, 167n32
land forces *see* armies
land warfare 4, 22–3, 31, 44–5, 66, 75, 108–9, 111, 124; *see also* armies *and* Clausewitz, Carl von
lasers 53–4, 57, 68, 94–5, 102, 104, 148
launch locations 82–3, 85
lawful targeting, principle of 70
Law of Armed Conflict 69–71, 143, 147, 161
Law of the Sea, Convention on the 182n26
lesser powers 28, 67, 103, 108, 159–60, 180ch14n5; advantages of being 117; defined 116; possible actions of 116–18
Liberia 46–7
limited aims 101–3, 120, 158, 170n15
Limited Test Ban Treaty 141, 182n17
limited war 27; compared to unlimited war 27
lines of communication: at sea 24, 26,

51 175ch6n8; in space *see* celestial
lines of communication; in the air
51; on land 24, 51

Mahan, Alfred Thayer 19, 23, 163;
disadvantages of using 19–20, 148,
161; on naval strategy and theory
19–20, 23, 31, 89, 98, 124
"maneuver space" 105, 179ch11n6
Manned Orbital Laboratory 42, 73
Mao Tse-tung 108; compared to Sun
Tzu 180n12; on concentration of
forces 108–9; on guerrilla war 124–6
Marine Corps, US 46, 151, 153
maritime, definition of 19;
differentiated from "naval" 19
maritime communications 22–4,
170n27, 172n82, 174ch6n1 and n4;
see also sea lines of communication
maritime strategy and theory: as defined
by Corbett *see* Corbett, Sir Julian S.;
best strategic framework for space
3, 19–20, 32, 154, 163; compared
to air power and sea power 19;
compared with land warfare strategy
23; subset of wartime strategy
23; weaknesses of using for space
strategy 31–2
maritime trade 19, 22–3, 25, 30, 46,
73, 91, 98
measures of effectiveness: and efficiency
55; and formulating strategy
54–5, 58–9; and non-physical
communications 56–8, 121; and
physical communications 55–8, 121;
and those employing both types of
communication 57–8
media, Western: being
counterproductive 65–6; and
influencing others 65;
microsatellites 68, 77, 90, 95, 113, 122,
179n17 and n18
militarization, definition of 181n5
military necessity, principle of 70, 147,
161, 179ch12n7
military strategy 4; requiring support of
space forces 50; subservient to grand
strategy 6, 44, 69; subservient to
national leaders 44
Milosevic, Slobodan 48
minor actions 23, 41–2, 155, 160,
170n15; for political effect 42–3,
174n33

missile defense 17, 101, 104
"mission essential" 71, 144
Mitchell, William "Billy" 14, 47, 148,
161, 163
Moon Treaty 139, 181ch15n9
mutual assured destruction 145

Napoleon Bonaparte 16, 45–6, 100
National Aeronautics and Space Act
140, 181n6
National Aeronautics and Space
Administration (NASA) 7, 38; past
programs 7
national interests x, 3–4, 13, 18, 22, 36,
41, 44, 62, 73, 87, 95, 127–8, 140,
143, 145, 160
national power: defined 35; instruments
of 4, 5, 35, 41, 60, 79, 141, 153,
156, 166n13; linked to national
security 5, 36, 41–2, 154
National Reconnaissance Office 7
national security 5, 35–6, 41–2, 62,
128, 140, 146, 154, 161
National Space Policy (1996) 127, 140,
180ch14n2
national strategy *see* grand strategy
naval: defined 15–16; differentiated
from "maritime" 15–16
Naval Research Lab 50
naval strategy and theory: as defined
by Corbett *see* Corbett, Sir Julian
S.; as defined by Mahan 19–20,
23, 31, 89, 98, 124; and sea power
15–16; weaknesses of using for space
strategy 18–19
navies: and ability to win wars alone 23,
46–7; and air forces 46; and armies
as one weapon 22–3; and hiding
disposition 31
Navy, US 58, 151, 153
Nelson, Horatio 172n84; and Napoleon
Bonaparte 16, 46; battles 16, 46; on
role of cruisers 30
network centric warfare 114, 150,
180n22
Nile, Battle of the 16, 46
non-destructive methods 96, 99
non-governmental organizations 35, 60
non-military methods 106, 116, 118–
20, 159–60, 163, 172n4
non-overt methods 121
non-physical communications *see*
communications: non-physical

non-state actor 106, 116, 152
North Atlantic Treaty Organization 48, 117
nuclear weapons in space 12, 41–2, 141, 168n48, 173n25, 180ch13n5, 182n23

offensive strategy: and defensive strategy 25–7, 69, 74, 78–9, 93, 130, 156–7; disadvantages of 74, 171n41; misinterpretations of 20, 27, 74, 148, 163; more "effective" form of war 25, 74, 97, 156, 178ch10n2; when called for 25, 73, 92, 157
On War (Clausewitz): quotations from 4, 35, 69, 74–5, 78, 108–9, 125, 159, 170n8 and n9, 172n1, 174ch5n1, 176n1, 179n13
orbits: high-earth 8, 167n27; geostationary 8, 10, 38–9, 54, 62, 83–5, 95, 119, 147, 177n6; geosynchronous 8, 167n27, 178n5; "graveyard" 53, 77, 149; low-earth 8, 38, 52, 54, 83, 88, 125, 167n27, 174n12, 177n6; medium-earth 8; Molniya 83, 167n27; near-earth 8, 76, 78, 86–7, 90, 132, 141, 167n31, 169n31
Open Skies policy 40–1, 86, 169n36
Outer Space Treaty 11–12, 63–4, 139–141, 143, 147, 160, 167n40 and n44, 181n7, 182n23, n25, and n30

parasitic satellites 77
particle beam weapons 52–4, 57, 94, 101, 104, 148–9, 156, 162
peaceful use of space 11–12, 72–3, 127–8, 139–41, 143, 181ch14n9, 181n6
physical communications *see* communications: physical
Plenipotentiary Conference 118–19
policing systems 111–15, 133, 159
policy 5, 181n1; and strategy ix, 5, 10, 137–8, 164; and war 36, 137, 160
politics: and policy 35–6; compared with diplomacy 35–6; defined 36; role in war 22, 36, 43, 45
positions and regions of interest: in space 8–9; on the earth 9–10
prestige: and information 39; and pride 42–3, 84; and the United States 36, 58, 140, 182n12; and warfare 39, 41, 67; gained through space programs 39–40, 56, 57–8, 84
primacy 117, 145
principles of war 3, 4, 5, 165n7; timeless 4, 87, 154, 166n11
proportionality, principle of 161, 176n5, 179ch12n7
protracted war 22, 105, 121, 126

radiation *see* Van Allen belts
rate of communications 56–7, 121
Redstone program 50
Rules of Engagement: Standing 71; Supplemental 71–2, 144
Russia and its people 48, 59, 62, 64, 68, 82, 147, 175n14, 179n17

sanctuary, space as a *see* schools of thought: sanctuary
schools of thought 16–19, 130–3, 169n34; control 17–18, 132–3, 165ch1n1, 169n41, n42, and n43, 175n1; high-ground 17–18, 41, 85–7, 132; sanctuary 17–18, 72–3, 86–7, 131, 169n35 and n36; survivability 17–18, 72–3, 131–2; weaknesses and limitations of 18–19, 131–3, 181n19
sea control 3, 16, 19, 132, 175n1, 176n13; *see also* command of the sea
sea lines of communication (SLOCs) 22–6, 29, 51, 73, 91, 98, 100, 109–12, 132, 174ch6n4, 175ch6n8; compared with lines of communication on land 24
sea power theory 18–19, 81, 132; compared with naval strategy 15–16; defined 15–16; roles and missions 16; weaknesses of using for space strategy 18, 132–3; *see also* maritime strategy
self-defense, right of 140, 143, 148–9, 176n3 and n8; collective 70–1, 76, 128, 140; individual and unit level 70–1; national 71
self-protection methods 76
separate space service 150–2, 162
shielding 76–7, 88, 102
Solar and Heliospheric Observatory 9
Some Principles of Maritime Strategy (Corbett): acclaim for 20; quotations from 22–31, 51, 75, 90, 98, 103,

109–10, 126, 158, 170n9, n13, n17, and n27
Soviet Union and its people 36; Communism being superior 39–40, 120, 173n19; dissolution of 65; space programs 41, 58, 61, 90, 140, 182n12; shaping legal regime 84; *see also Sputnik I*
space (outer space): activities in 7–8, 35, 38; as a "maneuver space" 105, 179ch11n6; defined 6; different from the air medium 15, 72; how people feel about it 141–2; indivisible with air medium 15; influence in 37; legal use of 10–12, 181n7; lowest boundary of 6, 166n20; presence in 37; shared use of 10–11; used for peaceful purposes 11–12, 72–2,139, 141, 143
space-based weapons *see* weaponization
space cadre x, 165n1
Space Commission Report 127–9, 163, 180ch14n2, 180ch14n5, 182n32
space communications 51–2, 156,174ch6n4 and n5
space control *see* schools of thought, control
space forces and operations: achieving strategic effects 49; affecting the enemy and populace 49; compared with air forces and operations 15, 17, 31, 154, 168n23; compared with naval forces 15, 17, 31, 52, 154; ineffective in achieving victory alone 49, 155; interdependent with other methods of warfare 49, 55, 100, 130, 155; less survivable *see* schools of thought: survivability; supported by land, sea, and air operations 49–50; supporting of land, sea, and air operations 41–2, 49–50, 101, 130, 151
space policy: and those that can shape it 35–7, 40; recommendations 142–53, 160–13
Space Power 2010 6
space power theory 3, 14, 163, 165ch1n1 and n2; *see also* space strategy
Space Race: and the United States 36–9, 120, 140, 182n12; good economically 38
Space Shuttle 52, 56

space stations 82, 84, 94, 112, 125; *see also* International Space Station
space strategy: and air power 13–15, 18, 168n22 and n23; and land warfare strategy 66; and maritime strategy 21, 32, 66, 89, 91, 97–8, 105, 109, 154, 164; and naval strategy 13, 15–16, 18; and role of national power 43; needing a holistic scope 15, 19–20, 23; subset of general military strategy 49–50, 109, 114, 130, 151, 155; supporting national strategy x, 3, 50, 153
Space War College 151–2, 162–3
space warfare 6: as a distinct warfare area 49, 72, 114, 151; deserving its own context and lexicon 21, 130, 154; nature of 36, 72, 141; objective of 51, 66, 84, 91, 108, 111, 148, 156, 159
Sparta 45
Sputnik I 39–40, 120, 173n19, 174n33
Starfish Prime 180ch13n5
strategic advantage 80, 85–6, 105, 108, 125–6
"strategic defense" 76
Strategic Defense Initiative 42, 73, 101, 104
strategic positions 162: choke-points 81–4, 90–1, 111, 157, 159, 170n1, 177n1; defined 80, 87; high ground 86–7, 149; high-value positions 84–5, 90–1, 177n11; inherent value of 75–6, 157; those with negative value 87–8, 90
strategy: and doctrine 129, 166n12; and measures of effectiveness 53–4, 58–9; and policy ix, 5, 10, 137–8, 164; balancing ends and means 4, 107, 181n2; defined 4, 181n2; during peace and war 4, 44, 50, 155; those of maritime and space being similar 31–2, 35, 49; *see also* space strategy
strategy mismatch 103
Sun Tzu 44; compared to Mao Tse-tung 180n12; on deception 178n13; on importance of information 40; on non-military methods of winning 36, 118, 172n4; on theory of war 172n2
surprise and initiative 26, 41, 89, 98, 130, 171n53
survivability *see* schools of thought: survivability

tactics 4, 5, 6, 68; and technology 4, 31, 68, 78, 94, 154; comparing those of air and space warfare 31–2, 154
Taylor, President Charles 46–7
technology, role of: differences between space and naval warfare 31–2; similarities of space and air warfare 32, 154; and strategy 4, 114; and tactics 4, 31, 68, 78, 94, 154; uses of 8, 114
telecommunications 7, 10, 37–8, 54, 56, 60, 64, 117, 119, 123, 166n25
"temporary passage" 148
terrorists: compared with insurgents 124; possible actions of 125, 160
Theater Missile Defense 101–2, 104
theory 4–5, 21–2, 154, 166n10
Third World countries 119
Thucydides 45
time: and effectiveness of communications 56–7; and offensive strategy 89; as strategic advantage 88–9
Tonga dispute 95, 178n5
"transparent force" 122–3; see also effects, military
Treaty of Versailles 41
trinitarian analysis of war 45, 48, 102, 174ch5n1 and n12, 175ch8n8

United Nations and its Charter 11, 61–4, 119, 138–9, 141, 142–3, 146–7, 160, 176n3 and n8
United States: and command of space 144–5, 152, 161; and peaceful purposes 11–12, 139, 141, 143; and prestige 36, 58, 140, 182n12; and the Space Race 36–9, 120, 140, 182n12; and weaponizing space 141, 146–7; dependency on space 7, 130; space programs 40–1, 61, 64, 101; military strategy 45–6, 129, 132, 152; on vulnerability of space-based attack 173n31; shaping legal regime 84, 139; see also Cold War

unity of effort, principle of 114
University of Surrey Space Centre 113, 179n17
unlimited aims 102, 158
unlimited war 27, 101, 103–4; compared with limited war 27
USSR see Soviet Union

V-2 missile program 41
value of space 16–18, 51, 60, 66, 80, 91, 155–6
Van Allen belts 8–9, 77, 88, 123, 180ch13n5
Vanguard program 50, 58
vulnerability 118, 169n37; see also schools of thought, survivability

war: and escalation 98–9, 141, 145, 147; being about people see trinitarian analysis of war; defined 22, 36, 137, 172n1; limited 27; luring the enemy into battle 29; and politics and policy 22, 45, 137, 160, 170n8 and n9, 172n1 and n2, 181n4; at the operational level 166n17; at the strategic level 32, 47, 49, 166n17; at the tactical level 32, 47, 49; protracted 22, 105, 121, 126; role of friction and uncertainty 114, 179n19; unlimited 27, 101, 104
Warden, John A. 14
weaponization of space x, 13, 16–17, 69, 127–8, 130–1, 139–41, 144–8, 160–1, 164, 169n43, 181n5
weapons-free sanctuary 17, 131, 141, 147, 161, 164; see also schools of thought, sanctuary
weapons of mass destruction (WMD) 12, 141, 182n23
White, General Thomas D. 14–15; see also air power
World War I 41
World War II 41, 46–8